ROYAL HISTORICAL SOCIETY
STUDIES IN HISTORY

New Series

CORNWALL POLITICS IN THE AGE OF REFORM

CORNWALL POLITICS
IN THE AGE OF REFORM
1790–1885

Edwin Jaggard

THE ROYAL HISTORICAL SOCIETY
THE BOYDELL PRESS

© Edwin Jaggard 1999

First published 1999

A Royal Historical Society publication
Published by The Boydell Press
an imprint of Boydell & Brewer Ltd
PO Box 9, Woodbridge, Suffolk IP12 3DF, UK
and of Boydell & Brewer Inc.
PO Box 41026, Rochester, NY 14604–4126, USA
website: http://www.boydell.co.uk

ISBN 0 86193 243 9

ISSN 0269–2244

A catalogue record for this book is available
from the British Library

Library of Congress Cataloging-in-Publication Data
Jaggard, Edwin, 1942–
 Cornwall politics in the age of reform, 1790–1885/Edwin Jaggard.
  p. cm. – (Royal Historical Society studies in history. New series,
ISSN 0269–2244)
 Includes bibliographical references and index.
 ISBN 0–86193–243–9 (hardback : alk. paper)
  1. Cornwall (England : County) – Politics and government.
 2. Elections – England – Cornwall (County) – History – 19th century.
 I. Title. II. Series.
 DA670.C8 J27 1999
 942.3'7081 21 – dc21   99–036470

This book is printed on acid-free paper

Printed in Great Britain by
St Edmundsbury Press, Bury St Edmunds, Suffolk

FOR PAM, MELISSA
AND SARAH

Contents

List of Tables

List of Maps

Acknowledgements

This study of county electoral politics originated in the United States, before being continued in England and Western Australia. In an intellectual sense Richard Davis of Washington University, St Louis, has accompanied me on every step of the journey. Over the years his advice, encouragement and hospitality have been unstinting and I am deeply indebted to him and to Elisabeth. Derek Hirst was an exacting and inspiring teacher, besides being a generous critic during the early stages of the research. On the British side of the Atlantic my debts are many. At the Cornwall Record Office, Colin Edwards was the first to guide me through the maze of Cornish family papers. With her infectious enthusiasm and interest the county archivist, Christine North, has helped in numerous ways, and maybe now I can repay her by rising to the challenge of Sir Christopher Hawkins. David Ivall directed me to several little known but useful sources. Les Douch, former curator of the Royal Cornwall Museum, patiently answered endless questions about people and places, while the museum's librarian, Angela Broome, provided friendly company during a memorably cold, dripping summer, and has since been helpful in many ways.

Elsewhere, the staff of the Gilbert White Museum in Selborne, the Devon and West Devon Record Offices, the Somerset Record Office, the Devon and Exeter Institution, the Bodleian Library, the Bishopsgate Institute, Alliance House, the Greater London Record Office, the Institute of Historical Research, the Local History Library, Redruth, the Reid Library, University of Western Australia, and Jenny Marshall, former Faculty of Arts librarian at Edith Cowan University, have provided valuable assistance. Without the generous financial aid provided by Washington University the initial research would never have begun. Since then two small grants awarded by Edith Cowan University have enabled me to revisit England to bring the research to a conclusion. I am grateful to the Professional Development and Research Committees of the Faculty of Arts, for assisting with funding and, equally important, for time away from administrative duties.

I also wish to thank the Nicholas Kendalls (now sadly deceased), Lord and Lady St Levan, the late Mrs Joan Colquitt-Craven, Mrs Philip Rashleigh, Lieutenant Colonel J. A. Molesworth-St Aubyn MBE, Sir John Carew Pole Bt, DSO; and Roger Penhallurick for drawing the maps which grace these pages. The editors of *Albion, Parliamentary History, Journal of British Studies, Southern History, Journal of the Royal Institution of Cornwall* and *Cornish Studies*, have kindly given their permission to reproduce in modified form sections of articles published in their journals. The jacket design is based upon a selection of election posters held at the Cornwall Record Office which are reproduced with their permission.

Peter Mandler, the Royal Historical Society's advisory editor for this period, whose painstaking editorial comments and corrections have transformed the manuscript, continually offered encouragement when it was badly needed. Others who at different times read and commented on various chapters include Iain Brash, who first stimulated my interest in electoral politics, Kevin Barry, the late John Phillips, Les Douch, and those at Edith Cowan University who have taken an interest in the research. In particular, members of the former School of Social and Cultural Studies have borne my preoccupation with Cornwall with remarkably good humour.

Encouragement and help of a different kind came from Loryn and Chris Green who kindly provided a London bed whenever needed. In Cornwall Jean and Roy Lapham were unfailingly generous to an antipodean 'emmet', as were Paul and Pam Treseder of the Marcorrie Hotel, Truro. For more than several years Christine Harvey, most capable and loyal of secretaries, typed and retyped successive drafts, without once complaining about my scrawl. Recently I have appreciated the patience and skill of Christine Linehan who prepared the manuscript for the press, and Anne Batt who compiled the index. However I owe most to Pam, who never imagined that when she embarked on a long-ago flight to the USA, the journey would take so long and reach such a conclusion. Without her love and encouragement this book might have remained a dream.

Edwin Jaggard
May 1999

Abbreviations

Bodl. Lib.	Bodleian Library, Oxford
BL	British Library
CRO	Cornwall Record Office
RIC	Royal Institution of Cornwall

Introduction

In 1814 in the town of Truro in Cornwall two apparently unrelated events occurred. Firstly, as a consequence of the death of John Lemon, there was a vacancy in the town's parliamentary representation. Lemon had been one of Truro's MPs since 1796, the year in which the Boscawen family of Tregothnan temporarily lost control of the borough's representation. Lemon had been a popular figure with extensive business interests in and around Truro, and his election was a rebuff to the dictatorial patron who had previously controlled both seats. With Lemon's death the Boscawens reasserted their electoral ascendancy – at least until 1831.[1] Secondly, the Truro Shipping Company was established. Its Articles of Agreement were signed by more than twenty local business, professional and tradespeople, among them John Ferris currier, Thomas Whitford mercer, John Cuming confectioner, Samuel Randall pipe-maker, Robert Blee iron-monger and Samuel Milford draper. Milford was a Quaker, many of the other signatories were Methodists. Most of these middle- or lower middle-class men became staunch opponents of the Boscawens' manipulation of the parliamentary representation of Truro.[2] While there is no direct evidence to prove the assertion, they were almost certainly among the 130 townspeople who signed a petition in 1818 promoting the claims of two reformers in opposition to the Boscawens' nominees. Certainly, all who could do so unsuccessfully supported Whig reformers in the general elections of 1830 and 1831, before finally satisfying their long-held expectations in December 1832.

Such challenges, sometimes surreptitious, sometimes open, were an important element of late Hanoverian electoral politics, but in corrupt Cornwall, the one-time exemplar of the Namierite view? Surely not. After all, this was the *locus classicus* of the unreformed electoral system, a county where greed, personal rivalries, venality and political interference through the duchy of Cornwall were allegedly endemic in the reign of George III. The correspondent who wrote of a 1761 election in the infamous Penryn, "'tis said the money is drove abt in wheelbarrows' was grist to the Namierite mill, a refined version of which grinds on in the form of the magnificent *History of Parliament* project.[3]

---

1   The patron's control was successfully challenged again in 1820, but the 'rebels' retired in 1826.
2   RIC, 'Articles of Agreement, Truro Shipping Co., 21 Oct. 1814'.
3   W. Roberts, Jr, to Thomas Hawkins, 30 Mar. 1761, ibid. MSS Hawkins HH/13/76; R. G. Thorne (ed.), *The House of Commons, 1790–1820*, London 1986. Admittedly Roland Thorne and his dedicated team have not yet completed the final 1820–32 stage, but there

What the two events of 1814 in Truro illustrate in simplified form are the opposing view-points in a long-running historical debate about the nature and workings of the unreformed electoral system, the extent to which the 1832 Reform Act wrought changes in the system. According to one side in the debate the Boscawens' temporary setback at Truro was part of the on-going struggle in an era when the politics of patronage prevailed. Wealthy patrons – and there was an abundance of them in Cornwall – either nominated members in the boroughs under their control, or exerted their formidable influence to make sure their favoured candidates were successful. Either way voters were largely irrelevant, unless they had to be bought off as so frequently occurred in the Cornish boroughs of Grampound, Tregony and Penryn. As for ideological debate about national or county issues – parliamentary reform, commutation of tithes, Roman Catholic emancipation or agricultural protection – this was believed to be non-existent.

Ammunition for this side of the argument was provided initially by Oldfield's *History of the boroughs* (1792) prepared for the reformers of the Society for Constitutional Information.[4] Much of it was republished early in the nineteenth century, later in the same century by Joseph Grego, then explored once more in Edward and Annie Porritt's *The unreformed House of Commons* (1903).[5] Twenty or so years later came Sir Lewis Namier's magisterial study, *The structure of politics at the accession of George III*, apparently confirming the corrupt, influence-ridden nature of the unreformed electoral system.[6] The same picture was presented in the Namier and Brooke edited *History of parliament* volumes spanning 1754 to 1790, while the continuation of these features after 1832 was exposed firstly by Norman Gash and later by D. C. Moore, the latter using a questionable socio-historical model to argue for the enduring strength of what he termed 'the politics of deference'.[7] Among specifically Cornish studies focusing on corruption, venality and the over-riding importance of influence were those by W. P. Courtney, W. T. Lawrance, A. de C. Glubb and three short articles by P. Jennings in the *Journal of the Royal Institution of Cornwall*.[8]

are relatively few signs of their most recent conclusions being congruent with current research on the period.

4   T. H. B. Oldfield, *An entire and complete history, political and personal of the boroughs of Great Britain*, London 1792.

5   Joseph Grego, *History of parliamentary elections and electioneering in the old days*, London 1892; E. Porritt and A. Porritt, *The unreformed House of Commons: parliamentary representation before 1832*, Cambridge 1903.

6   First published by Macmillan in 1929.

7   L. B. Namier and J. Brooke, *The House of Commons, 1754–1790*, London 1964; Norman Gash, *Politics in the age of Peel: a study in the technique of parliamentary representation, 1830–50*, 2nd edn, Hassocks 1977; D. C. Moore, *The politics of deference: a study of the mid-nineteenth century English political system*, Hassocks 1976.

8   W. P. Courtney, *The parliamentary representation of Cornwall to 1832*, London 1889; W. T. Lawrance, *Parliamentary representation of Cornwall: being a record of the electoral divisions*

Contrary to this, and representative of the opposition view-point in the debate, members of the Truro Shipping Company and people of similar background, played a conspicuous part in Truro politics before and after 1814, most notably in their persistent opposition to the patronage of the Boscawen family. This late Hanoverian participatory activism suggests a political milieu very different from that outlined earlier. And, those whose object has been to question the Namierite view by exposing voters' capacity for independent thought and vigorous debate over national issues, have effectively employed county studies to test their judgements. Richard Davis (who according to one reviewer attacked Moore 'with all the zeal of an inquisitor rooting out heresy') examined Buckinghamshire, R. J. Olney Lincolnshire, and T. J. Nossiter Northumberland and Durham.[9] Only Davis spanned the pre- and post-Reform Act periods, uncovering elements of consistently independent political behaviour well before 1832. Despite their different methodological approaches all three proved that the world of electoral politics described by Gash and Moore was more preoccupied with issues and principles, and more divided by partisanship than they would have acknowledged.

More recently similar activism has been exposed by Frank O'Gorman and the late John Phillips who have analysed both sides of the same electoral coin.[10] Phillips demonstrates from pollbook analysis of a handful of scattered boroughs (mostly with more than a thousand voters) how 'England contained a vibrant political nation well before 1832, much of it unenfranchised, but continued to suffer from corruption and coercion after 1832.'[11] O'Gorman is convinced that after the First Reform Act 'the substance of electoral life, already participatory, partisan and popular, continued'.[12] One electoral system gave way to another remarkably similar to itself. Where the *History of Parliament*'s constituency surveys are often permeated with the politics of personal relationships, intrigue and money, Phillips and O'Gorman detect the appearance of partisanship arising from public debate as popular participation in electoral politics grew.

The evidence produced by Phillips and O'Gorman in support of their view-points is very persuasive. More importantly, their conclusion in some

---

and boroughs of the county from 1295 to 1885, Truro 1925; A. de C. Glubb, *When Cornwall had 44 MP's*, Truro 1934; P. Jennings, 'Notes on the parliamentary history of Truro, part iv (1761–1787)', *Journal of the Royal Institution of Cornwall* xix (1913), 230–40; 'Part v (1787–1820)', ibid. xix (1914), 433–9; 'Part vi (1820–1832)', ibid. xx (1915), 95–106.

9   R. W. Davis, *Political change and continuity, 1760–1885: a Buckinghamshire study*, Newton Abbott 1972; R. J. Olney, *Lincolnshire politics, 1832–1885*, London 1973; T. J. Nossiter, *Influence, opinion and political idioms in reformed England: case studies from the north east, 1832–1874*, Hassocks 1975.

10 Frank O'Gorman, *Voters, patrons and parties: the unreformed electorate of Hanoverian England, 1734–1832*, Oxford 1989; John A. Phillips, *The Great Reform Bill in the boroughs: English electoral behaviour, 1818–1841*, Oxford 1992.

11 Ibid. 302.

12 O'Gorman, *Voters, patrons and parties*, 393.

ways parallels Davis's judgement on the broad sweep of Buckinghamshire electoral politics from 1760 to 1885, a period of profound change originating before the First Reform Act.[13] Even so, this and more specific conclusions have been compared with very few counties, as have the findings of Phillips, O'Gorman and James Vernon whose innovative study of mid Victorian popular politics suggests national parties and influence were periodically overwhelmed by local considerations.[14] In fact their judgements may be a distortion of the real situation because their evidence came from geographically scattered sources rather than one or a cluster of counties. Nor were the three particularly concerned about the ramifications of any possible nexus between county and borough politics. Consequently, the most general justification for this study is to test both sides of the debate mentioned earlier, within a specific local context. The purpose is to define the ways in which remnants of patron-dominated, often corrupt, political activity coexisted with strong loyalties to and belief in political ideologies, partisanship, and concern for national issues.

The choice of Cornwall to demonstrate how widespread and resilient 'participating, partisan and popular' strands were in the nineteenth century may seem surprising. After all, this was the county where borough representation was the plaything of scheming patrons, where voting and bribery were synonymous. A Cornish clergyman Richard Tyacke explained in January 1829:

> The rich man, openly and unscrupulously, bribes and corrupts the pooer [sic] voter to second his views, – his promise is undermined, his word is tempted, and money, basely proferred, strives to eradicate every principle of honor [sic] from his breast. Thus the patron, the representative of their rights, and whose higher grade in society influences, as a natural consequence the manners and actions of his inferiors.[15]

Observations similar to these still pervade the latest volumes of the *History of Parliament*, creating the false impression of an electoral system far more static than it was, in Cornwall and elsewhere. A glance in *McCalmont's parliamentary poll book* at Cornwall election results after 1832 reveals how the aristocracy and gentry did not have everything their own way. The obvious and crucial question is to what extent they were being challenged before 1832, and by whom? Closely related to this is the location of political power within Cornwall society and its gradual shift downward from the aristocracy and wealthy gentry, throughout the nineteenth century.

There are other justifications for a county analysis of the dynamics of the unreformed electoral system and its successor. The gradual transformation of Cornwall from a Tory into a Liberal stronghold makes it possible to explore

---

13 Davis, *Political change*, 227.
14 James Vernon, *Politics and the people: a study in English political culture*, c. 1815–1867, Cambridge 1993.
15 Diary of Richard Tyacke 1826–9, entry for 20 Jan. 1829, CRO, AD 715.

the origins of Liberalism in the early nineteenth-century parliamentary reform movement, as well as the erosion of Conservatism in the mid Victorian period. The often remarked-upon strength of Wesleyan Methodism along with the relative weakness of the Established Church was another dimension of the eventual Liberal hegemony. Religious issues, particularly those of concern to Dissenters, frequently intruded into electoral politics, beginning with Roman Catholic emancipation and opposition to colonial slavery. The concerns of agriculturalists were always prominent too, 'farmers' politics' being of central importance in many county elections between 1815 and 1885. Bitter family rivalries and a people whose relative lack of class consciousness distinguished them from many of their counterparts elsewhere in England, are also part of this exploration of one county's electoral politics.

It must be emphasised that this is 'not simply a work of regional piety', the mere filling of another gap in the complex nineteenth-century political mosaic.[16] Several historians have made a persuasive case for analysing the ebb and flow of politics in a single county. 'It is useful, for instance, to test generalisations about the nature of landed interests and the voting habits of tenant farmers by reference to specific examples. Generalisations about electoral behaviour at specific general elections can also be examined.'[17] Cornwall therefore is a laboratory, a peculiarly appropriate testing place. According to one school of thought the 1832 transition from one electoral system to another should have been least pronounced in the county because the politics of patronage and manipulation were so deeply ingrained. Instead issues and opinions, the rivalries of political parties and the volatile interaction between social classes constitute the foundation of what follows.

[16] Nossiter, *Influence, opinion and political idioms*, 1.
[17] Olney, *Lincolnshire politics*, p. vii.

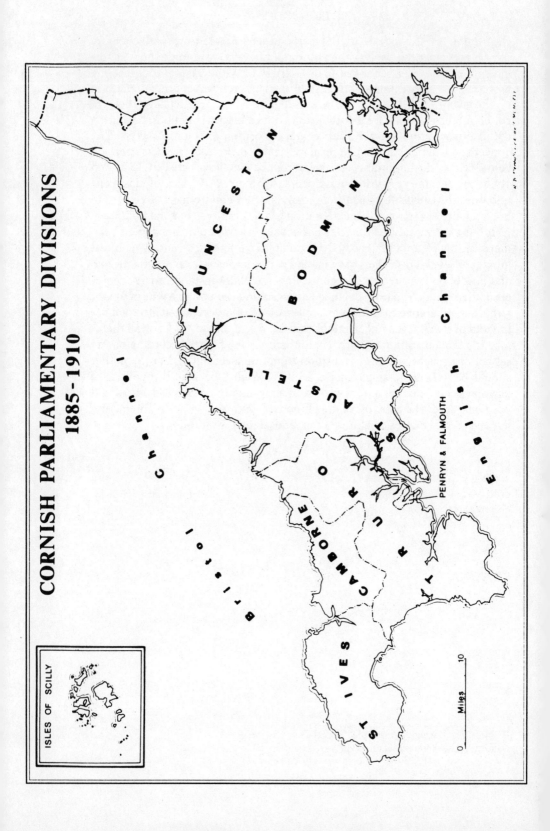

CORNISH PARLIAMENTARY DIVISIONS
1885–1910

ISLES OF SCILLY

Bristol Channel

LAUNCESTON

BODMIN

ST AUSTELL

CAMBORNE

TRURO

PENRYN & FALMOUTH

ST IVES

English Channel

Miles
0   10

1

Economy, Society, Politics

The Cornish landscape

In the British general election of 1790 Prime Minister William Pitt consolidated his control over government. Outwardly the election seemed uneventful, typical of many in the Hanoverian period when most seats were uncontested. Nevertheless this should not obscure the vibrancy of political life in those towns where the lines of partisanship were clearly drawn, or constituencies such as Cornwall (county) where a hard fought and sometimes bitter election centred upon local animosities and national issues. Almost one century later the Third Reform Act, the accompanying redistribution of seats and the ensuing general election allegedly heralded the dawn of 'mass democracy', a far cry from the relatively limited popular participation and widespread politics of patronage of Pitt's era. The years between these two events spanned a period of unparalleled economic, social and political change in England, affecting counties remote from London and the heartland of the Industrial Revolution further north. In this sense Cornwall was in the mainstream of English life after 1790, despite an unusual combination of economic activities – agriculture, mining, fishing – the occasionally idiosyncratic behaviour of elements among the population, and the powerful social control exerted by Methodism. In general terms Cornish electoral politics were also part of this mainstream; however, in the 'Age of Reform', the century after 1790, several distinctive characteristics emerged. The first step towards understanding these commonalities and differences is, therefore, to explore the environment from which they emerged.

When studied on a map Cornwall's comparative isolation from the remainder of England is obvious. Land's End is more than 300 miles from London, as far distant as Northumberland, Kirkcudbright in south-western Scotland, and the Irish Republic's County Wexford. Cornwall is very much part of the 'Celtic fringe', those distant and peripheral regions including Scotland, Wales and Ireland, where cultural distinctions have long been and remain evident. When measured from west to east Cornwall spans approximately eighty miles while the width is never more than half that distance. Geographical isolation is accentuated by the fact that Cornwall alone of English counties shares its borders with only one other – Devon. Because of this remoteness, most marriages among the Hanoverian aristocracy and gentry were unions of families within the county, prompting the eighteenth century aphorism, 'All Cornishmen are Cousins.'[1]

An obvious physical feature of the county is the ever-narrowing cornucopian shape, the coast being washed on the north by the Bristol Channel and on the south the English Channel. With the Tamar river providing a natural eastern boundary Cornwall is almost separated from the remainder of England by water; no location in the most remote parish is more than eighteen miles from the sea. Furthermore, the often forbidding granite hillsides ooze, drip or gush forth water. Deep underground the disused mines and a handful of productive ones – a reminder of one of the county's staple industries – quickly flood without constant pumping. Downwards from leaden skies, upward from the earth and to and fro with the daily tides, Cornwall is inundated with water.

After travelling on foot through the county in 1851, Walter White wrote of the landscape:

> The generally soft features of Devonshire are exchanged for a landscape of stern and unfinished aspect. Trees are few; and you see a prominent characteristic of Cornwall – a surface heaved into long rolling swells, brown and bare, not unlike what we should fancy of waves from the adjoining ocean solidified, cut up into squares by thick stone fences, which in many places are thickly covered with brilliant yellow stone-crop, growing from the crevices.[2]

This evocative description was not entirely accurate, for it overlooked the obvious regional variations. The land mass, mostly granite, splays outward and downwards from a comparatively high central spine. 'Much of the ridge consist of great stretches of barren and treeless moorland, strewn with huge boulders, and exposed to the fierce winds that blow from south and west across the heights.'[3] From this wild and remote terrain, a great deal of it never farmed by man, the land dips and curves towards the coasts. Generally the more fertile soils are found in sheltered valleys, but there is also a visible contrast between the rolling agricultural eastern landscapes and the stark, mine-scarred terrain west of Truro. Two centuries ago the difference was even more marked for the western region was the heartland of the great mining districts and population centres, Camborne, Chacewater, Carnon Valley and West Penwith being the more important among them.

Below ground the contrast is equally important because the most prolific mineral lodes are concentrated in the western Carmenellis Mass bounded by the towns of Redruth, Penryn and Helston, and in the hundred of Kerrier

---

1 See V. M. Chesher, 'Some Cornish landowners, 1690–1760: a social and economic study', unpubl. BLitt. diss. Oxford 1957, 9–10.
2 Walter White, *A Londoner's walk to the Land's End, and a trip to the Scilly Isles*, London 1851, 167.
3 RIC, 'Victoria county history of Cornwall' (draft), 2.

covering the westernmost portion of the county from St Ives to Land's End.[4] Within the streamer-like mineral veins running from east to west were – and still are – deposits of tin, copper, lead-zinc, iron and occasionally small quantities of silver and gold. Tin was the first to be mined on a large scale, beginning in Phoenician times. Not until the sixteenth century did underground mining commence, but exploitation of the lodes was limited by relatively inefficient pumping and draining technology. Later, in the eighteenth century when Trevithick, Boulton and Watt harnessed steam power to the never-ending pumping, the great thumping engines emptied thousands of gallons per hour. Consequently deeper lodes could be explored, and copper was found at greater depths.

In the course of his travels through the county in 1793–4 George Worgan reported the locals saying of the Cornish climate, 'that it will bear a shower every week-day and two upon a Sunday'.[5] Bone-chilling dampness and rain are ever present as is the wind. More than seventy years before Worgan Celia Fiennes noticed an important difference between the northern and southern coasts. Referring to the former she wrote 'they are very bleak in their countryes especially to this northern ocean and the winds so troublesome they are forced to spin straw and so make a caul or net worke to lay over their thatch on their ricks and out houses'.[6] Particularly in winter successions of gales blast the terrain, explaining why the wooded and more luxuriant vegetation is found in sheltered valleys along the south coast, and in eastern regions.

If, due to the pronounced maritime influences, Cornwall's climate may be summarised as mild, changeable, windy and above all moist, there are virtues, somewhat overstated by one early seventeenth-century observer:

> The air being cleansed with frequent Winds and Tides, is very pure and healthful, so that the Inhabitants are rarely troubled with any infectious Diseases; . . . The Seasons of the Year are something different from those in other Parts; the Spring is more backward, the Summer more temperate, Autumnal fruits later, their Harvest rarely being ripe enough for the Barn till near Michaelmas . . .[7]

It should also be noted that in these environmentally conscious times the atmosphere has an unusual clarity because of the constant westerlies.

Before 1790, and for at least another sixty years until Isambard Kingdom Brunel daringly spanned the Tamar with the Saltash bridge, Cornwall was little visited by tourists or curious travellers. Indeed as late as 1854 J. R. Leifchild believed more Englishmen had been to continental Europe than to

---

4   The most authoritative source on Cornish mining in this period is John Rowe, *Cornwall in the age of the industrial revolution*, Liverpool 1953.
5   G. B. Worgan, *General view of the agriculture of the county of Cornwall*, London 1811, 3.
6   *The journeys of Celia Fiennes*, ed. Christopher Morris, London 1947, 264.
7   Quoted in Daphne du Maurier, *Vanishing Cornwall: the spirit and history of Cornwall*, Harmondsworth 1978, 41.

Truro – because of the character of the county. Judging it by mid Victorian economic criteria Leifchild was convinced there were few attractions: it was 'neither a remarkable agricultural or manufacturing county', without coal and with very little iron. He and some of his predecessors thought the almost primitive 'means of inland communication' were another disincentive.[8] For example Defoe believed that the Cornish environment was hardly conducive to comfortable travel by horse or coach.[9] Scoured by continual use and heavy rains, deep potholes made the roads almost impassable, and untrimmed hedgerows added to the hazards. On moonless or misty nights the unwary traveller could easily lose his or her way, blundering into unfenced mine shafts. Tottering bridges plus the watery perils of fast rising tides wherever roads crossed tidal marshes, as they did, for example, between Marazion and Penzance, added to the dangers. Therefore it is understandable that prior to 1850 it was often far safer for the Cornish to travel by ship to Plymouth or Exeter, before embarking on the bone-rattling coach journey to London. Not until Brunel's time did Cornwall begin to benefit from the transport revolution.

The economy: farming, fishing and mining

Of the variety of ways in which families earned their livelihood, agriculture employed most people. No group in nineteenth-century Cornwall society was more politically obstreperous than the farmers, particularly those in the region east of a line drawn between Newquay and Truro. From the depression immediately after the Napoleonic Wars to the massive slump of the 1870s they were a critical element in county electoral politics, vocal, sometimes well-organised, and likely to shift across the political spectrum according to their economic circumstance and/or interests. Beset in the first period by low prices, high taxes and unyielding demands for tithes they joined the gentry Whig reformers in their campaign for parliamentary reform. This, the farmers correctly reasoned, could lead to stringent government economies and an easing of their tax burden, so they rallied behind their leader Penhallow Peters who was a farmer–reformer of mountainous physical presence and blunt opinions. Half a century later in East Cornwall it was the 'glib and slippery yeoman' William Snell who played a part in swinging farmer support behind the Conservatives, in the appropriate circumstances.[10] In 1872 at a Lostwithiel meeting Snell and his fellow farmers bluntly told the gentry that support for Conservative candidates would be conditional on the latter's

8   J. R. Leifchild, *Cornwall, its mines and miners*, new impression, New York 1968, 1.
9   Daniel Defoe (intro. G. D. H. Cole), *A tour through the whole island of Great Britain*, London 1927.
10 For Peters see ch. 2; for Snell see chs 6, 8.

opinions being acceptable to the farmers. Why then was there this continuity of farmer activism?

Partly it arose from Cornish agriculture itself, which at the beginning of the nineteenth century employed more families than any other industry in the county. 'In 1794 one third of the county was in a regular course of husbandry', and, according to Worgan, 'Cornwall not being a dairy county, the generality of farmers having an idea that there is nothing like corn sacks for making money, they are very fond of the plough; consequently the tillage for white crops is large.'[11] Well into the nineteenth century Cornish farmers believed the corn mow should pay the rent, so it was inevitable that arable farming predominated. Wheat and barley were most frequently cultivated, the former in the eastern hundreds of Pydar and Trigg, especially in a swathe of parishes from Wadebridge through to Bodmin. Barley was grown in much the same areas, as well as in isolated pockets along the north and south coasts. Oats were similarly widespread but grown away from the coasts, predominantly in East, Stratton and Lesnewth hundreds – all far closer to the Devon border than to Land's End.[12] Nowhere in the county in 1801 did potatoes make up more than one quarter of arable crops, even in western mining hundreds like Penwith and Kerrier where there were many small holdings.[13]

If the crops grown were similar to those in many other counties in England, the landholdings, the system of rents, and the relationships between landlord and tenant were not. The open field system had probably vanished from most of Cornwall by Tudor times: 'there were but few comparatively level tracts of five or seven hundred acres like those which made open field farming practicable in the plains of eastern England'.[14] Typically there was a complicated mixture of large and small fields, a sharing out of the relatively small patches of fertile ground, and, for a host of reasons, wide dispersal of estates. Early in the nineteenth century the Rashleighs of Menabilly had landholdings spread across more than fifty parishes in mid and west Cornwall – and they were not unusual. Consequently tenants more often dealt with stewards or agents than their landlords.

Independence from landlords was accentuated by the rental system. Until the end of the eighteenth century the majority of estates were let on three-life leases for ninety-nine years. Normally the tenant was entirely responsible for the upkeep of the tenement and also for payment of the land tax, hence landlords were freed from burdensome costs of upkeep and repairs. Furthermore, instead of annual rent tenants paid large entry fines when the lease was first taken, plus a small customary rent. Therefore landlords received the greater part of their profits when leases were issued. More importantly, if the

---

11 Worgan, *General view of agriculture*, 53.
12 Mark Overton, 'The 1801 crop returns for Cornwall', in Michael Havinden (ed.), *Husbandry and marketing in the south west, 1500–1800*, Exeter 1973.
13 Ibid.
14 Rowe, *Cornwall*, 212.

customary rents covered expenses in a normal year, fines provided a reservoir of capital for the landlord. Under this financial system farmers had greater flexibility in their dealings with their landlord or his steward.

The result appears to have been a less deferential relationship between owner and tenant than elsewhere in England, one in which the farmers seemed to have considerable freedom. Rarely in the estate correspondence of the leading Cornish families are there references to the coercion of tenants, although large landlords were certainly conscious of their innate influence. Reginald Pole Carew, for example, did not hesitate late in 1832 to advise his tenants about whom they should vote for in the forthcoming county election in East Cornwall.[15] One of them, Charles Jefferey, differed from his landlord; Jefferey and his brother opposed Lord Valletort, a possible Tory candidate, because he would not agree to the abolition of slavery in British colonies. Despite Pole Carew's persuasiveness Charles Jefferey retained his independence of mind on that issue as well as proposed alterations to the Corn Laws, on which they also differed. There is more than a suggestion of the combination of scattered land holdings, the rarity of parishes where one or two landowners dominated the lives of the people, inherent self reliance encouraged by Methodism, and the traditional Cornish independence of mind producing farmers willing to freely voice their opinions.

Generally, in the eighty years after 1790 Cornish agriculture flourished, especially in the central western areas where improving landlords such as Sir Christopher Hawkins and Sir Francis Basset resided. Yet despite this prosperity and through no fault of the agriculturists, from the 1780s onwards Cornwall became increasingly dependent on imported corn. In 1750 the county's population was 140,000; in 1800 it was 192,000 and by 1841 342,000, the highest rates of increase being in the western mining districts – Illogan, Gwennap, Camborne, Breage, Kenwyn and Kea.[16] In earlier years the county's eastern farmers had the capacity to satisfy the demand, but gradually it outstripped their efforts. Towards the end of the eighteenth century occasional poor harvests elsewhere in England, in conjunction with the laws of supply and demand, often encouraged these farmers to ship grain out of the county in order to benefit from higher prices. When their western counterparts contemplated similar action in times of food scarcity, starving miners ('tinners') and their families took the law into their own hands, expressing their outrage through food riots.

These men and women rejected the right of farmers and merchants to speculate on grain prices, arguing instead that the produce of the county

15 ?Sept. 1832, Antony House, Torpoint, MSS Carew Pole CC/63/7.
16 These approximations are based on N. J. G. Pounds, 'Population movement in Cornwall, and the rise of mining in the 18th century', *Geography* xxxiii (1943), 37–46, and Sheila Ryan Johansson, 'The demographic transition in England: a study of the economic, social and demographic background to mortality and fertility change in Cornwall, 1800–1900', unpubl. DPhil. diss. Berkeley 1974.

should always be sold at reasonable prices to its inhabitants and only afterwards should any surplus be exported.[17] If this did not happen, and particularly if deliberate hoarding of grain was suspected, so driving up prices, food riots soon followed. Then the irate participants, many of them women, either seized corn brought to ports for export, 'liberated' supplies from those farmers who were holding stocks in expectation of rising prices, or forcefully interfered in the price-fixing process in local markets. Such riots were 'far from being a blind unreasoning protest':[18] the frequency of their occurrence – 1789, 1793, 1795–6, 1801–3, 1812, 1831, 1847 – suggests the tinners had faith in their effectiveness, hence they were willing to pressure their social superiors who were the arbiters of law and order, rather than obsequiously accept starvation. At times during the Napoleonic Wars Cornwall's magistrates must have wondered whether hungry tinners or the French posed the greatest threat to their society.

Over the previous two hundred years the economic activity most readily identified with Cornwall had been mining, being almost as old as the county itself:

> Long before the ancestors of the Cornish gentry crossed over to England with William the Conqueror, and later rode west of Tamar to settle there, . . . long before Saxons wrought havoc and Romans built roads; back in the Bronze Age, some 1800 years BC, the tinners were at work in Cornwall.[19]

Their ancestors found tin among the sand and stone being washed down in streams from the granite spine of the county. Mixed with copper it formed bronze which could be employed for a variety of purposes, or by itself could be turned into pewter. The Cornish peninsula soon supplied all Europe's needs, its tinners becoming a distinct element within the local population. In the sixteenth century, as surface deposits dwindled tinners began to follow the lodes underground, hewing drives, levels and adits in pursuit of the precious metal. Inevitably underground mining, first of tin, later copper, required more capital than streaming so the result was the appearance of 'adventurers' in the industry, plus 'tributers' and 'tutworkers'. Together they gave mining an employment structure fostering a degree of independence among the underground workforce, besides tending to blur class differences.

Regardless of social status anyone with money to invest could be an adventurer; that is, they could buy a share in a tin or copper mine:

> All sorts and conditions of men were willing to venture in such concerns – landowners who had hopes of exploiting the underground wealth of their own estates but who lacked adequate fluid capital to start operations, professional

17 John Rule, 'Some social aspects of the Cornish industrial revolution', *Exeter Papers in Economic History* ii (1970), 71–106.
18 Ibid. 104.
19 Du Maurier, *Vanishing Cornwall*, 99.

men, especially lawyers who often held landlords in the palms of their hands, not a few clergymen who hoped to gain the money to buy better livings for themselves or their sons . . . some doctors, blacksmiths and carpenters who could do with the extra work mining operations afforded them, and above all merchants.[20]

In return for the capital they contributed (and most spread their money around several mines) the adventurers shared the profits. The so-called cost book system meant they met regularly every month or two to do this, or if further expenditure was required for underground development work or equipment, to supply additional capital in proportion to their share. For shrewd middle-class men or their industrious, self-employed working-class counterparts, successful investment was sometimes a stepping-stone to upward social mobility. Conversely, for the landed gentry it was an appealing way of diversifying their financial interests. Many of the wealthiest landed families gained much of their income from extensive mining interests; thus the Basset family controlled two of the largest mines, Cook's Kitchen and Dolcoath, plus many others in the Camborne area, while the Boscawens were the principal land- and mine-owners in Gwennap and Chacewater.[21]

Below ground there were similar opportunities for the working miners to back their skills and judgements in pursuit of profitable returns. Most were not wage employees: tributers were miners who in groups of two, three or more, contracted to lease a pitch (an area of the mine with mineral bearing lodes) and to receive an agreed proportion of the value of the ore raised over a specified period. Leases, verbal agreements between miners and mine captain, were usually finalised on a monthly basis; often tributers bid against each other for the pitches. This competitive system not only encouraged initiative and skill: depending on the richness of the ore in the pitch it could also bring substantial rewards. Tutworkers were on contracts to undertake development work – sinking shafts, driving new levels – again working in small groups and competing against each other through the monthly bidding process. Both systems meant few men were simply labouring miners, totally subservient in an economic sense to the adventurers or the mine captains.

The eighteenth-century mining industry was the chief reason for Cornwall being in the vanguard of the industrial revolution. With buoyant tin prices and discoveries of deeper copper lodes there were powerful incentives for adventurers to speculate; however deeper shafts and drives also reinforced the need for more efficient pumps with greater capacity. By 1775 more than forty steam engines had been erected at various mines to keep water levels down. Jonathan Hornblower and Richard Trevithick, Sr, were in the forefront of this application of steam power to pumping technology, and by the end of the century Trevithick's inventive son was developing further refinements.[22]

20 Rowe, Cornwall, 23.
21 Ibid. 83.
22 Ibid. ch. iii.

However during the interim years as copper prices slumped and costs such as coal needed to be reduced, Cornish adventurers also bought steam engines manufactured by Boulton and Watt, thereby involving themselves in tremendous acrimony and litigation over premiums owing to the manufacturers.[23] Despite this and the feuds of rival engineers the technological breakthroughs were significant, allowing output of ores to increase steadily at the beginning of the nineteenth century.

Controlling the flourishing mining industry were the Stannaries, a code of laws drawn up in the reign of Edward III, and giving tinners unique privileges. The fundamental principle of Stannary organisation was that in return for taxes levied on their product tinners enjoyed rights of legislation for, and jurisdiction over, the management of their industry. By the end of the eighteenth century the Stannary parliament was all but moribund, as were the supporting systems of courts. The duchy of Cornwall received all taxes and its impact was most visible at the quarterly coinages held at the designated towns of Liskeard, Lostwithiel, Truro, Helston and Penzance. There the sale of tin blocks from the mines took place after each block had been stamped by duchy officials, the insignia proving payment of coinage duties. For days before the coinage great blocks of tin littered the principal street in each town, often obstructing passers-by but also providing tangible evidence of the county's mineral wealth.

Besides agriculture and mining the other staple industry was fishing, although as the nineteenth century progressed the summer visitations of the fickle pilchards became more erratic. Almost all the small, isolated coves and larger ports on both the north and south coasts were the scene of fisheries, an activity involving entire communities (men, women and children) in the various processes of catching, stacking, salting and curing. Typically the industry revolved around small units of six or seven fishermen, there being no owner–employee relationships; instead the industry ran on a co-operative basis, from the 'huer' on the cliffs watching out for shoals of fish coming close inshore, to the highly skilled women who stacked fish in the cellars prior to their storage in hogsheads for export.[24] According to some writers this form of organisation encouraged individual enterprise among those living in small fishing villages. The inhabitants also found the Church of England to be unsympathetic and avaricious, fish tithes being a frequent cause of tension.[25] Not surprisingly, from the mid eighteenth century onwards more and more of these communities found spiritual satisfaction in Wesleyan Methodism.

In areas such as Mount's Bay, where hundreds of fishermen operated from Marazion, St Michael's Mount, Penzance and Newlyn, the industry ran year long. Both seine and drift nets were widely used; by law the seiners stayed

---

23 Ibid.
24 A first-hand description of this is provided in Wilkie Collins, *Rambles beyond railways: or notes in Cornwall taken a-foot*, London 1851, ch. vii.
25 Rowe, *Cornwall*, ch. vii.

inshore while the drifters worked several miles out to sea, although Cornish fishermen often 'interpreted' regulations to their own satisfaction. This occasionally led to tensions and even political harassment, such as that which occurred in 1791 when a group of drifters operating in Mount's Bay were served with writs by an attorney acting for Sir John St Aubyn. It was alleged they were fishing too close to shore. Curiously, all those selected for this act of vindictiveness (for the fishermen, along with dozens of others, were obeying the local convention on the night in question) had voted for Francis Gregor and Sir William Lemon, not St Aubyn, in the recent 1790 county election. As one of the victims remarked, the incident was 'a most flagrant party matter', although a long-standing struggle over the apportionment of fish tithes was another ingredient in the conflict.[26]

In their unique way the fishermen were small businessmen carrying a heavy capital investment, for the cost of boats, nets, casks and salt meant they were burdened with high overheads. Even a generous government bounty did little to ease their difficulties in those lean years when the fish failed to appear. To guard against this possibility many fishermen were also miners and/or husbandmen – subsistence farmers grinding out a living on the edge of poverty. No wonder tithes were resented, leaving many villages far beyond the social control exerted by the Church of England, and producing a strong-mindedness (encouraged by Methodism) which had ramifications for electoral politics. Nicholas Kendall, candidate for East Cornwall in the 1852 general election, was advised by a friend:

> I have seen our Mevagissey [a south coast fishing village] canvassers today and they all say you must go there some day. The inhabitants are unlike all other people on the face of the earth and many of them think their dignity requires that the Candidates should ask them personally for their votes. I think the place is in general favourably disposed.[27]

Under those circumstances Kendall or any other aspiring MP had little choice if he wanted the voters' support.

For several centuries it was fishermen who were frequently involved in what was euphemistically called 'the trade', the smuggling of brandy, gin and other goods across the English Channel from France. Although conducted covertly, smuggling was regarded tolerantly by the county community who saw little harm in cheating representatives of a distant government at Westminster. Besides, all levels of society benefited: from the aristocracy and gentry downwards almost everyone had links with the smugglers. For many men the dual occupation of fisherman-smuggler was perfectly natural, with the inlets and small ports of Brittany being as familiar to them as the backs of their hands.

---

[26] William Hichens to the Revd H. H. Tremayne, 8 Feb. 1791, CRO, MSS Tremayne T 2343.
[27] Edward Coode, Jr, to Kendall, 28 May 1852, ibid. MSS Kendall KL.

Fishermen, as well as the Cornish people in general, were also the beneficiaries of shipwrecks, because the coastline was one of the great navigational
hazards of the British Isles. Disregard for the law reached its height when
ships loaded with valuable cargoes came ashore. Then, the news travelled
fast: within hours hordes of men and women from inland parishes would flock
to the scene, eager to carry off whatever goods or materials they could drag
from the surf. Defoe said this behaviour revealed the Cornish as 'greedy,
cruel, and eager for prey', and almost a century later the spread of Methodism
had done little to dampen enthusiasm for benefiting from the tragedies of
others. Hence the reply of the man when told by his wife that Wesley had
condemned wrecking. 'Wesley? What do'ee knaw 'bout wreckin'?'[28] Timber,
coal, sailcloth, rope, liquor, clothing, in fact cargoes of almost every type
could ease the daily struggles of the poorer people.

Features of society

There have been many general observations about the characteristics of
Cornish people and society. For example Celia Fiennes, quite naturally concerned with the comfort of her late seventeenth-century travels, felt 'The
people here are very ill guides, and know but little from home, only to some
market town they frequent, but will be very solicitous to know where you goe,
and how farre, and from whence you came, and where is the abode.' George
Worgan was very taken by the women whom he considered 'accomplished',
and who he thought would make excellent wives. He found the Cornish
urbane, hospitable, courteous, and forty years later the novelist Wilkie
Collins agreed, adding, 'The views of the working men are remarkably moderate and sensible.'[29]

However Collins also noted something unusual: the county was one
'where, it must be remembered, a stranger is doubly a stranger, in relation to
provincial sympathies; where the national feeling is almost entirely merged
in the local feeling; where a man speaks of himself as Cornish in much the
same spirit as a Welshman speaks of himself as Welsh'. Three years after
Collins, Walter White found 'a strong spirit of distinct nationality is still
cherished in Cornwall'. For him the Celtic influence was strong and the
people, he found, had 'a habit of thinking for themselves, as you will find by
their shrewd remarks, if you get into talk with them'.[30] Thomas Mills agreed

---

[28] Defoe, A tour, 245; John G. Rule, 'Wrecking and coastal plunder', in Douglas Hay and
others, Albion's fatal tree: crime and society in eighteenth-century England, New York 1975,
185.
[29] Journeys of Celia Fiennes, 261; Worgan, General view of agriculture, p. xi; Collins,
Rambles, 41.
[30] Ibid. 47; White, A Londoner's walk, 294; Thomas H. Mills, A week's wanderings in Cornwall and Devon, London 1863, 31.

with this, finding no servility among the labourers and working men, no obvious deference, and 'a greater seeming of equality among the different classes'.

Others have remarked on slightly different characteristics. Recalling the Cornwall of his childhood before 1914 A. L. Rowse observed the frictions and almost feudal enmities dividing neighbours: 'There never was a greater joke than "One And All" as the Cornish motto, for Cornish people, like all Celts, are notoriously individualist and incapable of co-operating.' On a larger scale there was constant feuding between towns – Redruth and Camborne, Fowey and Lostwithiel. The popular novelist Daphne du Maurier who lived most of her life in the county suggested that 'There is in the Cornish character, smouldering beneath the surface, ever ready to ignite, a fiery independence, a stubborn pride.' In *The making of modern Cornwall* Philip Payton makes a similar point about the eighteenth century: 'Cornwall was still perceived as a rough and lawless county, its tinners and farmers notorious for their parochialism, violence and hostility to outsiders.'[31] In these and other observations the terms 'independence of mind', 'parochialism' and 'strong opinions' constantly recur. Why was this so, and why was there an almost Antipodean egalitarianism?

Independence of mind suggests that in a political context the deference given by tenant-farmer to landlord, tinner-husbandmen to wealthy mine adventurer, fisherman to tithe owner was probably less than in such relationships elsewhere. The ability of the aristocracy and gentry to influence the political behaviour of forty-shilling freeholders, or after 1832 the ten-pound householders, was, as elsewhere, part of a reciprocal relationship. In Cornwall the difference was that that relationship was more open, less restricted, partly because the organisation of agriculture and mining weakened the face-to-face influence of landlords, or threw men of different social classes together as a result of common speculative interests. But this is only a partial explanation.

Too important to be overlooked was the absence of a powerful aristocracy, possibly arising from the stifling influence of the duchy of Cornwall as a landowner.[32] Whatever the reason Bateman found that in 1873 Cornwall ranked behind Essex, Hereford and Middlesex (excluding London) with the lowest percentage of aristocratic landowners, and equal highest in the category of commoners owning more than 10,000 acres, well-known families such as Rashleigh, Basset, Hawkins and Robartes being prominent among them.[33] The comparative weakness of aristocratic landowners may have been inimical to deferential relationships between people of different classes, as the weakness affected much of the population's attitude towards the state,

31 A. L. Rowse, *A Cornish childhood: autobiography of a Cornishman*, new edn, London 1983, 15; du Maurier, *Vanishing Cornwall*, 11; Philip Payton, *The making of modern Cornwall: historical experience and the persistence of 'difference'*, Redruth 1992, 85.
32 Chesher, 'Some Cornish landowners', 9.
33 J. Bateman, *The great landowners of Great Britain and Ireland*, 4th edn, London 1885.

authority and the law. Geographic remoteness plus a small and uninfluential aristocracy meant that they and their gentry allies carried relatively little weight as conduits between Westminster and locality. It followed that there was a certain ambivalence towards authority, a tendency exacerbated by many of Cornwall's major landowners busying themselves with their own commercial affairs which tended to be more wide-ranging than in much of England.

Prior to the eighteenth century the pre-eminent members of the aristocracy were the Grenvilles and the Godolphins, each of the families being absentee landlords. However by the mid eighteenth century their estates were shrinking and their power was usurped by a resident peerage – in eastern Cornwall the Eliots and Edgcumbes, in the west the Boscawens whose viscountcy dated from early in the same century, and Francis Basset, land-, mine- and borough-owner who was created Baron De Dunstanville by Pitt in 1796.[34] As we shall see, during the reign of George III each of these aristocratic families had valuable political interests within Cornwall.

In some ways the gentry were far more cohesive than their counterparts elsewhere. Defoe noticed how their 'estates, connections and interests were concentrated within the county, and its immediate environs'.[35] One explanation for this may be that although there were gradations of rank and possessions, they mixed on more or less equal terms. It was also due to marriage patterns; in most instances choice of partners was limited to other county families or those in neighbouring Devon. Consequently they were united by intricate networks of family relationships. Also, most of these families shared common economic or social interests and these were rarely outside Cornwall. Yet there was no bland uniformity. Long-established families such as the Carews, Vyvyans and Tremaynes clearly carried far more political weight than the Brunes of Padstow or clergymen like the Reverend Robert Walker of St Winnow. The distinction between the two groups provoked periodic tensions after 1800, especially in county politics.

Cornwall's gentry were not rigidly exclusive. Theirs was an open society providing great opportunities for social mobility, because the county experienced its own version of the Industrial Revolution earlier than elsewhere in eighteenth-century England and the possibilities for wealth acquisition were almost unlimited. Shrewd speculation in banking, trade, flour-milling, shipbuilding, mining, smelting, the law and money-lending allowed ambitious families to improve their social position. This was why upward mobility from the middle or lower ranks was far from being exceptional, and could occur relatively quickly. Perhaps the best example is Sir William Lemon, county MP from 1774 until his death fifty years later. Educated at Christ Church, Oxford, then provided with the educational and cultural benefits of the European Grand Tour, he married Jane Buller whose family had monopolised one

34 Namier and Brooke, *House of Commons*, 62.
35 Defoe, *A tour*, 234.

county seat for much of the eighteenth century. Yet Lemon's grandfather began life as a labourer. In three generations the Lemons were transformed into grudgingly respected gentry, the proud possessors of a baronetcy.[36] Even so, this mobility was not free from tensions. Some in Cornish society regarded newcomers like the Lemons as upstarts, especially when by the conventions of the time they over-reached themselves.

Overall the gentry and professional classes played a pivotal role in the county's expanding economic life. Not only did they lend money with an eye to estate enlargement through foreclosure on mortgages; their funds flowed into all kinds of activity besides mining. They were the county's financial movers and shakers, the deal makers and risk takers whose successes led in many cases into electoral politics. There, rewards of a very different kind were on offer.

Below the middle ranks was the great mass of the population – tinners, fishermen, small farmers, labourers – the lower orders for whom life was a continual struggle. But despite the precariousness of their situation, which occasionally drove them to riot or to become involved in smuggling and wrecking, they were hard-working and adaptable. When the expansion of underground tin mining occurred in the western hundreds of Kerrier and Pydar during the eighteenth century, thousands of families moved to the region from eastern agricultural areas. Fifty or more years later many of their descendants sailed off to Canada, the United States of America and South Australia, driven from Cornwall by mining's dramatic decline.

Some of the mining communities and remote fishing villages provided fertile ground for the itinerant preachings of the Wesleys. Charles Wesley visited Cornwall for the first time in 1743 and less than two months later his brother John followed, preaching in the far western parishes of Towednack, Zennor, Morvah, St Just and Sennen – all on the Land's End peninsula, the most isolated corner of the Church of England's Exeter diocese.[37] Wesley's message was warmly received by his audiences who had suffered from years of pastoral deprivation. Remoteness from Exeter and the poverty of many of the livings were only some of the Church's problems, making Wesley's work relatively easy. Notwithstanding these advantages Methodism struggled through a succession of slumps and revivals before becoming the cornerstone of life for many nineteenth-century Cornish middle- and working-class families. Wesleyan Methodists, Primitive Methodists, Bible Christians and other Dissenters eventually swamped the Church of England, especially in West Cornwall as table 1 reveals.

---

[36] The rise of the Lemon family is described by Michael Trinick in 'A new acquisition: a portrait of William Lemon', *Journal of the Royal Institution of Cornwall* n.s. ii, i (1992), 121–7.

[37] John C. Probert, *The sociology of Cornish Methodism* (Cornish Methodist Historical Association, Occasional Publication viii, 1964), 5.

Table 1
Places of worship, West Cornwall, 1851

(Bracketed figures show total worshippers at most numerously attended service)

Division	Church of England	Wesleyan Methodists	Bible Christians
St Austell	18 (1,920)	31 (4,568)	27 (2,531)
Truro	31 (4,634)	59 (10,034)	21 (2,484)
Falmouth	10 (2,312)	13 (3,635)	4 (260)
Helston	21 (2,194)	36 (3,198)	10 (650)
Redruth	19 (2,030)	54 (8,964)	7 (1,350)
Penzance	22 (4,315)	58 (9,628)	16 (1,039)

Sources: P. Hayden, 'Culture, creed and conflict: Methodism and politics in Cornwall, c. 1832–1879', unpubl. PhD diss. Liverpool 1982; *1851 Census of Great Britain: religious worship (England and Wales): reports and tables*, PP 1852–3, lxxxix.

Besides emphasising work, thrift and temperance, virtues dear to the hearts of employers desiring to direct people into the new work rhythms flowing from Cornwall's industrialisation, Methodism encouraged self help and individual improvement. It 'also displayed an egalitarian strand, reflecting the general lack of class consciousness in Cornwall and pursuing a theology which taught compassion, concern for the needy, the equality of men before God, a contempt for riches'.[38] Many Methodists believed their members should remain aloof from political debate but this was a naive hope. By the 1830s Methodism and Liberalism were becoming identified with each other, producing a nexus influential in Cornwall electoral politics throughout most of the nineteenth century.

Parliamentary representation

Late eighteenth-century Cornwall was notorious for its over-representation in the House of Commons. In 1790 the county returned forty-four members to Westminster, two for the county, forty-two for twenty-one small boroughs

---

[38] Payton, *Making of modern Cornwall*, 90.

21

dotted on the coast and countryside from Launceston in the north-east to St Ives in the far west. Several general rules governed county politics at the time and they continued to do so until the First Reform Act, or in one instance even beyond it. The first was the convention that the aristocracy could interfere in borough but not county politics, which was normally the preserve of the gentry. Secondly, the two county members should represent different political interests – Whigs and Tories. Thirdly, there was a constant concern that mining and agriculture, two of the major economic interests, should each have 'their' member. For example from 1806 to 1824 John Tremayne was the agriculturist's choice, Sir William Lemon the spokesperson for the mining interest. After 1850 in West Cornwall this notion of representation of interests sometimes divided the gentry.

Cornwall's twenty-one boroughs could be grouped into five geographic areas. In the north-east Launceston, Newport, Callington, Bossiney and Camelford were spread across the hundreds of East, Lesnewth, Stratton. The ports of Fowey, St Germans, Saltash, East and West Looe were clustered in the south east, Bodmin (the county town), Liskeard and Lostwithiel in the centre of the county. Further west was Cornwall's most notorious constellation of boroughs – Grampound, Mitchell, Tregony, Truro and Penryn – all within a radius of ten miles of each other. Finally, there was Helston and St Ives. Many of these boroughs were thriving centres of commercial activity, for example Truro, Penryn and Fowey were sizeable ports while Helston serviced an important mining district. Others such as Tregony and Bossiney were tiny, decaying villages, but the political affairs of almost all of them were manipulated by patrons. None of the late eighteenth-century Cornish boroughs was open: those who controlled them were either local families or outsiders such as successive dukes of Leeds (Helston), Northumberland (Launceston) or Buckingham (St Mawes).

For ambitious Cornishmen politics therefore held far greater rewards than a mere seat in the House of Lords or Commons. The ownership of boroughs could lead to a baronetcy (Sir Christopher Hawkins) or a peerage (Sir Francis Basset, Baron De Dunstanville) if the patron could deliver his members' votes on critical issues to the government of the day, or if he permitted the government to return known supporters in his seats. In addition, recognition of such service by the government allowed patrons much greater scope for dispensing favours among dozens of eager supplicants. For other patrons whose aims were not so high, 'participation in electoral processes brought recognisable dividends: contacts with the upper classes, the personal and social rewards of political involvement, such as status and recognition, and, not least, a sense of social duty'.[39]

Lastly, there were the voters and their families. Namier, the Porritts and others considered them to be little more than dependent and corrupt

---

[39] O'Gorman, *Voters, patrons and parties*, 17.

appendages to the electoral system, manipulated by patrons, or in the case of the rarely contested county, mere onlookers.[40] Few, if any, had opinions about the issues of the day. Instead they obeyed the rules of what Moore has referred to as the 'politics of deference'. However in recent years much contrary evidence has surfaced elsewhere in England, exposing not only the reciprocity inherent in the exercising of deference or influence, but the deep and continuing interest which people had in expressing their opinions on local or national questions. Many Cornishmen were stirred by the principles underlying Christopher Wyvill's Association movement. Some of the most prominent among them voted for Pitt's 1783 and 1785 proposals for parliamentary reform.[41] Meetings and petitions testified to the interest which was never far below the surface, for there was ongoing concern about borough corruption as well as the county's infamous over-endowment with seats. The propriety of the slave trade, various disabilities imposed on the growing number of Dissenters, Catholic emancipation, parliamentary reform and agricultural protection stirred the minds of many voters and non-voters.

Long before 1832 issues were important in Cornwall electoral politics because independent minded people from all classes of society refused to be deterred from expressing their view-points. This was the outcome of economic, social and cultural forces which combined to produce a political milieu rather different from much of eastern and northern England. John Phillips's 'vibrant political nation' certainly included unreformed Cornwall, long condemned as the apotheosis of a corrupt and unbalanced electoral system. It was far from being so, and after 1832 there was an intensification of trends identifiable well before that so-called turning point in electoral politics.

---

40 Sir Lewis Namier, *The structure of politics at the accession of George III*, 2nd edn, London 1957; Porritt and Porritt, *Unreformed House of Commons*.
41 Included among them was Christopher Hawkins whose borough-mongering career is described in ch. 3.

2

County Politics and Parliamentary Reform

The 1790 county election

After the general election of 1790 forty-one years elapsed before there was another contested election for Cornwall's two county seats. During that period the representation changed three times without a contest: in 1806 when Francis Gregor retired after sixteen years in the House of Commons; in 1825 when Sir Richard Vyvyan replaced the recently deceased and highly respected Sir William Lemon who was first elected for the county in 1774; and 1826, the occasion of Edward Pendarves's election after John Tremayne retired shortly before the poll. Throughout these years Cornwall was represented by a Whig and a Tory or Independent, usually one member having interests in the west of the county where mining predominated, the other in the agricultural east. Ostensibly the pattern of representation seemed little different from the English norm: contests were rarities, the county gentlemen, or at least a select group among them met informally to arbitrate on claims for the seats, and according to Oldfield the county was 'as independent as any in England'.[1]

Yet this apparent stability was deceptive, for tensions evident in the 1780s were influential in the 1790 county election, and again in 1826. They were generated by the political activities of a small group of lesser gentry, some of whom, as supporters of Christopher Wyvill and Pitt, in January 1783 called a private meeting in Truro to express their support for parliamentary reform. Among the activists were Francis Gregor who in 1790 became a county MP, Christopher Hawkins, later a notorious borough-monger, and Robert Gwatkin who provided a thread of continuity between this period and the county's reform movement emerging in the early nineteenth century.[2] Others linked to this late eighteenth-century group included Jeremiah Trist, his fellow clergyman Robert Walker (another county reformer) and the prominent Veryan farmer John Penhallow Peters. Most agreed upon the necessity for Catholic emancipation, relief for dissenters and parliamentary reform, and all supported Gregor in the 1790 county election.[3] Later they were

---

1   Thorne, *House of Commons*, I: *Introductory survey*, 40.
2   Courtney, *Parliamentary representation*, p. xxii.
3   The relationships are explained in Christine North, 'The Trists of Veryan', *Journal of the Royal Institution of Cornwall* n.s. viii (1980), 191–223. Walker and Peters were among the county reformers' leading spokesmen until 1832.

divided by their political opinions (Gregor became the anti-reformers' most articulate opponent), but in 1790 their common motivation in the county election was to oppose the machinations of Sir Francis Basset and support Pitt.

Gregor's success and Pendarves's almost expense-free replacement of Tremayne in 1826 point to several hitherto unnoticed characteristics of Cornwall county politics. One was the occasional appearance of deep divisions among the country gentlemen who managed the county representation. In 1790, and again in 1826, it was the lesser gentry who challenged the hegemony of their wealthier counterparts, particularly their right to decide who would be the knights of the shire. The 'three baronets', Basset (Lord De Dunstanville), Sir John Molesworth and Sir John St Aubyn were their initial targets; in 1826 they clashed with De Dunstanville and his wealthy gentry allies. Each general election also had its ideological dimension: support for Pitt and his policies and later a successful move to have Cornwall represented by a Whig (Pendarves) and a Tory (Vyvyan or Tremayne).

Another peculiarity arising from the above was the occasional clash of several powerful groups: the aristocracy whose territorial influence could never be discounted; the wealthy country gentlemen whose status and prestige allowed them a prominent role in county politics; and the lesser gentry, some of them comparative newcomers to the ranks of the county families, who played an influential part not only in 1790 and 1826 but also earlier in 1774 when Sir William Lemon defeated the representatives of the old interest.[4] Finally, in over-represented Cornwall with its forty-four MPs before 1832 there was always an informal understanding that members of the local aristocracy who were entangled in borough-mongering should refrain from interfering in county affairs. When Basset ignored this in 1790 he was quickly put in his place. A parallel in 1825–6 may have been his and the first earl of Falmouth's provocative backing of the ultra-Tory Vyvyan and Tremayne, for both Basset and Falmouth had borough interests. The significance of these common links is that they point to the development of popular politics in Cornwall.

The 1790 British general election was of little apparent consequence, there being no major alterations in the numerical strength of the various parliamentary groupings dominated by Prime Minister William Pitt. Cornwall's county election was very different, for it became a trial of strength among various elements within the gentry. The sitting members, Sir William Lemon and Molesworth, claimed to be typically independent country gentlemen in their Westminster behaviour. In fact they were no such thing. Both were Foxites, causing some anguish in a county which preferred at least one of its members to be a supporter of the administration. More importantly, in the

---

4 From 1714 until 1772 the county representation rotated among four families, the Carews, St Aubyns, Molesworths and Bullers. Through his marriage ties to the Bullers, Lemon was able to break the monopoly.

context of Cornwall politics Molesworth's 'independence' was open to question. At the time of his election in 1784 he was widely regarded as being Basset's man, that is someone whose success was the result of manipulation by Basset. The latter thought this 'ridiculous' and 'absurd', but added that his estates gave him as much right to take part in the election 'as any of the greatest and proudest of my opponents'.[5] The trouble was that in the same election Basset openly ran candidates in five boroughs, two at Truro, Tregony, Mitchell and Penryn, one at Fowey, thereby challenging the borough empires of Lords Falmouth and Mt Edgcumbe.

As mentioned previously one of the accepted conventions of local electoral politics was that borough-mongers did not take a prominent part in county elections. Basset contemptuously disregarded this, with serious consequences. By the end of 1784, with the general election out of the way, Philip Rashleigh noted, 'This county is so much distracted with Party, that a situation among the Tartars would not be liable to such Convulsions. Even our Justices at their Sessions cannot give their Opinions Calmly.'[6] It seemed obvious to many people that Molesworth would face a contest at the next general election unless he severed his political links with the egotistical Basset.

The 1790 contest effectively began in August 1789 when Francis Gregor commenced canvassing in West Cornwall, prior to a county meeting to discuss the representation. Gregor was a declared Pittite. He took advantage of his wife's recent large inheritance to fund an expensive campaign (it eventually cost him more than £20,000), found allies in the Eliots of St Germans and Lord Falmouth who resented Basset's meddling, and enjoyed the tacit co-operation of Lemon whom everyone agreed was above the contest.[7] According to Basset, Gregor's weakness was his modest social stature: 'His vanity has, however, on this occasion, betrayed him beyond his usual prudence, and induced him to aspire to a station for which his connections and situation in life evidently never intended him.'[8] Gregor ignored the slur.

Meanwhile Molesworth's indignant reaction to the canvass was to retire immediately from the impending contest, whereupon Basset had no hesitation in supporting the candidacy of another cousin, Sir John St Aubyn. Like Molesworth his previous election for Truro and later Penryn on the Basset interest in 1784 conveyed the impression that he would not be his own man at Westminster. A contemporary pamphleteer correctly observed:

5   Basset to Reginald Pole Carew, 12 Jan. 1784, MSS Carew Pole CC/J/14.
6   Rashleigh to Pole Carew, 11 Oct. 1784, ibid.
7   Memoirs of Loveday Sarah Gregor (1851), CRO, MSS Gregor, G 1952, 195–205.
8   'A letter to the free and independent electors of the county of Cornwall' from 'A Cornish Man' (almost certainly Basset), St Aubyn papers, St Michael's Mount, Marazion.

there are Reasons to conclude from Experience, if he be elected, that as he owes his principal support in this Contest to his Patron at Penryn, he must, as before act under the direction of that Patron; and the Freeholders in this County, hitherto independent, may in future be disgraced by submitting to the Authority of a Dictator in the Choice of their Representative.[9]

Other questions besides personalities intruded. For example, there was the prospect of Gregor's successful candidacy returning the county to the preferred *status quo* of members' loyalties being divided between the administration and its opponents.

Table 2
General election results, West Cornwall, 1790

Parish	Lemon	St Aubyn	Gregor
Newlyn in Paul	37	3	34
St Ives	42	21	22
Paul	24	6	19
Penzance	54	33	23
Madron	12	7	6
Marazion	14	12	2
Mousehole	12	4	8
Totals	195	86	114

In the pamphlet warfare much was made by St Aubyn's friends of Pitt's allegedly ruinous taxation policies ('Besides from our Windows he block'd up the Day' and 'For he means to tax our Tin, Fish and Copper').[10] Furthermore, religious issues intruded. From October 1789 there was an active committee composed of delegates from the many congregations of Cornwall Dissenters which worked hard for the repeal of the Test and Corporation Acts. Dissenters were advised to question all candidates about their views on civil and religious liberties and no doubt did so during the extensive canvassing. Gregor's responses are unknown, but ultimately he was the beneficiary of the Methodist vote for Wesley himself publicly recommended him.[11] Because he went to great lengths to identify with the interest of the miners and fishermen Gregor was referred to in some quarters as a tinner, and also earned the appellation of 'the fishermen's friend'. No doubt this helped his cause in western Cornwall where the Basset–St Aubyn interests were strongest.

When the voting concluded the final result was Lemon 2,250 votes, Gregor 1,270, St Aubyn 1,136, an outcome in line with canvassing figures.[12]

9   CRO, MSS Carlyon CN 3211/4.
10 Handbill, 'The craft-splitter; or the minister's man', St Aubyn papers.
11 Thomas Shaw, *A history of Cornish Methodism*, Truro 1967, 29.
12 Canvassing notes 1790, MSS Carew Pole CO/CC/9.

As for Gregor winning votes in fishing villages and parishes, table 2 high-lights the point.[13] All the parishes were in western Cornwall where St Aubyn was well-known. However Gregor canvassed in person and sympathised with fishermen's grievances while St Aubyn, MP for Penryn, apparently remained in London leaving agents to canvass for him. Overall in the western hundred of Kerrier in which these parishes and villages were to be found, St Aubyn outpolled Gregor by 259 votes to 175, but the former would have expected his margin to have been far greater. Probably it was this disappointment which in February 1791 prompted St Aubyn to have writs served on ten fishermen who were breaking the law but not the local and accepted conven-tion, by fishing too close to shore in Mounts Bay. Each of the men had voted for Lemon and Gregor. Those St Aubyn supporters fishing in the same waters were left in peace.[14]

Ultimately though it was superior canvassing which helped Gregor most, along with the invaluable support of many of the lesser gentry. Neither they nor many freeholders could stomach Basset's naked ambition: one writer con-temptuously labelled him 'a shallow, babbling rivulet'. 'The truth is', he added, 'that the haughtiness of his Temper keeps pace with his Ambition, and his want of Judgement is equal to both.'[15] The open collaboration between the three baronets added to the disenchantment as did the obvious sympathy of St Aubyn and Basset for Fox and the prince of Wales, who, for various reasons including heavy-handed interference in several boroughs, was not the most popular of the dukes of Cornwall. St Aubyn's defeat was more than a rebuff for Basset. It was a reassertion of the principle of separation between county and borough electoral politics, the necessity to have one member voting with the government of the day, and a reminder of the usually latent strength of the lesser gentry.

Change in county politics

Having indulged in more than a little acrimony among themselves in 1789–90, the gentry reunited and remained so for more than a decade. In 1806 when Francis Gregor learned his popularity was waning he was at the same time becoming prone to increasingly severe attacks of gout. He there-fore decided to retire, and John Tremayne of Heligan was the unanimous choice as his replacement.[16] Unlike his predecessor Tremayne was far more independent in his politics, one outcome being that until 1824 the county members divided their support between government and opposition. Canon

13 Pollbook, CRO, MSS Pendarves PD 208.
14 William Hichens to Revd H. H. Tremayne, 8 Feb. 1791, MSS Tremayne T 2343.
15 Address to Freeholders, March (?) 1790, MSS Carlyon CN 3211/5.
16 The retirement was propitious for the general belief was that Gregor would be defeated if he recontested his seat.

Rogers, a prominent member of the Cornish gentry once remarked of Lemon, 'I have long ceased to be surprised at any opposition vote of Sir W. Lemon; he is just as systematic an opposer of the measures of government whether right or wrong, as the most devoted tool of administration is in favour of them.'[17] Lemon's death in December 1824 and the ensuing machinations to replace him brought to the fore a deep ideological split within the gentry.

Even before Lemon's death rumours were afoot that the youthful Sir Richard Vyvyan and Edward Pendarves, a well-known reformer, were contemplating contesting the county at the next general election.[18] As soon as the vacancy occurred both confirmed their intentions, Vyvyan's candidacy causing concern in some quarters about a Tory takeover of county representatives. These fears soon materialised when Pendarves changed his mind, deciding to conserve his financial resources for the forthcoming general election. Vyvyan and Tremayne knew this Tory hegemony would be highly unpopular with the Cornish Whigs for it was a blatant attempt to return to the 'Old Monopoly' of the eighteenth century. Furthermore, when the Pendarves challenge materialised Tremayne decided his future course of action would be to imitate his late father-in-law's position in 1790. On the grounds of long and faithful service to the county (although he was also worried about the expense) he would claim to be above the contest, refusing to canvass and leaving the politicking to others. Unfortunately his apparent diffidence about his future plus the collapse of canvassing arrangements (for example Vyvyan's friends actively sought the second votes of Tremayne's plumpers) left him vulnerable, forcing him to withdraw after the nomination day.[19] So eighteen months canvassing, public debate and unprecedented press coverage by the two county newspapers, the *West Briton* and the *Royal Cornwall Gazette*, ended in a surprising victory for Pendarves.

As suggested earlier there were similarities between this election and 1790. For example, like Gregor before him Pendarves was judged to be socially unfit for the high office he sought. De Dunstanville opposed him 'not only on political grounds but because I think he has no pretensions whatever to the distinguished place which he wishes to fill'.[20] It was an opinion shared by others and was symptomatic of another hallmark of 1790, a deep split in the county gentry. Those of greater wealth and political prominence rallied in support of Vyvyan and/or Tremayne. Pendarves's allies were of a quite different calibre although family relationships brought the influential Rashleighs of Menabilly into his camp. The Lemon–Tremayne parallel proved to be spurious because one or two Tories with long memories recalled that

---

17 Canon Rogers to William Rashleigh, 24 Jan. 1820, CRO, MSS Rashleigh R 5313.
18 See W. B. Elvins, 'The reform movement and county politics in Cornwall 1809–1852', unpubl. MA diss. Birmingham 1959, ch. iv.
19 *West Briton*, 16 June 1826, 3.
20 De Dunstanville to Pole Carew, 13 Sept. 1825, MSS Carew Pole CC/N/58.

Lemon did canvass personally in 1790, at the same time offering covert assistance to Francis Gregor.

What is indisputable is that the events of 1825–6 were a watershed in county politics, breaking the succession of gentry manipulations, of compromises and representation by imposition. These methods became increasingly unpopular with many Cornishmen, because of the remarkable activism of a gentry group who provoked a greatly heightened level of political awareness and participation among the rural middle classes. As 1826 showed, the eventual product was the election of one of the most prominent reformers and the total frustration of the county's political wire-pullers – most of whom were Tories. The county election also thrust issues into prominence in a way never seen before, transforming public debate. How then did this happen?

Emergence of the parliamentary reformers

The origins may well lie in the late eighteenth-century interest in reform sparked by Christopher Wyvill's Association movement. Among Wyvill's Cornish supporters were the Reverend Robert Walker (1754–1834), vicar of St Winnow near Lostwithiel, and Robert Gwatkin (1757–1843), a small landowner whose seat, Killiow, was close to Truro.[21] Both turned their backs on Pitt in the 1790s after voting for Gregor, and both became involved in the county reform movement beginning in 1805.

Neither Walker nor John Colman Rashleigh (1772–1845) had played a conspicuous role in county political life before 1805, the year in which peculation in the Admiralty sparked a public outcry. In Cornwall as elsewhere, parliamentary discussion of the degree to which Lord Melville, Treasurer of the Navy, was aware of the fraud prompted a group of magistrates, all of them minor gentry, to demand that the sheriff summon a county meeting. Most of the requisitioners merely wished to express indignation at the recent exposures, making it a typically 'Country *versus* Court' assembly, but among the magistrates were Trist and Gwatkin. The former was now a staunch Tory but Gwatkin, a reformer, may have been responsible for drawing in Walker and Rashleigh, encouraging their help in the drafting of the petition as well as a motion demanding Melville's impeachment.[22]

Rashleigh was related to one of Cornwall's best-known landed families, being a cousin of William Rashleigh of Menabilly, the independent MP for Fowey from 1812 to 1818. Much of his early life was spent outside Cornwall. After attending Trinity College, Cambridge, Rashleigh led a rather feckless life until he was stirred by the political questions being raised by the French Revolution. He wrote:

---

21 The biographical details are from Elvins, 'Reform movement'.
22 *Royal Cornwall Gazette*, 20 May 1805, 1.

I, though never at any time a Republican enlisted myself into the ranks of the popular party which though never, that I know, meditating the abolition of monarchical government or establishing an actual equality – certainly were more democratic in their leanings than even the most liberal of Whigs could be said to be.[23]

Soon political questions dominated his life; he joined a debating society and the Society of Friends of the People, a Whig group favouring temperate rather than radical reform, though it had many radical members. Later he drifted into the often conflicting political orbits of Major Cartwright (whom he considered 'a perfect fanatick in politics') and Sir Francis Burdett, apparently remaining in touch with both until their deaths. Cartwright was for many years a neighbour of Rashleigh's brother-in-law, Thomas Holt White of Enfield, Middlesex, and it was through White's involvement that Rashleigh was drawn into assisting Burdett in his campaign for a Middlesex seat in 1802.[24] It should be added that Holt White was a founding member of the Friends of the People and remained a dedicated reformer thereafter. Of Walker we know little, except that he was an innovative farmer and shared the reforming opinions of his contemporary, Gwatkin.

This then was the background to Colman Rashleigh's political début at the county meeting of 1805. He and Walker argued that Lord Melville should be impeached – that he should be answerable to the Commons, the people's representatives. Many Tories present were aghast at this, one unwittingly aiding the case by angrily exclaiming:

The people of this County should be the last to complain of violation of the Acts of Parliament. There is little else to be heard of in Cornwall but the breaking of acts, defrauding the revenue, and people cheating their next door neighbours. Surely the House of Commons knew what they were about better than half-a-dozen gentlemen assembled at the Fag-end of the Kingdom?[25]

This was hardly calculated to bring a chorus of approval from the listening freeholders and Rashleigh's impeachment motion, supported by Walker, was passed with near unanimity. Both men showed that they were willing to give the lead on contentious public issues. Their outspoken criticisms heralded the birth in Cornwall of an opposition party whose existence was confirmed four years later.

Once again it was a national scandal, this time over the sale of commissions by the duke of York's mistress, which aroused the country.[26] Many

23 CRO, Sir John Colman Rashleigh, 'Memoirs of Sir Coleman Rashleigh Bt: in four parts, (1772–1847)' (typescript), 1, 39.

24 Rashleigh's correspondence with Thomas Holt White may be found in the Gilbert White Museum, Selborne, MSS Holt White, 302–19.

25 *Royal Cornwall Gazette*, 1 June 1805, 3.

26 The Cornish reaction to the scandal and the emergence of the reformers in county politics may be found in Elvins, 'Reform movement', ch. ii.

believed that through the powerful borough patrons the king's ministers were controlling debate in the House of Commons. Therefore the crucial question of the representational system moved to the forefront of public discussion. Such was the case in Cornwall where, to the consternation of the Tories, for the first time since 1782 a group of reformers requested a county meeting. Heading them were Rashleigh, Walker and Gwatkin, all men of relatively small property, but nevertheless gentry and magistrates.[27]

Also among the signatories were John Trevanion, Edward Stackhouse, Henry Peter, Nicholas Kendall, William Hocker and several other reformers. Most of the group were under forty in 1809, lived within a radius of fifteen miles of each other in central southern Cornwall, were of similar economic and social status to Rashleigh, and had been university-educated. The same could be said of Peter's sons William and Robert, and the Reverend Darrell Stephens, who also took a prominent part in the reform movement during the next twenty years.[28]

From one point of view the 1809 meeting was similar to that of four years earlier, because there was public conflict between Tories and Whigs over the petition to be sent from Cornwall. There were also important differences, notably the Tories' preparedness for opposition at the meeting. In fact one aristocrat boasted that it was 'intended to put down for ever the factious spirit which had begun to show itself in Cornwall'.[29] Another difference was in the wording of the petition, which naturally enough reflected the concerns of the originators. According to them corruption within departments of state could be attributed to 'the defective state of the representation', so reform was the only solution to such abuses. Moreover, they claimed the state of the public mind demanded constitutional reform.[30] Led brilliantly by Rashleigh who used the scandal as an opening to present his arguments for moderate reform and to highlight the evils of the corrupt borough system, with suitable Cornish examples, the reformers had the best of a debate lasting almost five hours. Unfortunately for the Tories De Dunstanville, one of their leaders, made a poor and rambling speech during the course of which he disparaged many of his audience. Speaking of the people's rights at the time of Magna Carta he asserted that 'the ancestors of the greater part of those who hear me, were probably at that time, slaves attached to the soil and possessed of no rights or privileges'.[31] The reformers and many freeholders present did not forget this, and it widened the growing political rift in the county.

Writing much later Colman Rashleigh looked back to this county meeting in May 1809 as a political landmark:

[27] Gwatkin's appearances among the reformers were spasmodic in later years. However he also openly supported the anti-Boscawen reform party in Truro in the 1830s.
[28] William Peter was MP for Bodmin from 1832 to 1835.
[29] 'Memoirs of Coleman Rashleigh', pt ii, 37–8.
[30] *Royal Cornwall Gazette*, 20 May 1809.
[31] Ibid. 2.

The meeting laid the foundation of those unremitting and systematic exertions of the popular party in Cornwall through good and evil report and in the teeth of nearly the whole aristocratic interest and the most unscrupulous use of a prostitute press which after twenty one years struggle were crowned by complete success.[32]

He was right, for this new political party remained a cohesive force until the First Reform Act. What Rashleigh failed to mention was that from 1809 onwards he became the acknowledged leader and foremost spokesman of the reformers. What then were the grounds upon which he and his supporters based their arguments?

Between 1809 and 1832 Rashleigh, Walker and later William Peter were the principal speakers at a succession of county meetings. In addition Rashleigh rehearsed his major arguments in letters to his brother-in-law Holt White, so there is no shortage of evidence about their ideas. Among the clearest of them was one, first elaborated in the 1790s by the Society for Constitutional Information and the Friends of the People (FOP), that the existing borough system was grossly defective. The latter organisation went to great lengths to show that through the power of nomination and influence 154 individuals returned 307 Members of the House of Commons. Because of this degree of control by borough patrons Rashleigh, among others, claimed that political power was in the hands of an oligarchy. It was a theme he developed in 1809, at another county meeting in 1811, and frequently in the years that followed. He contended

that by the limitations and distribution of the elective franchise the people are neither fully nor fairly represented: that from the description of those communities which possess the power of returning a majority of the House of Commons; from the nature of the Influence exercised over them in elections and nominations: from the degree of weight which they possess, and from the lands in which that weight in truth rests 1st the people are not only not adequately represented, but not represented at all: their share in the public voice being entirely countervailed and stifled . . . by an oligarchy; by a corrupt oligarchy: the number of patrons etc being so few as to make it an oligarchy.[33]

Like FOP, Rashleigh, Walker and other reformers frequently distinguished between legitimate and illegitimate aristocratic influence, the latter arising from fear and misuse of the power of wealth which ultimately contributed to the unrepresentative nature of the Commons. Conversely, legitimate influence should be preserved and vindicated.[34] An anonymous contributor to the *Gazette* in 1809 (probably Rashleigh) wrote:

[32] 'Memoirs of Coleman Rashleigh', pt ii, 37–8.
[33] J. C. Rashleigh to T. Holt White, [1819?], MSS Holt White, 316.
[34] Christopher Wyvill, *Political papers chiefly representing the attempt of the county of York, and other considerable districts to effect a reformation of the parliament of Great Britain*, York 1794, iii. 231–2.

I will allow . . . that besides the representation, the influence of large properties *will have* – in the nature of things *must have* great weight. The possessor of
large property whether Peer or Commoner [who uses his influence wisely] . . .
deserves to have great weight . . . . But if he makes use of the powers of large
property, to purchase that elective franchise of others, for the purposes of personal ambition or family aggrandisement, he must not be allowed to plead this
as a natural or constitutional influence of property.[35]

Elimination of rule by oligarchy, and illegitimate aristocratic influence,
shorter parliaments (without commitment to a specific length) and electoral
redistribution to eradicate some of the more gross anomalies, were the
reformers' chief concerns. Economical reform was far too mild, while Rashleigh believed Cartwright's radicalism, resting on the triad of annual parliaments, secret ballot and universal suffrage, was highly dangerous.[36]

In terms of ideology it was parliamentary Radicals like Burdett and
Thomas Brand with whom the Cornish reformers were most compatible.
They applauded Brand's motions for reform in May 1810 and 1812. Similarly,
in June 1811 when the Friends of Reform met at the Freemasons' Tavern in
London, fourteen Cornishmen attended, Rashleigh, Walker, Gwatkin, Trevanion and Stackhouse prominent among them. Major Cartwright was
present too, not because he hoped such a gathering would agree to his radical
programme first published in 1776, but because he was currently absorbed in
promoting a reform party in parliament. With Burdett and Brand also in
attendance the meeting argued that the House of Commons did not speak
the sense of the nation and that reform of the House was as essential to the
independence of the crown as it was to the liberties of the people.[37] Later
Rashleigh and Stackhouse joined Cartwright's Hampden Club, eager to
support him, Burdett and others in their endeavours to promote reform.[38]

However this did not mean that the Cornish tail was being wagged by the
Westminster dog. Between 1812 and 1815, while Cartwright and Burdett
compromised on a petitioning campaign embracing equal electoral districts,
annual parliaments and the vote for all those subject to direct taxation, Rashleigh and his friends continued to attack 'oligarchy', corruption and electoral
abuses, as well as unreservedly supporting Catholic emancipation and repeal
of the Test and Corporation Acts. By contrast with the insipid Whiggery of
many in parliament Rashleigh promoted a far more vigorous ideology,
although he never flirted with extreme radicalism. So in 1815 when Burdett
identified himself with the advocates of universal suffrage, he wrote, 'and as
to his [Burdett's] opinions on reform . . . they are wild, crude and untenable;
nor will it do for us to have anything to do with him. We must look elsewhere

---

[35] *Royal Cornwall Gazette*, 3 June 1809, 3.
[36] N. C. Miller, 'John Cartwright and radical parliamentary reform, 1808–1819', *English Historical Review* lxxxiii (1968), 707.
[37] *West Briton*, 21 June 1811, 1, 4.
[38] 'List of Members of the Hampden Club 1812', MSS Holt White, 455.

for a leader'.[39] Three years later, following the general election of 1818, Rashleigh reiterated these comments, pinning his hopes on George Tierney (a former member of FOP) leading the struggle in the House of Commons.[40] By this time too he was thoroughly disenchanted by the 'radicalism' of the Hampden Club.[41] Yet, though occasionally Rashleigh and his friends were heartened by events at Westminster, more often the parliamentary Whigs' indecisiveness forced them along their own path. They never wavered in their determination to encourage popular support for their principles. At the same time, the extremism of Henry Hunt and William Cobbett held no attraction for a gentry group who hoped above all else that the Westminster Whigs would stop vacillating and put themselves at the head of a campaign for reform.

In spite of their fixity of principles Cornwall's reformers were willing to adapt to changing circumstances. Thus in 1813, as will be seen presently, they took advantage of an acrimonious debate within the county on religious questions, attending and speaking at a county meeting called by the Tories. One year earlier when Sir William Lemon and his colleague John Tremayne (who represented the county's leading Tories) were re-elected unopposed, the reformers used the proceedings on election day to embarrass Tremayne and forcefully present their arguments for reform.[42] Then, from 1815 to 1822 they initiated a series of meetings on the property tax, government economy and retrenchment, economic distress, the assassination attempt on the Prince Regent, Peterloo, the Queen Caroline affair and reductions in tithes and rents. At these gatherings the reformers generally addressed themselves to the topic of the day before offering reform as the ultimate solution to most grievances, particularly those which weighed so heavily upon agriculturalists. During the comparative economic prosperity of the mid twenties the only public forums at which reformers appeared and spoke were the county by-election of 1825, the general election one year later and various town anti-slavery meetings. Then the crisis over Catholic emancipation in December–January 1828–9 revitalised them; between 1830 and the end of 1831 they called several county meetings, whipping up popular feelings and excitement as their long-awaited goal drew closer.

Unwavering adherence to the moderate reform espoused by FOP in 1793, skilful utilisation of the corruption and anomalies in Cornish borough politics, unity and powerful leadership, were the hallmarks of the Cornish reformers. Colman Rashleigh led by example, usually making the most telling speech at any meeting he attended, and tirelessly demonstrating how unrepresentative was the existing constitutional system. He often employed historical precedents to bolster his arguments, especially an elaborate version of

[39] Rashleigh to Holt White, 2 Apr. 1815, ibid. 310.
[40] 15 Aug. 1818, ibid. 314.
[41] 25 Jan. 1817, ibid. 312.
[42] *West Briton*, 23 Oct. 1812, 4.

the American catchcry 'No Taxation Without Representation', but always he, Walker, William Peter and others fell back on the Whig ideals of the early 1790s. These became their creed, and in a county so rife with electoral corruption it was understandable that many clear-thinking men among the small town and rural middle ranks found it attractive. How then did the gentry reformers build up a widely supported movement?

From December 1812 until late in January 1813 the Cornish press was preoccupied with an often emotional debate over Catholic emancipation. So determined were the principal Tories to resist a relief act that they called a county meeting, one of the very few times they were to do so between 1805 and 1832. Colman Rashleigh and the reformers attended in force. More importantly, they urged many non-freeholders to journey to Bodmin to judge the issue for themselves. During the meeting the prominent Tory solicitor Charles Rashleigh (Colman's cousin) explained that while riding into Bodmin he had met one of his tenants, the captain of a tin mine. Rashleigh questioned him about why he was attending when not a freeholder. The man replied that Colman Rashleigh had ordered him to be present. Charles Rashleigh triumphantly crowed amid the mounting uproar, 'how was it to be supposed that such persons could be masters of the subject; the idea of a captain of a tin mine, followed by his labourers, coming forward to vote for Catholic emancipation, was absurd in the extreme'.[43] In reply his cousin contended that any person who paid the county rate should be eligible to attend, and that 'the unsophisticated understanding of the tinners would lead them to as safe political conclusion as the understanding of any person present'.[44] The meeting quickly bogged down on this point, but like the landmark of 1809 this was a turning-point for the reformers. Thereafter they began a protracted and finally successful campaign to open county meetings to freeholders *and* inhabitants.

The elimination of attendance restrictions at the largest public forums was one of several tactics used by the reformers in order to broaden their support. They realised such a step was essential if they were to maintain credibility and continue to attract large audiences to their meetings. Consequently they shrewdly developed two other lines of attack which complemented the first. In 1810, frustrated by the evident and unabashed Toryism of Cornwall's single newspaper, the *Royal Cornwall Gazette*, they established the rival *West Briton*, Edward Budd, a reformer and Wesleyan lay preacher, becoming the editor.[45] The other tactic was to enlarge their support by establishing strong ties with an influential but hitherto mute segment of the population – the yeomen and tenant farmers. By publicly sympathising with their post-war grievances and proposing remedies they forged an alliance which was instrumental in electing Edward Pendarves as a county member in 1826.

---

43 Ibid. 29 Jan. 1813, 2.
44 Ibid.
45 Elvins, 'Reform movement', ch. ii, pp. 1–7.

Within a year of the first public arguments about attendance restrictions at county meetings, the issue, like reform, clearly divided Cornish Tories and Whigs. In June 1814 the lord lieutenant, Earl Mount Edgcumbe, the other Cornish peers, De Dunstanville, Falmouth and Eliot, as well as Reginald Pole Carew, William Rashleigh, Francis Gregor and several more well-known Tories headed a requisition for a county meeting to address the Prince Regent on the restoration of peace with France. Only 'Noblemen, Gentlemen, Clergy and other Freeholders' were invited to attend, a provocative step as far as the reformers were concerned.[46] They immediately applied to the sheriff, Rose Price, a one-time reformer, for a counter-meeting including *inhabitants* of Cornwall. He refused. So Rashleigh and his allies, after first seeking legal opinion, decided to summon the meeting on the basis of their authority as magistrates. Thus two meetings took place, on 11 and 16 July, each group re-emphasising its previous stand. The Tories quoted precedent in their defence; for at least two centuries they said, meetings had been restricted to freehold-ers. To that Trevanion, Rashleigh and Walker replied that no legal usage or statute could be quoted to defend the *status quo*, therefore custom should be ignored.[47] They did that with a vengeance in the years ahead, and judging by press reports their action was popular with non-freeholders.

Having established the precedent in 1814 of calling meetings on their authority as magistrates if the sheriff refused a request, and of inviting free-holders and inhabitants, the reformers used this to their benefit. In February 1817, following the Spa Field riots and opposition to a meeting from the Tory sheriff W. A. Harris, they nevertheless proceeded, Colman Rashleigh outlin-ing the direct connection as he saw it between recurring economic distress, the suspension of Habeas Corpus and the evils of the 'rotten borough' system.[48] The same procedure was followed for a county meeting in 1819 to recommend an inquiry into Peterloo, and again in February 1821 when, under the pretext of demanding the restoration of Queen Caroline's name to the liturgy, the reformers petitioned for 'a rigid system of economy and retrenchment in every branch of the public expenditure, a full enquiry into the present distress especially of the agricultural interest, and an immediate consideration of the state of the representation'.[49] Parliamentary reform pre-occupied most speakers and thereafter it was always raised before freeholders and inhabitants at county meetings, regardless of the ostensible purpose.

By the early 1820s the Cornish reformers had made their point. Through legally sidestepping the sheriff's authority if he rejected a requisition, they could assemble whenever the need arose. More importantly, by insisting upon the admission of freeholders and inhabitants they not only enlarged the audience to whom they could explain their principles, but also earned the

---

[46] *West Briton*, 15 July 1814, 1.
[47] Ibid. 12 Aug. 1814, 1.
[48] Ibid. 7 Mar. 1817, 1; 14 Mar. 1817, 1, 4.
[49] Ibid. 23 Mar. 1821.

gratitude and support of those previously excluded. In turn many of the tenant farmers who were now drawn into political debates played an active rather than a merely passive role. This is illustrated by the county meeting of April 1822, for the requisition was signed, not by the principal Tories or Whig magistrates, but by nearly 500 freeholders and leaseholders who wished to consider ways of relieving distress among farmers and 'to take into consideration the defective and unequal state of the Representation of the people to which the burthens and privations under which they suffer are principally to be attributed'.[50] In fact the farmers, having been encouraged to become political activists, were now prepared to proceed with or without the reformers.

The same meeting underlined another salient feature of county politics – the reluctance of the Tory magnates to offer political leadership other than at elections. Colman Rashleigh pointedly drew attention to this when, during the course of his speech, he observed that the absence of the reformers' opponents

> will be deeply felt and long remembered. The landed Aristocracy were the natural leaders of the People. When the Yeomanry and the country were breaking down under the burthens, how were the people to act when those who from their stations should lead them, deserted them in their dilemma?[51]

It was a rhetorical question, for the answer was obvious to everyone listening. Only the reformers appeared genuinely interested in the plight of the farmers – and only they were prepared to initiate county meetings. Why did the Tories, the traditional leaders of a community in which the farmers were an important element, allow their position to be undermined?

The answer lies in the fact that until 1809, despite periodic but short-lived challenges, the Tory aristocracy and wealthy gentry directed county politics and opinion. They had been the 'popular' side within the landed classes, and they also dictated the frequency and topics of public debate. Petitions despatched from Cornwall to the monarch or parliament were more often than not reflections of their viewpoints. However in the first decade of the nineteenth century they began to lose the initiative to the reformers, opponents whom they labelled 'factious', 'Jacobinical' and 'obscure persons'. The Tories were willing to contest any issue so long as it was primarily a struggle within the ranks of the aristocracy and gentry. But once the reformers made attendance restrictions at county meetings a central issue, and once meetings convened by reformer-magistrates were opened to the 'lower orders', they refused to attend. Their stand was one of principle; the Tories believed that the meetings were illegal. Charles Rashleigh's contempt for the lower orders (so publicly expressed in 1813) was shared by all the principal members of the party –

---

50 Ibid. 29 Mar. 1822, 1.
51 Ibid. 5 Apr. 1822, 3.

and this was another reason for non-attendance. They had no wish to be associated with those whose opinions they regarded with disdain. Thus in 1825 Lord De Dunstanville wrote, 'it will be a disgrace to have a member forced upon the County by a party chiefly composed of the lower orders'.[52] Finally, the county leadership of the Tories was undermined because they feared the numerical strength of those supporting the gentry reformers. There was the real possibility that they could be publicly humiliated at public meetings, particularly those on reform. Reflecting on the past in 1832 Pole Carew admitted that 'I have never been a friend of the measure of attending the county meetings when we have always been beaten and shall infallibly be beaten as long as this popular delusion and phrenzy lasts.'[53] It was these attitudes which led the Tories (probably unwittingly) to neglect the farmers' interests, so making the farmer–reformer alliance a certainty.

If the series of county meetings had a significant impact upon emergent public opinion, the *West Briton* constantly reinforced the reformers' position. It was, from its foundation, a mouthpiece for them. Colman Rashleigh and the Reverend Robert Walker were certainly among the original proprietors, and within months the paper was on a sound financial footing.[54]

No records survive of the comparative circulations of the two papers before 1831 when the *Gazette*'s yearly total was 27,000, the *West Briton*'s 50,900.[55] Under Budd, the first editor, the paper continued to outsell its rival until his death in 1835. Throughout he never wavered in his support of parliamentary reform, or shrank from attacking the *Gazette* with skill and gusto. Furthermore the *West Briton* brought many examples of Cornish borough corruption to the public's attention, while the editorials were invaluable for propagating reform principles. Universal suffrage and annual parliaments were sternly disapproved of and generally Budd was content to agree with the Whig ideals espoused by the principal reformers. During general elections the manipulations of various borough-mongers, particularly Lord Falmouth and Sir Christopher Hawkins, were mercilessly exposed, and there was always a detailed coverage of the progress of radicalism and the reform movement elsewhere in England. Unquestionably some of what the *West Briton* printed was blatant propaganda and exaggeration: nevertheless by 1825 its political reporting was far more accurate and detailed than that of the *Gazette*. In short the *West Briton* kept the question of parliamentary reform continually before the Cornish reading public in a way that public meetings, however numerous, could never do; and it probably won over many waverers on what might otherwise have remained a relatively abstract issue.

Yet it would be wrong to regard the *West Briton* as a single issue paper. Evidence suggests that, important as were the public roles of Rashleigh, Walker,

---

52 Elvins, 'Reform movement', ch. iv, n. 70.
53 Reginald Pole Carew to Lord Falmouth, 18 May 1832, MSS Carew Pole CC/N/65.
54 Elvins, 'Reform movement', ch. ii.
55 Ibid. appendix 4.

Trevanion, Pendarves (who usually chaired the reformers' county meetings) and William Peter, it was the editor Edward Budd's obvious concern about the causes and effects of post-war economic distress which did much to forge the farmer–reformer alliance. Through the columns of the *West Briton* he attacked the levels of government expenditure, taxation and the undue burdens which tithes and local rates placed upon Cornish farmers. Equally significant was the paper's encouragement of farmer activism. The outcome was that the agriculturalists concluded that their complaints and the reformers' objectives were complementary.

Whether or not Cornwall's reformers consciously wooed the farmers into an alliance is debatable. Obviously the campaign over county meetings opened an avenue of complaint to them, drawing the farmers into political discussions. After 1815 the reformers helped that process by taking up their various concerns (often economic) as a prelude to the principal objective – parliamentary reform. Yet, these developments notwithstanding, there were two other circumstances which aided the union. One was the economic hardships endured by the agriculturalists between 1815 and 1822, the other the energetic proselytising of the yeoman farmer and political activist John Penhallow Peters whose support for reform was evident as early as 1783.

The course of the national post-war depression is so well-known that except for several Cornish peculiarities it needs little discussion. Unlike their contemporaries elsewhere Cornwall's farmers did not become agitated about the malt tax. Certainly barley was widely grown in the eastern hundreds, but perhaps because only moderate amounts were destined for the maltsters, opposition to the tax was sporadic and geographically isolated. The same may be said of the currency issue. Peel's act of 1819 produced no more than occasional comment. With agricultural protection a very different situation developed. Under the leadership of Penhallow Peters the Cornwall Agricultural Association adopted a solidly protectionist attitude: through his efforts and those of the association's secretary John Bligh, Cornwall became affiliated with George Webb Hall's Central Agricultural Association, a short-lived national protectionist pressure group. Although it enjoyed support in many agricultural counties the association achieved little, Hall's arguments about the benefits of protection finally being discredited before a parliamentary select committee in 1821. Despite this Peters and the Cornish farmers rallied to Hall's support by expressing their appreciation of his efforts at a Truro meeting in December 1821.[56] The farmers decried the judgements of the select committee and dispatched another petition, before turning away from protection to complain about more immediate problems – the levels of tithes and rents. Once again it was Penhallow Peters who led them, just as it was he who played a pivotal role in the farmer–reformer alliance.

Peters, a farmer on the Veryan peninsula, was a mountainous figure who regularly held court at the Red Lion Inn, Truro, during farmers' ordinaries.

[56] *West Briton*, 14 Dec. 1821, 1.

Once described as 'a sane madman' he was no one's fool, either as a farmer or as a politician; he pioneered the crossing of Leicester and Cotswold sheep, and was instrumental in drastically increasing Cornish wool yields through regular sales of his long-wool Leicester rams. Politically his position was defined by his fervent Whiggery and by the realisation that parliamentary reform could lead to a government more responsive to agriculturalists' complaints. Therefore it was natural that he should join the gentry reformers in their protests after the meeting of 1813, when they not only supported the Catholic claims, but also began their campaign for the rights of inhabitants to attend.[57] Henceforth Peters's name was usually among those of reformers requesting meetings and he became the unofficial leader of the farmers.

His pivotal role between reformers and farmers began to emerge in 1816. Two county meetings were held to approve petitions to the government demanding economy, retrenchment and relief for the alarming rural distress. Peters was prominent at the second meeting in October and it was reported that the farmers too were there in force. Colman Rashleigh told them that only through an independent parliament could financial changes be secured, and no doubt the message was heeded.[58] In the same year Peters, obviously a natural leader, used both Cornish newspapers to address himself to the gentry, clergy and farmers of Cornwall on the annual burden imposed by tithe payments. He initiated a petition and undertook a well-supported campaign against the tithes, arguing that they were unfair and promoted divisiveness within the community.[59] One of the most interesting aspects of this episode was the decision by Peters and his principal allies to channel surplus funds into the Cornwall Agricultural Association. Peters, George Simmons and John Bligh, all farmers, were leading members of that organisation and Simmons, like Peters, was on the list of requisitioners for both county meetings in 1816. Here were the seeds of a future alliance.

From then until 1822 it seems that the embryonic union was carefully nurtured by Peters, Bligh and Simmons on the one hand, and the gentry reformers on the other. Repeatedly Peters organised the rural middle classes, the climax coming in 1822 when many freeholders and leaseholders requested the sheriff, David Howell (another reformer), to call a county meeting. No reformers signed, yet the connection was unmistakable; the farmers stated that they were 'labouring under unexampled distress from the unprecedented low prices of all Agricultural produce, and oppressed by an excessive weight of Taxation, which added to the payment of Rent, Rates, Tithes, and an enormously increased Poor Rate, has become intolerable'. Pleading for urgent relief they then added that the House of Commons should seriously consider parliamentary reform.[60] It was an open invitation for the reformers to join the

---

[57] Ibid. 29 Jan. 1813, 1.
[58] Ibid. 18 Oct. 1816, 3.
[59] *Royal Cornwall Gazette*, 8 June 1816, 1.
[60] *West Briton*, 29 Mar. 1822, 1.

farmers at the meeting – which they did. And although Peters proposed the list of resolutions, as we have already seen it was Colman Rashleigh who dominated the meeting, supported by Walker, Trevanion and William Peter. The farmers enthusiastically endorsed their reformist ideals and from then until 1832 their support for parliamentary reform never wavered. Politically, the consequences were far-reaching.

1826: the farmer–reformer alliance triumphs

With Sir William Lemon's death in December 1824 the ensuing by-election in January, followed by the general election of 1826, gave both farmers and reformers the opportunity to demonstrate their political strength. Edward Pendarves initially decided to contest the county by-election against the Tory Sir Richard Vyvyan, but the realisation of a possibly expensive general election in 1826 made him reconsider and withdraw. Then at the nomination meeting on 26 January 1825 Penhallow Peters and Abraham Hambly unexpectedly proposed Pendarves on behalf of the yeomen and tenant farmers. They pointedly remarked that 'the yeomanry know their rights and strength and will never allow two members to be thrust on them by the aristocracy in this way'.[61] Despite Pendarves's protestations the farmers insisted that he go to the poll, but after an evening of arguing Pendarves persuaded them to bide their time. So, throughout the prolonged canvassing and campaigning of 1825–6 there was a remarkable show of strength by the farmers in his favour. Independence from aristocratic influence and parliamentary reform were the farmers' catch cries and Pendarves eagerly identified himself with both while the sitting member, Tremayne, vacillated and Vyvyan, regarded by everyone as the representative of the 'aristocratical interest', laboured under what had now become an electoral handicap. The outcome was that in mid 1826, shortly before the election, it was acknowledged on all sides that should there be a poll Pendarves would head it, the contest being between the ultra-Tory Vyvyan and the moderate Tremayne. As the latter was reluctant to empty his pockets for an expensive election he withdrew at the last moment.

This process of reversion to shared Whig and Tory county representation produced a major upheaval in Cornwall electoral politics. Beforehand Pendarves made sure that questions of principle came to the fore, something hitherto unknown. Richard Retallick, a watch and clockmaker from Liskeard in east Cornwall, was sure that 'Myself with the greater part of the freeholders here have given Mr Pendarves an unqualified support although all the attorneys in the town except Mr Anstis and Mr Geach, Conveyancer are against us. It may be said of the Freeholders that they vote from principal [sic].'[62] In this instance parliamentary reform was the principle, now obviously a potent

61 Ibid. 28 Jan. 1825, 2.
62 Retallick to William Rashleigh (copy), 4 Jan. 1825, CRO, MSS Rashleigh R 5313.

force in county politics. Yeomen and freeholders alike had every reason to demand independence from aristocratic domination, a sentiment bluntly expressed by one of them in a letter to the *West Briton* in February 1825: 'Aristocratic pride once informed the Yeomanry at a public meeting *at* this County that "their ancestors were slaves attached to the soil" but ere long they will prove that they know their rights and that they dare maintain them.'[63] This was why parliamentary reform remained such a topical issue in Cornwall until 1832.

On reform there were three clearly defined positions. Tremayne's stance had long been clear; since 1816 he had periodically reaffirmed his belief in the necessity for vigorous pruning of government expenditure. When agricultural distress reached disturbing levels in 1819–21 he was more than ever convinced of this but would go no further. In his case conviction was rarely followed by action. If Tremayne's views seemed cloaked with an air of diffidence, Vyvyan's opinions were firm and clear. As the representative of the Tory landed interest he could see no evidence of constitutional weakness, even in Cornwall! At the nomination day on 15 June 1826 William Peter referred to the 'Thatched House party' behind Vyvyan, then asked his listeners to

Look at the greater number of boroughs in the County – look at Truro, completely under the beck of a certain noble Lord in the neighbourhood, – look at Mitchell, under the same noble Lord and a Baronet, – look at Helston, St Mawes, St Germans, and many others in the County, under whose dominion are they? Would you reduce the County to this state?[64]

Such arguments had long been the battle cry of the reformers and if Peter hoped to provoke Vyvyan he was successful. Amid a cacophony of hisses, taunts and jeers Vyvyan proudly announced that he was no reformer, principally because he was certain the House of Commons had never been purer than it was in 1826! He assured his listeners that no matter when and how the general question was brought before parliament, he would oppose it.[65]

As a long-standing parliamentary reformer Pendarves's position was well-known, so he was content to allow Peter to make the running, which he did to good effect. It must be remembered that this was the first occasion since the general election of 1812 when parliamentary reform was discussed with the Tories at a public meeting. To draw an unequivocal condemnation from Vyvyan was a minor triumph; it must have made a great impact on the farmers, and reform was one of the topics of discussion which demonstrated that, like it or not, candidates now had to address themselves to the questions of the day.

Catholic emancipation also occupied all candidates, for several reasons.

63 *West Briton*, 4 Feb. 1825, 2.
64 Ibid. 17 June 1826, 2.
65 Ibid.

Besides many Anglicans Cornwall's population included a very substantial proportion of Wesleyan Methodists, Bible Christians and followers of those churches comprising 'Old Dissent'. As the subsequent furore over emancipation in 1829 revealed, there were strongly held views on both sides of a question which had periodically been in the forefront of local political debate since 1813. At that time Pendarves and other leading reformers such as Rashleigh had unequivocally supported Catholic claims, so in many people's minds he was identified with the emancipationists. At the beginning of his protracted election campaign Pendarves reiterated his support for Catholics, but later muted his opinions in the interests of widening his appeal among the freeholders.

Vyvyan's tactics were completely different. He was unshakeable in his belief that any concessions to the Catholics would endanger not only the Established Church but also the constitution itself. His arguments had a particular urgency because of the successful passage of Sir Francis Burdett's Catholic Relief Bill through the House of Commons in 1825. Parliamentary support for the Catholics' position was obviously widening, and the events at Westminster were well publicised in Cornwall, generating great interest. Therefore Vyvyan worked hard in the press and elsewhere to encourage the 'no popery' cry, endeavouring to draw out statements from Tremayne (who was known to be equivocal on the justice of the Catholics' claims) and Pendarves. The latter refused the bait, his silence probably arising from fear of alienating vital supporters, including some farmers. George Bosustow, one of William Rashleigh's tenants, was certain the issue was causing problems: 'I am fearful Mr Pendarves will lose a good number of his supporters in consequence of his not promising to vote against the Catholic Bill, and his opponents has [sic] taken every advantage to represent it in the worst possible manner.'[66]

One unexpected result of Vyvyan's efforts, ably assisted by the veteran Tory Reginald Pole Carew, was to provoke comment from a surprising quarter. Since campaigning for Gregor in 1790, Sir Christopher Hawkins (he had been given a baronetcy in 1791) had remained aloof from county politics. The political affairs of St Ives, Helston and Mitchell gave him more than enough challenges; however, he took a keen interest in the youthful Vyvyan's career. Besides being shrewd enough to foresee a backlash against a revival of the eighteenth-century 'Old Monopoly', Hawkins publicly disagreed with Vyvyan on the possible effects of Catholic emancipation. For almost forty years he had argued (mostly privately) that neither Church nor State would be in the slightest danger should existing penalties be lifted. Now in March 1826, in a carefully worded letter to the *West Briton*, he made his position clear. Carew immediately launched a sarcastic counter attack hoping to obscure the Tory schism, but it merely emphasised what was already known –

---

[66] Bosustow to Thomas Robins, 14 Mar. 1826, CRO, MSS Rashleigh R 5319.

the county's Tory wirepullers were far from unanimous on this crucial question.[67]

The plight of 'Negro' slaves in British colonies was another issue which Pendarves repeatedly publicised. The term 'Negro' has been retained rather than changing to 'African-Americans', as it reflects contemporary usage. At the time of the founding of the London Society for the Abolition of Slavery in 1823 the *West Briton* began publicising the evils of 'Negro' slavery. Almost immediately meetings began county-wide, Wesleyan Methodists, Baptists, Independents and other Dissenters taking a prominent part in the movement, with Pendarves lending his support. From January 1826 anti-slavery meetings and associations proliferated and Pendarves chaired several of them, leaving no doubt in anyone's mind that here was another great question which he and his fellow parliamentary reformers would pursue until success was achieved.[68] Naturally Pendarves's public stance forced Vyvyan and Tremayne eventually to publicise their opinions too. Both were lukewarm abolitionists who failed to provide any leadership to the campaign.

Finally, what was the impact of the prolonged canvassing and campaign on the Cornish Tories? To understand this it must be realised that well before the election the traditional leadership role was being eroded by their own inaction. In the grim post-war period when Cornwall's farmers were confronted with plummeting prices, rising poor rates, and the greatly resented burden of tithes, their vociferous complaints against the Liverpool administration became evident in meetings, petitions and local newspapers. It was soon apparent that Cornwall's most powerful landowners, particularly the aristocracy, were not prepared to exercise their traditional leadership role upon which much of their political influence had been based. None took up the farmers' grievances. Falmouth, De Dunstanville, Lords Mt Edgcumbe and St Germans, together with their gentry allies such as Reginald Pole Carew, Francis Glanville, F. H. Rodd and others shunned county meetings, convinced that Whig reformers were lurking behind every requisition, whether or not their signatures appeared. Besides pressuring Tory sheriffs to refuse the meetings, they called none, so after 1816 they unwittingly but inevitably began to abdicate their leadership role. Who then could the yeomanry and tenant farmers turn to but the reformers? The Tories' ill-considered step of replacing Sir William Lemon with Sir Richard Vyvyan, leaving the county represented by two Tories for the first time since the previous century, demonstrated an arrogance resented by many farmer-freeholders. For them the events of 1825–6 confirmed their faith in the alternative leadership.

Equally serious was the fatal division within the Tories over support for Tremayne or Vyvyan, a rift which in various forms was to plague them for the next half century. At the core of the problem was Tremayne's family con-

---

[67] Hawkins's opinions were published in the *West Briton*, 13 Jan. 1826, 1, and 24 Mar. 1826, 2. Carew's reply to the former appeared in the *Gazette*, 21 Jan. 1826, 3.
[68] See ch. 3 for elaboration on this.

nections, which resulted in support from a remarkable cross section of the political spectrum. De Dunstanville, a leading Tory and married to Tremayne's sister-in-law, was foremost among his friends. Ties to the Whig Lemon family ensured their backing too. The Lemons, through marriage, brought the borough-mongering Bullers into the alliance, side by side with the reformers Colman Rashleigh, Penhallow Peters and Trevanion who justified their support on the grounds that Tremayne's long service to Cornwall, his 'always straight and independent conduct' and his unshakeable honesty in 1812 when he affirmed his opinion not to vote for reform, all made him eligible.[69] Prominent in the Vyvyan camp were most of the aristocracy plus Pole Carew, Rodd, Glanville and the rest who had opposed the reformers since 1809. Pendarves believed Tremayne was too independent for the 'High Tories' and if Falmouth and Pole Carew were representative of such a group then this was certainly the case. Catholic emancipation was in the air; the Protestant constitution was under attack; so an 'ultra' like Vyvyan was preferable to an independent country gentleman who sometimes revealed a disconcerting flexibility in his thinking.

It might well be argued that between 1805 and 1826 Cornwall's gentry reformers achieved comparatively little. At the national level this is certainly true. They had no spokesman in parliament, for Sir William Lemon was a passive though consistent reformer, and they apparently exerted no influence over the vacillations of the parliamentary Whigs. However in Cornwall their impact was far-reaching. Divorcing themselves from the twin radical demands for annual parliaments and universal suffrage, they presented the county with what Christopher Wyvill, Major Cartwright and Sir Francis Burdett at various times advocated – a gentry-led reform movement. Deriving much of its impetus from irregularities in the existing constitutional system, from the beginning it was firmly organised and led. In fact the *Gazette* grudgingly admitted this as early as October 1812 after Colman Rashleigh, John Trevanion and the Reverend Robert Walker had severely embarrassed John Tremayne on the hustings. Financially very few of the reformers could afford to stand for the county, but light purses were no hindrance to continuous political activism which annoyed and frustrated the leading Tories.[70] By utilising county meetings, the *West Briton* and post-war distress of the agriculturalists, they took the cause of parliamentary reform to the people of Cornwall. Many among the rural middle classes needed little persuasion to take a far more active, or as 1825–6 revealed, decisive political role.

Naturally enough in the aftermath of the 1826 general election reformers and farmers were jubilant. While the latter busied themselves on the land, the gentry reformers, knowing that rural prosperity would provide them with few opportunities for public meetings, now took a new direction. They

---

69 'Memoir of Coleman Rashleigh', pt iii, p. 33.
70 Pendarves could afford to contest a county seat in 1826 only because of a fortuitous inheritance.

became enmeshed in small town anti-slavery societies – Rashleigh, Pendarves, Walker, William Peter and the others using these groups to engender political activism in several of Cornwall's largest boroughs. At a series of borough public meetings in January 1829 they also spoke out strongly for Catholic emancipation, and their eventual reward was the appearance of a dynamic small town reform movement. Well before the general election of December 1832 it was obvious that the spirit of Whig liberalism had gripped Cornwall.

3

Change in the Unreformed Boroughs

Patterns in borough politics

Apparently distinguished by little other than a well-deserved notoriety, Cornwall's twenty-one pre-reform boroughs have provided excellent examples of the inadequacies of the late eighteenth- and early nineteenth-century electoral system. Everywhere Cornish-born or outside patrons manipulated parliamentary representation, corruption and venality were openly displayed, properties were sometimes destroyed to reduce the number of voters, and worst of all there was an indefensible over-representation of the county in the House of Commons. This well-known story has been endlessly repeated so that one result has been the near obliteration of any evidence suggesting the need for modification or reassessment. Careful study of the *History of Parliament's* relevant constituency volume in *The House of Commons, 1790–1820* does little to alter the long-held Namierite view of the Cornish boroughs, but can there be a different reading of electoral politics before 1832, even if the evidence is sometimes circumstantial and fragmentary?[1] The central argument of this chapter is that Cornwall electoral politics differed in two ways from the usual portrayal: firstly county-wide trends have been disguised by atomisation, and secondly, early in the nineteenth century the growing prominence of local and national issues which gradually undermined the old Tory hegemony, has been overlooked.

An appropriate commencement point is the coherence of borough politics in the forty years between 1780 to 1820, when electioneering was convulsed by a series of attacks and dogged defence among those borough patrons who were members of Cornwall's aristocracy and wealthy gentry. Those constantly on the attack were Sir Francis Basset, later Lord De Dunstanville, and Sir Christopher Hawkins, while the objects of their frequent depredations were various members of the Boscawen, Eliot and Edgcumbe families, together with successive dukes of Leeds. The conflict arose from a generation of ambitious young men attaining their majority at much the same time and being concerned with their families' status and prestige, hence the unusual degree

---

1 Most reviewers were lavish in their praise of the volumes for the years 1790–1820 edited by R. G. Thorne. See, for example, Norman Gash, 'Between court and country', *Times Literary Supplement*, 24 Oct. 1986, 1181. One who tempered his praise with several caveats was J. P. Parry in 'Constituencies, elections and members of parliament, 1790–1820', *Parliamentary History* vii (1988), 147–60. Among his reservations was the absence of discussion on ideology and public opinion.

of antipathy, even feuding which soon manifested itself. Throughout the period the one-time schoolmates Basset and Hawkins were resourceful enemies, always plotting to achieve an advantage, and in 1810 fighting a duel over their borough interests. Basset's dislike of the Boscawen family of Tregothnan (probably intensified by Hawkins's friendship with them) extended to clashing views about who should sit for pocket boroughs (Cornishmen or family relations from elsewhere) and a protracted struggle over patents for steam powered pumps.

Besides the generational pattern with its accompanying personal conflicts, there were two well-defined categories of boroughs, those of relative patronal stability in eastern Cornwall and the remainder in the west which were subject to repeated changes. In the past various classifications of English boroughs have been employed, for example by size of the electorate or franchise type. Recently Frank O'Gorman has offered another categorisation, 'distinguishing the basic elements of control which both outweigh others and yet which determine the character of electoral relationships in a group of constituencies'.[2] His typology of electoral behaviour embraces venal, proprietorial, corporation, patronage and 'open' boroughs. Of Cornwall's twenty-one, eighteen fall into three categories – venal, corporation and patronage – but with notable differences between the groups. A different classification, based on the fact that all Cornish boroughs had patrons who could either nominate MPs or influence elections, is to identify them by patronal stability or instability. In so classifying Cornwall's boroughs it will also become obvious that by the 1820s the one-time protagonists who were then in their sixties had lost interest in the conflicts redolent of their more energetic years. Coincidentally, political activism in the boroughs became more prevalent.

In the search for patterns of change prior to 1832 another emerges, one which was county-wide and was composed of several inter-related elements. The previous chapter introduced the county reformers, led by Coleman Rashleigh and the Reverend Robert Walker. Their energetic pursuit of constitutional reform, together with support for parliamentary measures to ease the economic plight of the farmers during the post-war depression, undoubtedly widened their base of support. The well-known rivalry between their newspaper, the *West Briton*, and the Tory controlled *Royal Cornwall Gazette* (the circulation of both steadily rose in the 1820s) must have stirred a growing political awareness among not only farmers but also shopkeepers, miners and fishermen. After fifteen years of such activity this may well have been the reason why in the 1820s national issues including reform intruded into several towns in a way rarely seen before. Colonial slavery, relief for Catholics and tithe reform all sparked controversy. What also must not be overlooked, after 1805, are the apparently spasmodic manifestations of politi-

2 O'Gorman, *Voters, patrons and parties*, 27.

cal activism separate from the reformers' usual activities. The outcomes of these associated developments could be seen by the end of the 1820s: as the number of Cornish-born MPs declined and the influence of non-Cornish patrons increased, borough politics were more lively and more ideologically oriented than ever before. For the first time there were signs of continuous participation by the small town middle classes.

Patronal rivalries

The key to understanding Cornwall politics from 1780 onwards is the generation of young men from landed and commercial families who came of age in that decade. The biographical details of most are supplied in the three 'Members' volumes of *The House of Commons, 1790–1820*, but a portrait of the generation provides far greater insights than the individual summaries. Because of their frequently conflicting ambitions these young men born between 1757 and 1761 dictated the patterns of electoral politics for almost half a century. Furthermore they unwittingly provoked Whig opposition for, like their contemporary William Pitt, most, in time, became Tories.

Francis Basset was born in 1757, Christopher Hawkins, George Boscawen, Edward James Eliot, John St Aubyn and William Molesworth in 1758, Francis Gregor in 1760, John Eliot in 1761, and slightly later than the rest but nevertheless important in this context, Richard Edgcumbe in 1764. The aristocratic families were the Boscawens and Edgcumbes, the only two in Cornwall in 1780 (their peerages was an eighteenth-century creation), who in 1784 were joined by the Eliots who received a barony. The Molesworth and St Aubyn families possessed baronetcies; the remainder were wealthy commoners. In terms of electoral politics in 1780 the Boscawens controlled the representation of Truro and Mitchell, with interests at Tregony and St Mawes, the Edgcumbes were firmly ensconced at Lostwithiel, Bossiney (one seat), Fowey (one) and Grampound (one) with a lesser interest at Penryn, while the Eliots controlled Liskeard, St Germans and Grampound (one). As for the Molesworths and St Aubyns, together with the Carew and Buller families they monopolised the two county seats for most of the century. Therefore of the nine only Basset, Hawkins and Gregor were without political footholds.

With the exception of the Eliot brothers all attended schools outside Cornwall (Basset, Hawkins and Molesworth were at Eton together) and the majority went up to either Oxford or Cambridge. Three, Edgcumbe, St Aubyn and Basset, also enjoyed the cultural and social benefits of the Grand Tour, while Edward Eliot visited France in 1783. A common thread among four of them, was that they inherited their family estates before attaining their majority – Basset in 1769, Hawkins 1770, St Aubyn 1772 and Molesworth 1775 – so when they came of age at the end of the 1770s all had the financial means to pursue political ambitions, if they wished. There were also family ties; for example Molesworth, St Aubyn and Basset were first cousins and shared common political ambitions during the 1780s. Also, typical of many Cornish families, three of the group married heiresses or co-heiresses. On the other hand Hawkins remained single while St Aubyn eventually married one of his long-time mistresses who earlier had borne eight of his fifteen illegitimate children.

This then was the generation responsible for sparking a series of political upheavals commencing in 1780. In a sense Boscawen, the two Eliots and Edgcumbe may be regarded as defenders of the patronal *status quo*, eager to maintain the property and political interests they inherited. Conversely Basset and Hawkins were 'men on the move' possessing sufficient money to support their political ambitions and eager to stake a claim. Molesworth and St Aubyn were used by Basset as allies (pawns might be a more appropriate term) while Gregor remained aloof, preferring to consolidate his friendly links with neighbours such as Hawkins and Boscawen.

There were other rivalries within the group, between Hawkins and Basset in particular. Whether their mutual antagonism began as early as their schooldays is hard to determine, but both inherited their estates before their fifteenth birthdays and Basset certainly chafed at the restraints imposed by his trustees and others. For example in November 1773 he wrote from Eton to his guardians 'I desire to know whether I am to come down at Christmas or no – because if I am not I shall know how to behave – for I have too long stooped tamely to what you have been pleased to impose upon me – my final determination is to bear it no longer.'[3] He always regarded himself as a cut above Hawkins for the Bassets had a long and distinguished history until their fortunes declined in the last half of the seventeenth century. At that time minorities and economic troubles arising from the Civil War had allowed the Godolphins and Boscawens to pre-empt them in county affairs. Afterwards, successive owners of the Tehidy estate and its associated mining interests seemed intent on rebuilding the family's fortune and status, a task to which Francis Basset applied himself with great energy.

His contemporary Hawkins was from a very different background, being only two generations removed from an unscrupulous, highly successful attorney whose fortune was due largely to the profitable manipulation of mortgages.[4] By the mid eighteenth century the family was well established at Trewithen near Probus in central Cornwall, with extensive estates and several profitable mines. During the eighteenth century a member of the family represented the nearby borough of Grampound; however, nothing could disguise the fact that when compared to the Bassets the Hawkins personified the upward mobility of 'new wealth'.

As challengers to the county's political *status quo*, Basset and Hawkins

---

[3] Basset to his guardians, 7 Nov. 1773, RIC, Menwinnion Farm Book, Men/38.
[4] Hawkins's father Thomas was MP for Grampound (close to Trewithen) from 1747 to 1754.

soon made an impact. 'Virile, rigid, sensing infringement of his rights or offence where neither was meant, he [Basset] seemed driven by an inner urge to fight, without much thought of the purpose.'[5] He was egotistical and enormously ambitious, indeed even more so after he received a baronetcy in 1779 for organising 600 tinners to repel a suspected sea-borne invasion of the county by the French. A peerage was his goal, plus control of the lucrative patronage attached to the duchy. In the general elections of 1780 and 1784 as a supporter of the Fox–North coalition he challenged the Boscawens at Truro and Mitchell, the duke of Leeds at Penryn, and the Edgcumbes. In 1784 he continued his assault on the Boscawen and Edgcumbe interests for he and his candidates contested five boroughs, and he was strongly identified with his cousin Molesworth's successful bid for a county seat at a by-election. Even more ostentatious was his shuffling of 'his' MPs, St Aubyn and Reginald Pole Carew at Truro and Penryn, resulting in 1790 in the control of Tregony, shared control of Mitchell (with the Boscawens) and both seats at Penryn.

In 1793–4 Basset changed political sides, becoming a Pitt supporter, and after much pressuring and political bargaining he was created Baron De Dunstanville in June 1796. Thereafter it is generally believed his interest in borough politics declined. With a considerable amount of patronage at his disposal (that of the duchy had earlier fallen into his hands and he also had the right of appointment to numerous positions at the port of Penryn), he had consolidated his position as a formidable rival to George Boscawen, third Viscount Falmouth. But evidence of declining interest is hard to find. At Penryn, for example, Davies Giddy, who adroitly managed to ingratiate himself with both Hawkins and De Dunstanville, told the attorney Christopher Wallis 'that his Lordship had, meant to, and woud [sic] give up his Interest there, and woud retain his Interest to be used hereafter as he saw occasion, so that I coud [sic] not form any opinion at all from his conversation'![6] In fact until 1832 (and beyond) De Dunstanville retained a measure of control over Penryn's parliamentary representation. Meanwhile the ubiquitous Giddy was his MP at Bodmin from 1806 to 1832. Add a serious bid in 1815 to buy the properties conferring votes in the freeman borough of Camelford, thus rebuffing Viscount Falmouth, and there is persuasive evidence that De Dunstanville's rivalry with Hawkins and the Boscawens lingered on long after 1800.

Christopher Hawkins began his political career in rather more circumspect fashion than the thin-skinned Basset. When in February 1784 Hawkins had ambitions of contesting the county against Molesworth, he asked his neighbour Falmouth for an assessment of his prospects, and his support. Falmouth equivocated; on the one hand he knew 'that I should be assisted by most of the Cornish Gentlemen who would be filled with indignation at the Idea of an ambitious young Man's [Basset] presuming to dictate to the

5   Namier and Brooke, *House of Commons*, 62.
6   RIC, Journals of Christopher Wallis, journal 5, entry for 13 July 1805.

County, and to choose his Member there as he does at his Boroughs'.[7] On the other hand there was the expense Hawkins would incur. 'And will he meet with the Support that he ought to have to expect success, from the Freeholders in our Neighbourhood, and from the Gentlemen of the County, so little known as he is from the retired manner in which he lives?', Falmouth wondered.[8] Eventually Hawkins ignored the county contest, preferring to be elected for Mitchell – on the Boscawen interest.

This highlights a remarkable paradox, for while the third Viscount Falmouth strongly opposed parliamentary reform, Hawkins, later to become the arch-borough-monger, favoured it. One year earlier (January 1783) he had been among a small group of West Cornwall gentry who had declared their support for Wyvill's proposals, including the abolition of fifty treasury boroughs and the addition of 100 county members.[9] Hawkins's adherence to these principles survived the 1784 general election. In April 1785, along with Sir William Lemon and the Eliot brothers who at the time were members for Liskeard, he supported Pitt's second unsuccessful motion for constitutional reform. One month later he attended a London meeting at the Thatched House Tavern, the reformers' usual meeting place. Throughout the remainder of the 1780s and into the next decade Hawkins continued to hold far more liberal opinions than many of his Cornish contemporaries: he sympathised with the injustices imposed on Dissenters by the Test Acts and was anxious to pursue the most expedient way of introducing changes without arousing fatal opposition from defenders of the Church–State establishment.[10] Hawkins also remained in touch with Wyvill, quietly disseminating the contents of his pamphlets among his neighbours.

For his faithful support of the prime minister from the time he entered parliament Hawkins was rewarded with a baronetcy in 1791. Thereafter, in pursuit of a much coveted peerage, he became a 'bitter aggressor', beginning his borough campaign by undermining the Boscawens at Mitchell in 1796, and in the same election returning his two nominees at Grampound. Then followed prolonged assaults at Penryn, Helston, Tregony and St Ives, a career of borough acquisition outstripping anything Basset attempted, although he employed different means. Hawkins remained a 'loner', unhindered by the sometimes unhappy alliances which bound other gentry families through marriage or commercial links. His energies were initially directed towards the boroughs closest to his seat at Trewithen (Grampound, Tregony, Mitchell). Because all three were scot and lot or householder boroughs Hawkins avoided any involvement in the kind of factional politics which bedevilled corporation boroughs such as Truro, factions of course meaning alliances. He and his

---

7   Falmouth to Revd H. H. Tremayne, 12 Feb. 1784, MSS Tremayne T 2328/1.
8   Ibid.
9   Courtney, *Parliamentary representation*, p. xxii.
10   North, 'Trists of Veryan', 196–201.

agents were also experts at subterfuge, often outwardly supporting a rival interest but secretly pursuing very different goals.

The result? In 1816 Oldfield listed his 'empire' as Grampound (2 seats) Penryn (2), Mitchell and St Ives each one seat.[11] Prior to this Helston had also briefly fallen into his hands. So at various times he outwitted Falmouth, the Eliots, Basset, Richard Barwell and the duke of Leeds. Unhappily for Hawkins the long-sought peerage remained beyond his grasp, probably because in 1807 he was charged with bribery and corruption in connection with the Penryn election one year earlier. Nothing however could blunt his rivalry with Basset; by 1820 they had interfered in more than half of Cornwall's twenty-one boroughs, with mixed success.

What of the families earlier categorised as defenders of a previous borough order – the Eliots, Edgcumbes and Boscawens? The first two had been forced to withdraw to their interests in East Cornwall, the 'family boroughs' of St Germans and Lostwithiel being most firmly in their grasp. Meanwhile the Boscawens clung tenaciously to Truro where they were threatened from interests within the town rather than by an external challenger. Also, in an uneasy compromise with Hawkins, they retained one seat at Mitchell. Having been used by Basset, their egocentric cousin, Molesworth and St Aubyn retired into political obscurity for the remainder of their lives, though the latter sat as a Whig for Helston from 1807 to 1812. As for Gregor, the last of the nine, he enjoyed a successful career as a county MP, then in retirement became the most trenchant and articulate critic of the county reformers.

Patronage: instability and stability

The ambitious onslaught on the Cornish boroughs unleashed by Basset and Hawkins typified the situation described eighty years ago by Elie Halévy. Boroughs subject to patronal nomination or influence were, he suggested,

> by no means always a property of which the assured possession passed down in a family from father to son without the need of effort for its preservation. In many cases constant attention and almost infinite outlay was essential if the electoral fief were not to be lost. An important rival family, a 'nabob' returned from India with an enormous fortune, a local banker, a wealthy manufacturer, might at any time, if the proprietor were not willing to sell his electoral interest for ready money, declare war upon him, buy the voters, and outbid the patron, until the day came when the new patron would be threatened in his turn by the operation of the same factors.[12]

11 T. H. B. Oldfield, *The representative history of Great Britain and Ireland*, London 1816, iii. 152.

12 Elie Halévy, A *history of the English people in the nineteenth century: England in 1815*, London 1964, 105.

Table 3
Unstable borough patronage, 1790–1830

Bodmin	G. Hunt, Lord Camelford, De Dunstanville, Davies Gilbert, Lord Hertford (1)
Callington	Lord Clinton, earl of Darlington
Camelford	Sir J. Phillips, duke of Bedford, earl of Darlington
Fowey	William Rashleigh (1), earl of Mt Edgcumbe (1), George Lucy
Grampound	Eliots of St Germans, Sir Christopher Hawkins and others
*Helston	duke of Leeds, Hawkins, Sir John St Aubyn, duke of Leeds
Mitchell	Falmouth, then Basset (1), Falmouth (1), then Hawkins replaced Basset
Penryn	duke of Leeds, De Dunstanville, Hawkins, De Dunstanville
St Ives	W. Praed, Hawkins (1), Samuel Stephens (1), James Halse
Tregony	Richard Barwell, Hawkins, Darlington

Sources: Michael Comber, 'The Cornish boroughs and parliamentary reform, 1800–1832', unpubl. MA diss. Exeter 1976; James J. Sack, 'The House of Lords and parliamentary patronage in Great Britain, 1802–1832', *Historical Journal* xxiii (1980), 913–37.

* Most sources list the duke of Leeds as patron from 1790 to 1832. In fact the family's interest in the borough survived until 1841 when Sir Richard Vyvyan gained control. However prior to 1832 there was a series of successful challenges; Basset in 1790, Hawkins 1803–7 and Sir John St Aubyn 1807–12. In 1812 Leeds resumed his interest following his withdrawal in 1803.[13]

Before and after 1790 there were numerous instances proving Halévy's point, although, of course, continuity of patronal control was the rule in many other boroughs. Table 3 lists those boroughs experiencing instability during the period 1790–1830 – defined as the presence of more than one patron. Although the durability of patrons varied greatly – for example Hawkins controlled one St Ives seat from 1806 to 1829, Sir John St Aubyn Helston from 1807 to 1812 – most of these boroughs illustrate the continuous process of infiltration mentioned by Halévy. There were always eager buyers of borough properties, men wishing to ingratiate themselves with the government of the day by offering the support of 'their' members sitting for 'their' boroughs. Alternatively they regarded them as a financial proposition, selling the seats and sometimes seeking control of government patronage in return. Hence Reginald Pole Carew wrote in April 1802: 'Sir C. H. is come to Town on Purpose to repeat his general offer of nomination to all his seats – and is ready to give them without Reserve upon the easiest terms which such advantages can be conferred.'[14] In return Hawkins demanded control of the patronage

13 Thorne, *House of Commons*, II: *Constituencies*, 62–5.
14 Memo dated 6 Apr. 1802, Antony House, Torpoint, MSS Buller BO/23/70.

attached to the boroughs of Grampound and Mitchell. Contested elections and frequent challenges to voting rights were features of this category of boroughs.

Mitchell, a small scot and lot borough where the number of habitable properties was steadily reduced by the patrons to strengthen their hold over voters, illustrates the process of patronal change. Mention has been made earlier of Hawkins's re-election in 1790 on Viscount Falmouth's interest (by this time Basset had wrested the second seat from the Boscawens). After this Hawkins began to work towards eventual control. Hence Falmouth's letter to Thomas Curgenven, his Mitchell agent, in January 1796: 'I am informed that . . . the opposition at Mitchell continues, and that great pains have been taken to persuade the electors that Sir C. Hawkins stands there upon his own interest unconnected with any support of mine.'[15] He wanted that impression contradicted in the strongest possible terms, going on to observe, 'I intend to keep up to the utmost my interest in the borough, in conjunction with Sir F. Basset, and that Sir C. Hawkins comes in as my member, and never has nor never will consider himself as upon any other footing.' Within four months Basset had sold his Mitchell property to Hawkins, making the latter Falmouth's partner.

In August 1800 Hawkins and Falmouth reached agreement over the future representation of the borough. Eight years later, following Falmouth's death, Hawkins agreed with his heir and Charles Rashleigh, the St Austell attorney, 'that the Interest [in Mitchell] should be united and tho' the written agreement between the late Lord and myself [Hawkins] should be destroyed yet, the substance should be kept. This Lord F and myself pledged ourselves to observe.'[16] Having consolidated his position Hawkins retained it until his death in 1829. His nephew and heir John Heywood Hawkins, a forthright reformer, successfully stood for Mitchell in 1830. Unfortunately at the election one year later he found himself the victim of a coup by a Falmouth-nominated Tory, proving there was no honour among thieves.

The fourth viscount, who in 1821 became the first earl of Falmouth, justified this high-handed action by arguing that he had no copy of a written agreement between himself and the late Sir Christopher (in fact with his concurrence it had been destroyed in 1808).[17] Presumably then he felt free to take unilateral action. A more important justification offered by Falmouth was that, with the whiff of parliamentary reform in the air, as an ultra-Tory defender of the 'institutions of state' he could not sanction a parliamentary seat for anyone who would help in the destruction of the constitution. After all, as he explained to J. H. Hawkins, his father and Hawkins's uncle had exploited the unreformed system; therefore he, Falmouth, was being

15 Falmouth to Curgenven, 26 Jan. 1796, RIC, MSS Hawkins HH/14/92.
16 C. Hawkins, memo, Oct. 1808, ibid.
17 Falmouth to J. H. Hawkins, ?May 1831, CRO, MSS Hawkins J 2142/2.

Table 4
Stable borough patronage, 1790–1830

Bossiney (1)	earl of Mt Edgcumbe
East Looe	Buller family
Launceston	duke of Northumberland
Liskeard	Lord Eliot
Lostwithiel	earl of Mt Edgcumbe
Newport	duke of Northumberland
St Germans	Lord Eliot
St Mawes	duke of Buckingham
Saltash	Buller family
*Truro	Viscount Falmouth
West Looe	Buller family

Sources: Comber, 'Cornish boroughs'; Sack, 'Parliamentary patronage'

*As R. G. Thornepoints out, 'The Boscawens of nearby Tregothnan, Viscounts Falmouth, were recorders and patrons of Truro', except that in 1796 the third Viscount sold a life interest to John Lemon (who remained a member till 1814) and from 1818 to 1826 his successor endured the depredations of an independent group of townsmen who temporarily gained control of the Corporation. They seated two candidates in 1820.[18]

consistent in defending it.[19] There was a certain irony in this last twist before Mitchell was disfranchised.

In the boroughs detailed in table 4, however, there were relatively few contests because the patrons nominated members with impunity, and there were few, if any, challenges to their authority. Interestingly the boroughs were a mixed bag as far as franchises and numbers of electors were concerned. Two, Truro and Lostwithiel, were corporation boroughs, voting rights were with freemen in Launceston, Liskeard, Bossiney, the two Looes and St Mawes, Newport was a scot and lot, Saltash a burgage and St Germans a householder borough. Eight of the eleven had Cornish patrons, whereas in the unstable boroughs outsiders were far more conspicuous.

Nevertheless it would be wrong to regard each of these small towns as being entirely free from the sort of activity outlined earlier by Halévy. Truro, a borderline inclusion in the category, was not as secure as successive Lords Falmouth would have preferred, and there were occasional rebellions at Liskeard. In both instances, as we shall see later, the source of instability was elements among the townspeople wishing to make the borough more 'open'. It is also apparent that with the exception of Truro the stable boroughs were

18 Thorne, *House of Commons*, i. 87–8.
19 Ibid.

those farthest away from Hawkins's and Basset's estates in west Cornwall. Therefore the patrons were relatively safe from their attentions. Finally, between 1790 and 1830 Launceston, Newport, Bossiney, St Germans, St Mawes and Saltash almost without exception sent non-Cornishmen to the House of Commons at each general election. Among the unstable boroughs only Callington, Camelford, Tregony and Grampound could equal this.

If it is wrong to make simplistic judgements about the Cornish boroughs and their patrons, it is certainly right to stress how the notoriety of several helped keep the flickering flame of parliamentary reform alive at Westminster. Penryn, Grampound, Tregony (where Hawkins's dabbling was a common factor) and Helston were unsurpassed in this respect and their sins have been well-documented. Such consistently corrupt boroughs, by their repeated infringements of electoral law, educated members of the Commons to the necessity for change.

Helston, for example, was brought into ridicule after the 1812 general election when Hawkins was defeated. He petitioned unsuccessfully, and then his friend Henry Swann tried vainly to have the duke of Leeds prosecuted because of an agreement between him and the electors. Thwarted in this objective the briefly virtuous Swann (his career as MP for Penryn was one of infamy) decided the only remedy for a town where such illegal pacts were made was to disfranchise it.[20] John Cannon rightly portrayed this as a significant contribution to a faltering reform movement, for it reinforced the Whigs' growing attraction to the idea of piecemeal disqualification of boroughs.[21] Swann tried in vain, but a crucial development came in the House of Lords on the third presentation of the bill to disfranchise Helston. The prime minister, Lord Liverpool, expressed agreement with the principle it embodied, a minor landmark on the long road to 1832.[22]

After 1820, Helston having played some part in converting the first minister, it was the turn of Grampound and later Penryn to make the running. Each provided plentiful ammunition for the Cornish reformers and their Westminster counterparts. In the wake of the 1818 general election Sir Manasseh Lopes, one of Grampound's contending patrons, was convicted of bribery and gaoled. From 1819 onwards the borough's fate was continually debated in both Houses. There was, in February 1821, an unsuccessful proposal to give Grampound's seats to the neighbouring hundreds; then there were alternative schemes to enfranchise either Yorkshire or Leeds. The arguments were passionate and intense, but what was never really in dispute was the necessity to make an example of one of Cornwall's over-plentiful boroughs. Finally acceptance of the principle of piecemeal transfer of seats came to a climax and Grampound's two members were given to Yorkshire, 'and for

[20] These convoluted developments are summarised in Courtney, *Parliamentary representation*, 56–60.
[21] John Cannon, *Parliamentary reform, 1640–1832*, Cambridge 1973, 177.
[22] Ibid.

the first time for nearly three hundred years a parliamentary borough had lost its representation through delinquency'.[23] Professor Cannon argues that the significance was not so much in the breakthrough as in the disillusionment felt by Lord John Russell and the Whigs who, in a spirit of conciliation, had seen their original bill severely modified. For them the lesson from Grampound was that only a comprehensive programme of parliamentary reform would do in future.[24]

Challenges to the patrons

On 19 February 1820 the editor of the pro-reform *West Briton* resignedly wrote that

> we do not know a single instance, in which the election is likely to hinge on the political opinion or conduct of the candidates. For other matters engage the attention of the Electors of the Boroughs of Cornwall; and on far other grounds will the success of the different candidates be decided. To address the electors of these privileged marts of corruption, in the language of patriotism, would be as ridiculous as it would be unavailing.[25]

Meanwhile his counterpart at the *Royal Cornwall Gazette*, always alert to attempts to deprive Cornishmen of any of their forty-four seats, reminded the electors of some of the 'allegedly corrupt boroughs' that they might be offered temptations which could result in petitions, disfranchisement and, of course (although this was left unsaid), the loss of regular benefits.[26] The two newspapers seem to reinforce the current, widely held view that many Cornish borough electors participated in elections only to the extent of holding out their hands to receive payment for voting. Can voters and non-voters' involvement in electoral politics therefore be ignored because they rarely showed any independence of thought?

In this context it is worthwhile recalling the young Viscount Falmouth's comment in 1784 when Hawkins sounded out his prospects of success for the county: would he receive support from freeholders in the neighbourhood? Falmouth did not suggest freeholders could be pressured. They would make up their own minds, without directions from influential landlords. Obviously Falmouth was well aware of the independence of county voters. Two years earlier he made an equally interesting observation about their borough counterparts. When he found an arrangement between his father and Basset was to be broken by a 'turbulent, ambitious opponent', he decided to resist for 'tho I perceive the advantage Sir Frances [*sic*] has over me in many Respects,

23 Ibid. 180.
24 Ibid.
25 *West Briton*, 19 Feb. 1820, 2.
26 *Royal Cornwall Gazette*, 4 Mar. 1820, 3.

yet the circumstance of his Tenants not being likely to give both their voices to one man which would make their Votes his Property, has its due Weight'.[27] This suggests very clearly that even in a small, venal, scot and lot borough the tenants of a domineering autocrat (Basset) were far from being passive members of some kind of deference community. The electoral reality was that they rejected any notion of handing their second votes to their landlord, because that would deprive them of their highly valued independence. Falmouth appreciated this.

Before 1800 there were various signs of voter independence in boroughs, for example in Truro and Penryn. The Truro Corporation seems to have been particularly obstreperous at times. It responded positively to Wyvill's 1782 demand for petitions in favour of parliamentary reform, defying its new patron Francis Basset. One reason for disagreement between patron and corporation may have been the town's underlying preference for at least one local MP, preferably someone of standing who could promote the town's interests. This was to be a recurring theme in Truro elections.

Simultaneously Basset, who was MP for Penryn from 1780 to 1796, forwarded to Wyvill a letter from the town's portreeve and 100 electors who suggested the reform demands were unjust, unwise and ill-timed, adding, 'We trust you will not permit the idle and groundless censure of Cornish Boroughs, in general, to prevent you from giving us a fair and impartial hearing.'[28] Basset's covering note approved these sentiments, but even in his stronghold his control was not unchallenged. An opposition group, comprising the corporation and vestiges of the former Edgcumbe interest, proceeded to petition parliament for the enactment of the reforms, an action which enraged him.[29]

Little evidence survives of popular feelings in the Cornish boroughs from this time until 1820, apart from sporadic rebellions against the patrons in Truro and Liskeard. In the former much of the evidence is circumstantial; nevertheless, it suggests a surprising level of popular political activity. The origins lay in the shared concerns of the townspeople and corporation: a preference for at least one Cornish-born MP with first-hand knowledge of the town's economy and needs, and an intense dislike among many of the contemptuous way the Boscawens foisted their nominees on the borough at short notice. This explains why George Boscawen, third Viscount Falmouth, came to terms with John Lemon, Sir William's brother, in 1796. Lemon had valuable commercial and property interests in the town, so although he refused to support Pitt's government and therefore found it difficult to tap the springs of patronage, he was very acceptable on other grounds. Lemon maintained sufficient support among the corporation members to make his re-election a

---

[27] Lord Falmouth to H. H. Tremayne, 12 Mar. 1782, MSS Tremayne T 2323/1.
[28] For the correspondence between Basset and Wyvill see Wyvill, *Political papers*, 130–5.
[29] Ibid.

certainty. By 1812 there was genuine harmony among both parties; in fact, they dined together after that uncontested general election.

However the end of such geniality was close at hand:

This was the last time that both parties joined in common festivities; the agitation for parliamentary reform soon reached so acute a stage in Truro that friendships were shattered, the peace of the town was destroyed, and public life was debased by the bitterness of contending factions.[30]

Following Lemon's death in 1814 Viscount Falmouth wasted no time; he quickly nominated George Dashwood, a Buckinghamshire gentleman, to partner a relative of the Boscawens, Sir George Warrender ('Sir Gorgeous Provender' as he was nicknamed, being a noted epicure). For once the *Gazette* and *West Briton* agreed in condemning such manipulation, and the townspeople felt even more strongly, but Falmouth failed to heed the warning signs.[31]

Dashwood and Warrender were replaced in 1818 by Lord Fitzroy Somerset, later Lord Raglan of Crimean War infamy, and Edward Tomline, both total strangers. Only distantly related to the Boscawens their nomination evoked tremendous indignation, so much so that it bubbled over into an outright challenge by Sir Hussey Vivian and Colonel William Gossett. Each was a 'front-man' for powerful opponents of the Boscawens: Vivian's father, John, was an extraordinarily wealthy mining adventurer, and ambitious for his family; Gossett was the son-in-law of Ralph Allan Daniell, a Truro financier and member of the corporation whom Falmouth managed to offend by demanding Daniell pledge his votes to Somerset and Tomline.[32]

The election day was as eventful as any in Truro's long history. Besieged in the town hall by hundreds of vocal citizens the corporation reluctantly decided to shift proceedings to the marshy green nearby. There, jammed together on a tiny platform they gradually tilted ever lower into the slimy mud while acrimony and haranguing burst forth around them. As if any was needed, further motivation for the uproar came from the Falmouth faction's refusal to allow the mayor to read a petition signed by 130 townsmen who preferred Vivian, the local champion.[33] Besides Daniell and John Vivian the leaders of this outburst of middle-class resentment appear to have been Humphrey Willyams, a nearby landowner, Truro banker and corporation member, John Bennallack, a solicitor and mayor of Truro 1819–23, and John Edwards, another solicitor.

We can safely infer that their supporters were made up of local business, professional and tradesmen, the town's middle classes, but who were they? Many of those who in 1814 put their entrepreneurial instincts on record by

30 Jennings, 'Part v', 436.
31 Ibid.
32 Ibid.
33 *West Briton*, 12 June 1818, 1.

founding the Truro Shipping Company were later identified with parliamentary reform, and a lesser number with the campaign against colonial slavery. Among the signatories were John Bennallack, John Ferris currier, Thomas Whitford mercer, John Cuming confectioner, Samuel Randall pipe-maker, Robert Blee iron-monger, Samuel Milford draper and Martin Magor grocer.[34] Milford was a Quaker. Many of the others involved were Methodists, and the great majority of them cast votes for the two reformers, William Tooke and Sir John Lubbock, at the 1830 Truro election, and two years later for Tooke.[35] They were prominent too in a published list of those townspeople demanding a Reform meeting in Truro in January 1831.[36] These men were middle-class political activists; given their prominence in the town in 1814 and their later adherence to reform it is reasonable to assume they were among the 130 petitioners of 1818. Such, then, was the nucleus of the on-going opposition to the strict control of Viscount Falmouth.

Unhappily for the rebels their efforts in 1818 were unsuccessful. The Boscawen candidates were victorious by the narrowest possible margin (twelve votes to eleven). Unprecedented disorder and mob violence then erupted in the town, and it was obvious even to Viscount Falmouth that the next election would be equally hard fought. In the interval between 1818 and 1820 he therefore tried to reconcile John Vivian and Daniell to his family's role in Truro politics, without success. Hussey Vivian once again was the nominee of local interests and this time he mustered a majority of the corporation.[37] One year later, after a successful petition, Colonel Gossett joined him. In the aftermath of this slap in the face Falmouth quickly moved to regain control of a majority of the corporation, ensuring his success in 1826, but also knowing from experience there was now well-organised middle-class opposition in the borough.

The struggle against the Eliot family in their pocket borough of Liskeard pre-dated the Truro clashes. The voters were freemen elected by the corporation, so in effect Edward Eliot seated family and friends through the deference of the mayor, capital and free burgesses. He and his family before him totally dominated the corporation which ruthlessly checked more democratic tendencies. It was not surprising that, by the beginning of the nineteenth century, 'the impression was strong on the minds of many respectable inhabitants, that they were unfairly debarred of their rights and privileges'.[38] Discontent boiled over in 1802 when two distinct groups of townsmen petitioned against the election of John and William Eliot. According to the town's historian, 'The object was to break down the system of exclusion, and

---

34 RIC, 'Articles of Agreement, Truro Shipping Co., Oct. 21, 1814'.
35 Ibid. *Truro: further account of election proceedings in this borough . . . together with a copy of the poll,* Truro 1833.
36 *West Briton,* 28 Jan. 1831, 3.
37 Jennings, 'Part vi', 95–106
38 J. Allen, *History of the borough of Liskeard and its vicinity,* Liskeard 1856, 297.

to open the electoral privileges to the inhabitants at large.'[39] Apparently the spirit of reform was flourishing. The town's householders had long been exempted from all local rates due to the generosity of their patron, and to overthrow him would seem to have been an act of far-reaching folly, when the townspeople were motivated by ideals of some kind. The trigger for the opposition is unknown, but Joseph Childs, a young solicitor, was manager of the malcontents.[40]

The events which followed, beginning with two petitions opposing the Eliots in 1802 and ending in 1804 with the patron's power intact, are open to two interpretations. They can be judged as an attempt by Childs and his allies to free the borough from patronal control and widen the franchise, or to secure the prince of Wales as the new patron in place of the Eliot family. At the very least the evidence is open to conjecture, because there is a consistency to Childs's links to the reform movement. With Edward Budd he was one of the driving forces behind the formation of the *West Briton*, Budd having been known to Childs when he ran a boarding school in Liskeard before moving to Truro.[41] In fact Liskeard was considered as the possible place of publication for the newspaper. Liskeard's reformers, Childs among them, tried again to free the borough from the Eliot's control before the 1818 election, and one year later Childs joined reformers and farmers in demanding an enquiry into the Peterloo massacre.[42] Looking back on these years from 1856 when people then active in the town were still alive, John Allen claimed there were links between the town's reformers and Rashleigh's group. He implied that Childs was the point of contact, the result being one of the first interventions by the county reformers in borough politics. After 1820 such interventions became more frequent.[43]

Apart from the political partisanship gradually appearing in Truro and Liskeard before 1820 there were other random occurrences pointing to the reformers' preparedness to extend their activities beyond county meetings. The first actually to contest one of the boroughs was John Trevanion of Caerhayes Castle who in 1806 offered himself for venal Penryn. Trevanion was an impressive speaker whose arguments on topical issues including reform were much admired by his listeners. In a close contest he polled 128 votes, finishing behind the notorious Henry Swann (162 votes) and Sir Christopher Hawkins (137).[44] After a successful petition Trevanion replaced Hawkins, but only for a month or two before the 1807 general election. Meanwhile in 1806 at East Looe, one of the Buller family's pocket boroughs, Captain Hamelin Trelawny stood on the ground 'that the right of election lay in

---

[39] Ibid. 299.
[40] Ibid.
[41] Elvins, 'Reform movement', chs ii, iii.
[42] *West Briton*, 22 Oct. 1819, 3.
[43] Allen, *Borough of Liskeard*, 303, 513.
[44] Thorne, *House of Commons*, ii. 75–7.

residents paying scot and lot, not in the freemen', a claim rejected by the mayor.[45] Whether Trelawny's candidacy reflected an attempt by his family to renew their interest in the borough, a growing surge of reform feelings or a popular desire to challenge the Bullers, is problematic.

Fowey attracted the attention of two reformers, Colman Rashleigh and Joseph Austen. Rashleigh's political opinions cannot be questioned; he publicly espoused them for more than thirty years. Austen (he later changed his surname to Treffry) was different, someone whose personal ambition sometimes over-rode his principles. In 1811–12 Austen meddled in Fowey politics, perhaps with a view to overthrowing the Menabilly Rashleighs' control of one seat.[46] Support for parliamentary reform may have motivated him whereas it certainly was the reason why Colman Rashleigh briefly contemplated standing in 1812, in opposition to the interest of his uncle William. Success would have given Colman the opportunity to join Burdett and other parliamentary reformers at Westminster, but the first step was an expensive contest, one which he could not afford.

Two of the reform movement's sympathisers who sat in the parliament of 1807–12 were Charles Lemon (Penryn) and Sir John St Aubyn (Helston). Lemon, only twenty-three years of age when elected, came in on the De Dunstanville interest, probably because of an enduring friendship between the two families.[47] His success meant he joined his father Sir William Lemon and uncle John (Truro) in the House of Commons. Charles Lemon usually voted with the Whig opposition: he supported the 1810 motion for parliamentary reform and the Catholic Relief Bill of 1812.[48] Although Lemon then retired, he was elected for Cornwall in 1831 and twelve months later for West Cornwall, which he represented until he decided to step down in 1857. His parliamentary longevity was not matched by St Aubyn, De Dunstanville's hand-picked but unsuccessful county candidate in 1790. Seventeen years after this rebuff St Aubyn resumed his former interest in Helston, when he had the opportunity to share the borough patronage with the sixth duke of Leeds. Following his uncontested election as a Whig he, like Lemon, was another of the Cornish members who took a consistent line on parliamentary reform and Catholic emancipation, voting in favour of both.[49] On the basis of this record the county reformers tried unsuccessfully to persuade him to oppose John Tremayne for the county in 1812. No doubt St Aubyn remembered the expensive debacle of 1790.

When considered together these examples of intervention in borough politics suggest that before 1820 issues and principles were far from being non-existent in at least some of the boroughs, a conclusion congruent with

45 Ibid. ii. 71.
46 Ibid. 53–5; Comber, 'Cornish boroughs'.
47 Thorne, *House of Commons*, IV, V: *Members*, iv. 411.
48 Ibid.
49 Ibid. v. 83.

O'Gorman's view of Hanoverian electoral politics, particularly the view that elections were about much more than purely personal and mercenary considerations.[50] Just as interesting were the occasional assertions of voter independence. O'Gorman believes that in the scot and lot boroughs of St Ives, Penryn and Fowey independent sentiment was one possible reason for several early nineteenth-century contests.[51] Soon they merged into more frequent outbursts of genuinely popular feeling, especially in Cornwall's larger towns.

Changing forms of political debate

Without overstating the case, the 1820s revealed an important change in the level of political debate, because for the first time questions of national importance were discussed. This paralleled a similar trend in Buckinghamshire where 'Towards the end of the second decade of the nineteenth century, there was an important shift of emphasis. . . . The influence of national issues, which heretofore had been only occasional, now became constant and critical.'[52] Parliamentary reform, Catholic emancipation, repeal of the Test and Corporation Acts and the campaign for the abolition of slavery were the catalysts. The same phenomenon was observable in Cornwall, but with differing emphases: repeal stimulated little discussion or controversy, whereas debate over colonial slavery and emancipation resulted in numerous meetings and petitions. And, contrary to the view that Methodists generally steered clear of politics at this time, they and other Dissenters were often among the leaders of the growing agitation.

From a national perspective, James Walvin believes, 'It is hard to deny that the cause of the West Indian slaves became a popular issue both in the 1790s and in the mid 1820s, more popular indeed than many other issues which have attracted historians' attention.'[53] The campaign for abolition of slavery in British colonies, especially the West Indies, sparked hundreds of public meetings and petitions throughout northern England, the Midlands, counties close to London and ports such as Bristol which relied on the West Indies trade. Support came too from counties such as Cornwall where Methodists were most numerous. Add to this those Churches classified as 'Old Dissent' – Quakers, Congregationalists or Independents as they were known by the early nineteenth century, and Baptists – and the total was a formidable segment of the Cornish population. Their involvement in the anti-slavery campaign made it the most popular of all issues except parliamentary reform.

50 O'Gorman, Voters, patrons and parties, 385.
51 Ibid. 270.
52 Davis, Political change, 59.
53 James Walvin, 'The public campaign in England against slavery, 1787–1834', in James Walvin (ed.), Slavery and British society, 1776–1846, London 1982, 63.

The slave trade itself had been abolished in 1807, due largely to the efforts of William Wilberforce. For the next sixteen years the British anti-slavery movement was concerned to end the participation of foreigners in the trade. However in 1821–2 the emphasis changed. Beginning in Liverpool a campaign was mounted to free slaves in employment, while simultaneously there were demands for the equalisation of duties on West and East Indian sugar imports (the former enjoyed an important tariff differential).[54] This, it was assumed, would reduce the demand for West Indian sugar, leading to fewer slaves being required as labourers. Soon afterwards, in May 1823, the 'London Society for the Abolition of Slavery in our Colonies' was founded, the precursor to a widespread campaign which also assisted the stuttering movement for parliamentary reform. There was evidence to show that members for some rotten boroughs assisted the West Indian sugar interest to maintain its privileged tariff position. Therefore one of the consequences of electoral reform would be the inevitable erosion of the interest's power base, an argument having direct relevance to Cornwall.

Debate commenced in the county immediately after the formation of the London Society. The Wesleyan Edward Budd, editor of the *West Briton*, began publishing a series of articles on the evils of 'Negro' slavery and soon afterwards public meetings in Falmouth, Liskeard and Truro resulted in petitions to parliament.[55] Dissenters and particularly Methodists were drawn into the issue for several reasons: firstly, slavery challenged the doctrine of equality of all men before God, secondly it was held to be sinful and unChristian, and thirdly the continuing existence of slavery seriously hindered the work of missionaries. Local anti-slavery societies soon sprang up, chapels were used for meetings 'and on at least one occasion petitions for the abolition of slavery were placed by the chapel doors to be signed by a great number of people as they left the Sunday services'.[56] Several years later the *Cornubian* observed in the course of a fierce editorial against slavery, 'The Wesleyans are unanimous in seeking its amelioration.'[57]

After a further spate of county-wide meetings in 1824, a year later at Bodmin the 'Friends to the Cause of the Mitigation and Abolition of Slavery' was established. Among those attending were three leading parliamentary reformers, the Reverend Robert Walker, Abraham Hambly and the Reverend Darrell Stephens, all of whom were elected to the committee. In addition two Quakers, George Fox and John Allen, became secretary and treasurer respectively. Besides Dissenter/Wesleyan involvement, therefore, the other feature was the leading role of county reformers in these town-based societies.[58] Early

---

54 David Eltis and James Walvin (eds), *The abolition of the Atlantic slave trade: origins and effects in Europe, Africa, and the Americas*, Madison 1981, 37–8.
55 See *West Briton*, May 1823.
56 Hayden, 'Culture, creed and conflict', 79.
57 Ibid.
58 *West Briton*, 30 Dec. 1825, 3.

in 1826 Edward Pendarves chaired a meeting in a Dissenting chapel in St Ives, and another in Camborne, underlining the growing reformer–Dissenter link.[59]

Meanwhile a Launceston abolition meeting held at the same time had overtly political overtones. Supporters of the town's patron, the duke of Northumberland, attempted to stifle discussion and simply send off a petition without arousing too much furore.[60] Presumably the obvious topic of the town's political subservience to Northumberland had to be avoided at all costs. William Pearse, a woollen manufacturer, refused to be silenced, saying it was well known that the electors were reluctant to debate issues – they 'loved darkness rather than light'.[61] As 1826 wore on the meetings continued with Rashleigh, Walker and their friends usually prominent. The farmer–reformer alliance was now broadening its appeal, incorporating townspeople (many of them Dissenters) in the larger boroughs.

Truro was the scene of two anti-slavery meetings in March and April, both attracting men of various political viewpoints. At the first the reformers Budd and William Peter proposed or seconded resolutions but some lesser-known personalities appeared in the political spotlight.[62] Samuel Milford, a Quaker draper associated with the Truro Shipping Company and one of those who took a leading part on the reform side between 1830 and 1832, proposed the adoption of the petition. He was supported by the banker William Tweedy, another Quaker and like Milford a reformer. The Reverend William Moore (Independent) and the Reverend Edward Clarke (Baptist) also spoke forcefully against slavery; several years later they made no secret of their support for parliamentary reform. Truro's anti-slavery society, despite its seemingly apolitical nature, was full of men of liberal outlook. Sir Charles Lemon was president, Humphrey Willyams a vice-president – both were later Liberal MPs – while the town's dentist Nathaniel Stephens and other Boscawen opponents filled the committee.

Many of the meetings resulted in petitions to parliament. Seymour Drescher believes that such petitions were the product of an enormous amount of energy and public discussion.[63] If this was so in Cornwall, and if petitions were 'the political voice of the dispossessed', then it suggests that the level of small town political activism was rising.[64] Many of the inhabitants, including significant numbers of Dissenters, were being drawn into debate in a way not seen previously in Cornish towns. After 1826 the plight of colonial slaves temporarily faded from the political limelight, but reformers, Dissenters and

59 Ibid. 21 Jan. 1826, 2; 3 Mar. 1826, 2.
60 Ibid. 3 Mar. 1826, 1.
61 Ibid.
62 Ibid. 10 Mar. 1826, 2; 14 Apr. 1826, 2, 3.
63 Seymour Drescher, 'Public opinion and the destruction of British colonial slavery', in Walvin, Slavery and British society, 25.
64 Ibid.

others quickly rediscovered a familiar outlet for their activist energies: Roman Catholic emancipation.

Until 1829 this was the controversy overshadowing all others in the county, for the repeal of the Test and Corporation Acts made relatively little impact.[65] Several circumstances combined to make repeal a non-event in Cornwall. Generally Methodists were loyal to the Church of England and the Establishment because they regarded themselves as part of it. Therefore the Test Act was not a major concern, their perception being that they were different from other Dissenters. During the agitation preceding repeal the *Methodist Magazine* remained silent on the issue, although most Methodists welcomed the easing of religious persecution. Nor was Old Dissent in Cornwall prominently identified with repeal. Perhaps members of the Baptist, Congregational, Independent and other Churches failed to press the issue because they were well aware of Methodist ambivalence. Often Methodists joined other Dissenters in a show of solidarity on such issues, but not on this occasion. A mere nine petitions were presented to parliament, and there were few if any public meetings.

Emancipation was different. As long ago as 1813 it had prompted a county meeting where the aristocracy and leading gentry were virulent in defending the established constitution. Nevertheless the county reformers maintained their unwavering support for the Catholics' demands and by 1826 had the satisfaction of seeing a majority of the House of Commons consistently voting the same way. Influential peers in the House of Lords and, of course, the king were the stumbling blocks. Conflicting view-points appeared in 1825–6 during the county election campaign: Pendarves remained unobtrusively in favour because he had no wish to antagonise the Dissenter vote; Vyvyan, like Lord Falmouth his principal supporter, was a very determined opponent. The Whig–Tory division sharpened after the election, for in March 1827 Burdett's motion for emancipation was lost in the Commons by 276 to 272, the first defeat for such a motion in that house since 1819.[66] The rival view-points of the *West Briton* and *Gazette* also contributed to the growing debate.

Canning's brief 1827 ministry revived hopes of the issue being settled. Speculation increased after the shortlived Goderich ministry when the duke of Wellington became prime minister. He was soon confronted by the constitutional crisis stemming from Daniel O'Connell's successful election for County Clare and by September 1828 in Cornwall the *Gazette*, alarmed at the drift of events, was suggesting parish clergy organise petitions against

[65] The *Methodist Magazine* was mostly silent during the repeal campaign, and there was no pressure on Methodists, from within their own body, to take a stand on the Test Acts.
[66] Michael Brock, *The Great Reform Act*, London 1973, 51; G. I. T. Machin, *The Catholic question in English politics, 1820–1830*, Oxford 1964, 15.

emancipation.[67] There was even a call for a county meeting (which was ignored), provoking the *West Briton* to assert,

> Knowing that all the resident Peers, with ONE exception, and a decided majority of the Gentry were favourable to the final adjustment of the Catholic question, the Ultras have devised a plan for getting up so many petitions against the Catholics without openly and fairly taking the sense of the County, by calling meetings in different parts of the County for the same day.[68]

No editorial did more to highlight the irony of the Cornish reformers' position. For almost twenty years the paper had railed against the 'lordly lead' in Cornwall, the unremitting opposition of the aristocracy and leading gentry to parliamentary reform, Catholic emancipation and government measures to relieve agricultural distress. With only Falmouth and Lord Edgcumbe against emancipation the paper was now quick to ally itself with those it usually ridiculed. At the same time the *West Briton* also pleaded the case for the unreformed House of Commons' right to decide such a question. This *volte-face* was not missed by the *Gazette*. The reformers also found their alliance with the Dissenters under great strain, because some Wesleyan ministers and their followers chose to stand firm with the Established Church against any concessions to the Catholics.

Anti-Catholic feeling peaked in Cornwall in the first three months of 1829. Meetings and extensive press coverage characterised the controversy with voters and non-voters being subjected to highly political speeches against concessions by various members of the gentry and several Wesleyan preachers. On the other side were the reformers, astutely promoting their arguments to many of the same people with whom they had worked to abolish colonial slavery. To avoid a mass demonstration of feeling against them at a county meeting the opponents of emancipation chose to conduct a series of meetings in the second week of January. Despite being geographically divided the reformers and their allies were not deterred, seizing the chance to speak out at Bodmin, Lostwithiel, Launceston, Callington and Truro, leaving Helston to the Vyvyan-led opponents of emancipation.[69] William Peter and Colman Rashleigh were prominent at Bodmin, Peter moving the amendment to the motion to petition against concessions, Rashleigh supporting him.[70] Each argued persuasively and at length about the false dangers in the minds of many die-hard Protestants. David Howell, another well-known reformer, spoke for the Catholics at Launceston while Owen Trelawny put the case at Callington.[71]

---

[67] *Royal Cornwall Gazette*, 6 Sept. 1828, 2.
[68] *West Briton*, 2 Jan. 1829, 2.
[69] Ibid. 16 Jan. 1829, 2, 3.
[70] Ibid.
[71] Ibid.

By far the largest public meetings were held at Truro and Helston. As the two county newspapers were published in the former town and had been attacking each other on this issue for years, interest was understandably high. Unfortunately William Peter, the reformers' most articulate spokesperson for the Catholic claims, was prevented at the last minute from attending. This left Budd of the *West Briton* to stand up to a phalanx of high Tories, among them the earl of Falmouth. Budd, in the course of his speech, argued that Wesleyans were generally hostile to the Established Church. Quickly William Dale, a member of the Wesleyan Methodist Society, sprang to his feet before the packed audience. 'I rise, Sir, indignantly to *repel that insinuation* (Hear, hear) and to assert that Wesleyan Methodists feel no hostility to the Established Church, but, like their venerable founder, are firmly attached to the Church, and unshaken in loyalty to their King. (Loud applause).'[72] Dale's view was that the Dissenters' alliance with the high Tories was not so remarkable, because both groups were determined to protect the Protestant constitution. To a chorus of approval he denied that because the repeal of the Test and Corporation Acts had been completed without imperilling the constitution, Catholics could be similarly treated. They owed allegiance to a foreign head of state, held the principle of exclusive salvation, and claimed infallibility, therefore they menaced the state. Together with Dale, Falmouth ridiculed Budd's arguments in favour of emancipation. There were very few others prepared to debate with his lordship so ultimately the meeting reflected his Tory opinions.

The best attended meeting was at Helston where almost 2,000 people assembled in the Wesleyan chapel. Sir Richard Vyvyan, the county MP, took the chair and the Methodist ministers of Helston and Gwennap, major centres of Cornish Methodism, supported the principal motion opposing emancipation, 'the latter stating that though he came not to represent his Church yet he believed that the individuals who composed that body were of the same opinion as himself regarding the great question on which the meeting was assembled'.[73] Unquestionably these Wesleyans were opposed to Catholic emancipation, although De Dunstanville later argued that those in the Redruth–Camborne district were changing their minds in great numbers.[74] This then raises the question about the degree of public support for the opponents of emancipation, especially among Dissenters.

No doubt Linda Colley was correct in her recent assertion that 'It was the poorer, more marginal and less literate folk who were the most stridently and devotedly *anti*-Catholic in 1829.'[75] Evidence supporting this view-point may be found in hundreds of parish petitions from Cornwall. Yet there was considerable support for Catholic claims. At Bodmin the mover of the motion to

---

72 Ibid.
73 Ibid. 9 Jan. 1829, 3.
74 Elvins, 'Reform movement', 305.
75 Linda Colley, *Britons: forging the nation, 1707–1837*, New Haven 1992, 332–3.

petition against emancipation, John Wallis, was reported as saying that 'He was aware that on this subject public opinion was divided: a great many being averse to such concessions and others being favourable.'[76] Eventually 100 people voted for the petition, eighty opposed it and more than 100 'did not hold their hands'. Similarly one of the anti-Catholic speakers at Helston said he saw around him many friends 'whose private virtues he admired and respected' but they held different opinions to him 'on this great subject'.[77] A much smaller Penzance meeting was actually dominated by opponents of the petition, including the local Baptist minister. Apparently the 'exclusionists' came off second best at Launceston, too, where Howell successfully generated a counter petition prior to the meeting.[78]

Popular opinion was almost equally divided, as were views among Dissenting and Anglican clergy. At Callington the Methodist minister, Mr Wade, forcefully put the case for opposition to emancipation. Several Methodist ministers took a leading role in the Helston meeting, one from Gwennap suggesting 8,000 people were under his pastoral care and he guaranteed two-thirds would sign the petition.[79] Interestingly Dissenting ministers were less conspicuous elsewhere. Perhaps the exposure of local hypocrisy had left many of the more intelligent Dissenters wondering why they should support the die-hard Protestants. This was pointed out by Matthew Anstis at Liskeard. 'For many years we had been told by those who were now so desirous of holding meetings, that the great body of the people were incapable of forming an earnest judgement on public affairs, which should be left to the wisdom of parliament.'[80] Now neither the parliament nor the government were to be trusted, nor apparently were most of the Cornish aristocracy and leading gentry. Anstis went further, ignoring protests that he was being too blunt, to ask why many who had signed the requisition against the Catholics had, in 1826, elected two members for the borough who were known to be in favour of emancipation.[81]

The final twist in the emancipation saga occurred in Truro in March 1829. More than anything else it highlights the cynical way in which the unreformed electoral system could be manipulated, providing further stimulus to the town's unenfranchised reformers. When Lord Falmouth learned of his two parliamentary members' support for emancipation he was appalled. Confronted by the inevitable ultimatum from their patron to toe his ideological line, both members refused. Thereupon Falmouth wasted no time on the niceties of decorum or persuasion: on 5 March Sir Robert Peel introduced the Catholic Relief bill into the Commons; next day the Truro members

76 *West Briton*, 16 Jan. 1829, 2, 3.
77 Ibid. 9 Jan. 1829, 3.
78 Ibid. 16 Jan. 1829, 2, 3.
79 Ibid. 9 Jan. 1829, 3.
80 Ibid. 6 Feb. 1829, 2.
81 Ibid.

'retired'.[82] At the by-election immediately afterwards (the same day) Lord Encombe and N. W. Peach, total strangers to the town, were elected by the corporation. The deed was accomplished before mid-day, accompanied by a speech from a corporation Tory, Dr Clement Carlyon, justifying the change and wishing that all constituencies throughout the kingdom had a similar opportunity. The spurious justification for Falmouth's action – that it was in accord with the 'sense of the people' which should be considered on such an important question – was not lost on his growing number of critics. After all Falmouth consistently ignored 'the people' when the town elected its MPs.

Assessing change in borough politics

To any casual observer of Cornwall electoral politics transplanted from 1790 to 1829, few outward changes would be observable. Admittedly an 'outsider', Edward Pendarves, was one of the county members, someone whose family did not measure up in either income or status to those of the 'old interest' of the eighteenth century. And of course he was a parliamentary reformer, a man of decidedly liberal opinions. But then so, to a lesser degree, was his long-serving predecessor Sir William Lemon. Pendarves's presence was balanced by the ultra-Tory Sir Richard Vyvyan, descendant of a family with a long history of county representation and therefore very acceptable to the wealthy gentry. Grampound's lack of political virtue had recently been penalised, but the remaining twenty boroughs, like painted ladies, still flaunted their quirks and peculiarities. The Edgcumbes, Eliots, Boscawens and Bullers retained their electoral strongholds, although by 1829 the disposition of borough property among them was slightly different. While the borough MPs still included a familiar mixture of odd, well-known and obscure characters, fewer had direct links with the county. The observer might therefore be lulled into the belief that little had altered in almost half a century when in fact nearly the opposite was the case.

One important clue to the nature of the change was Charles Rashleigh's contemptuous outburst at the 1813 county meeting, when he protested about the presence of inhabitants (in addition to freeholders) eager to hear and participate in the debate on Catholic relief. Although he was a very successful solicitor, not a landowner, Rashleigh spoke for the county's powerful Tory oligarchy because he was their trusted agent in electoral matters and shared their reactionary opinions. Having seen the oligarchy challenged several times since 1805 by the reformers, Rashleigh sprang to the Tories' defence because he, like them, realised how probable it was that parliamentary reform would decimate Cornwall's representation in the House of Commons. Within eighteen months Rashleigh and those he spoke for such

---

[82] Ibid. 13 Mar. 1829, 2.

as De Dunstanville, Gregor, Pole Carew and Falmouth, had lost the debate about inhabitants attending meetings, one result being confirmation of the existence of two political parties, not only at county meetings but also in electoral politics in general. Whigs led by Colman Rashleigh had successfully embarked upon a campaign to build popular support among rural and town dwellers, by publicly criticising the existing Tory hegemony. This, it seems, was one catalyst for change in the Cornish boroughs.

Another, the farmer–reformer alliance, added to the impetus for change and brought the reformers' message more clearly into the towns. There the farmers regularly gathered for market days and the accompanying ordinaries (their market day dinners), discussing their concerns with the small business-men, shop- and inn-keepers who were equally dependent on the strength of the rural economy and therefore listened carefully. The third factor inducing change was the county press, the *West Briton* and the *Gazette*, because besides their weekly fulminations at each other they brought the rural and small town middle and working classes into contact with wider political horizons east of the Tamar. It was parliamentary reform in several towns, abhorrence of colonial slavery in most and conflicting views about Catholic relief every-where which produced a vibrant political milieu in Cornwall. This was assisted by the prolonged county election campaign of 1825–6, when more than ever before national issues were paramount and widely publicised.

Finally then, if England's *ancien régime* was essentially aristocratic, Angli-can and monarchical, with its unifying strength being the Established Church, the regime was under attack in Cornwall well before 1828.[83] In par-ticular the aristocracy's 'entrenched dominance' was always weaker than else-where because there were relatively fewer aristocratic families and a higher proportion of wealthy gentry. Outwardly, aristocratic borough patronage was little changed from the 1790s, but the Boscawens, Edgcumbes and Eliots were increasingly unpopular. Regularly scorned by the *West Briton* for their inde-fensible manipulation of borough representation in almost a dozen towns, they seemed destined by the beginning of the 1820s gradually to become dis-credited reminders of an earlier era. Furthermore, the grip of the Church of England was visibly weakening as the bishop of Exeter's 1821 visitation returns showed. Growing numbers of Bible Christians in the east, Wesleyan Methodists in the west, meant the battle between Church and Chapel was beginning to swing away from the Church. Associated with this was the linking role of the anti-slavery movement, connecting well-known reformers to Old and New Dissent, thereby bringing a new political constituency into association with the Cornish Whigs. Ultimately it was this alliance which provided the energy and ideological commitment identifiable in the small town liberalism of the 1830s.

[83] J. C. D. Clark, *English society, 1688–1832: ideology, social structure and political practice during the ancien régime*, Cambridge 1985.

4

County Politics and Change, 1830–1841

Stability in county politics?

On New Year's Day 1835, in the damp chill of a Cornish winter, Edward Boscawen, first earl of Falmouth, wrote from his seat at Tregothnan near Truro to Sir Robert Peel the Conservative prime minister. With a general election looming later in the month Falmouth was concerned to strengthen the Conservatives' position in West Cornwall by promoting the candidacy of his elder son Lord Boscawen Rose. It was a formidable task given that the two sitting members Edward Pendarves and Sir Charles Lemon were popular and had been unopposed in 1832.[1] However Boscawen Rose also faced unnatural difficulties:

> We had calculated upon much violence and the most determined opposition from the whigs and Radicals, but we could not have conceived that Mr Tremayne should have drawn Sir T. Acland and other men of property and influence here, into a league having for its object to stifle at once any conservative attempt upon the plea of wishing to secure the sitting Whig Sir Ch Lemon in his seat.[2]

Tremayne verified this, admitting that he had canvassed with the sole object of seating his Whig brother-in-law.[3] Both Tremayne and Acland were Conservatives of a kind. Their actions against the interests of their party meant there was little point in Boscawen Rose going to the poll.[4] What Falmouth hoped for was action by Peel to check Tremayne and Acland's interference, otherwise they would 'extinguish all chance of restoring either part of Cornwall to a sound state of feeling for many years to come'. Being unacquainted with the two 'renegades' Peel could do little to help.[5]

Eventually Boscawen Rose and his father decided not to proceed in 1835, but four years later when the short-lived Bedchamber Crisis offered the Conservatives some prospect of office, Falmouth again put his and his son's case to

---

[1] Falmouth to Peel, 1 Jan. 1835, Peel papers, BL, MS Add. 40409, fo. 17.
[2] Ibid.
[3] Ibid. fo. 20.
[4] Ibid. De Dunstanville's second marriage, in 1824, was to Harriet Lemon, Sir Charles Lemon's sister.
[5] Ibid. fos 20–1.

74

Peel.[6] He emphasised the contribution he had made to the Conservative cause in Cornwall, and the Western division in particular, since 1831. Canvassing expenses, and the necessity of maintaining a 'sound' press (the *Royal Cornwall Gazette*), were burdens Falmouth willingly undertook for the party.[7] Once again Peel had to disappoint his supplicant whose eldest son was finally elected for West Cornwall, unopposed, in July 1841.

The Boscawen–Peel correspondence wrongly suggests political manoeuvring of an old-fashioned kind in Cornwall, combinations of aristocratic and gentry influence carrying far more weight in county politics than the opinions of voters. In his letters to Peel, Falmouth omitted any mention of public issues, the state of the voter register, or formalised party organisation, implying instead that power still resided 'in the hands of some ten, twenty, or thirty country gentlemen of comfortable wealth and independent outlook who decided among themselves the representation of the county in parliament and were not easily amenable to any form of central influence'.[8] According to this viewpoint 'family connexion', neighbourliness and county sentiment – a sense of localism – over-rode party feelings. This was not the case in Cornwall, despite there being an absence of contested elections in the West between 1832 and 1841. Closer examination reveals how superficial this stability was, disguising changing circumstances from which even the earl of Falmouth was not immune. The outcome was an era when the county Conservatives slowly reasserted themselves, in 1841 winning three of the four seats they had conceded to their Whig–Liberal opponents nine years earlier.

Understanding this recovery means analysing the defeat from which it sprang, especially Tory attitudes and reactions to parliamentary reform. The changes in county politics after 1832 must also be exposed: for example an intensification of the general concern with such political issues as the abolition of church rates or opposition to free trade, and the appearance of party electoral organisations in each division. Finally, in the context of arguments about Cornish distinctiveness, it is appropriate to attempt to judge whether or not the pattern of county politics was notably different to that elsewhere in England during these years.

Another face of parliamentary reform

The origins of the 1832 Reform Act, and the various roles of those who were supposedly influential in framing it, have long been the subject of historiographical controversy. As part of his much more sweeping study, after examining the broad religious and political contexts in the decade or so preceding

6 Falmouth to Peel, 19 May 1839, ibid. 40426, fos 286–7. The four Falmouth nominees were elected for Truro (2) and Mitchell (2).
7 Ibid.
8 Gash, *Politics in the age of Peel*, 189.

reform, J. C. D. Clark found a slow erosion of what he termed England's *ancien régime* – a process set in train by several factors including dissenting disenchantment with the Church of England.[9] Until 1828–9 when repeal and emancipation triggered the final collapse, parliamentary reform was relatively insignificant; after 1829 it was the by-product of the religious upheaval. Another aspect of the controversy, one preceding by more than a decade Clark's conclusions, concerned county politics more directly. It arose from the occasionally fiery interchange between D. C. Moore and R. W. Davis about the merits of Moore's 'other face of reform'.[10] Just as Davis employed evidence from Buckinghamshire to question Moore, so Cornwall provides a rather different county perspective. Similarly it fails to conform to Clark's account of the genesis of reform. In both instances the key to the differences is the very public persistence of the Cornish reformers.

Turning firstly (and briefly) to Clark, the two preceding chapters emphasised how after 1803 parliamentary reform was at the forefront of public political debate in Cornwall, even if it rarely appeared on the order of business in the House of Commons. Cornwall's powerful Tory political wire-pullers were repeatedly attacked and embarrassed by a group whom they undoubtedly would have regarded as their social inferiors, among them several Anglican vicars including Robert Walker and Darrell Stephens. Using the various forums outlined previously, plus their alliances, the reformers slowly but inevitably politicised the county in the two decades before Repeal. Their victory in the 1826 county election did far more than prove this: it also revealed how the reformers had undermined the Tory hegemony. Later, repeal aroused little interest whereas emancipation sparked a short-lived furore, providing yet another opportunity for the reformers. Thus Clark's conclusion, that in the first decades of the nineteenth century 'Emancipation and Repeal took a great, and a growing, precedence over Reform',[11] is plainly wrong in the case of Cornwall, and maybe other counties. By the beginning of 1830 two decades of public debate were coming to a climax in a way never envisaged by Clark. Moreover the county's *ancien régime* did not explode with the fuse being lit by the ultras. As we shall now see, Clark's ideas about collapse and change at the end of the 1820s are further undermined by a search in Cornwall for Moore's 'other face of reform'.

Debate on this topic began when Davis in his book on Buckinghamshire electoral politics addressed himself to Moore's earlier conclusions about a county-based reform movement. The crux of Moore's argument lay in the English counties: there, in the 1820s, many country squires, already worried by the Tory government's policies on finance and agricultural protection

---

9 Clark, *English society*, esp. ch. vi.
10 D. C. Moore, 'The other face of reform', *Victorian Studies* v (1961), 7–34; Davis, *Political change*, 78–88; D. C. Moore, 'Is "the other face of reform" in Bucks an "hallucination"?', and R. W. Davis, 'Yes', *Journal of British Studies* xv (1976), 150–61.
11 Clark, *English society*, 409.

('cash' and 'corn'), regarded Wellington and Peel's about-face over Catholic emancipation as the final straw. From that springboard the disgruntled ultra-Tories launched themselves into a short-lived but crucial campaign for parliamentary reform. It took the form of a series of county and other reform meetings in the winter and spring of 1830. Joining with the rural Whigs who were equally concerned about 'cash' and 'corn' but not 'Catholics' (many of them, as in Cornwall, favoured emancipation), they pressed their demands for reform. The ultra-Tory gentry, firm in their anti-liberalism, had their sights set on those aristocratic borough patrons and other borough-mongers whose support for the duke of Wellington, they believed, had allowed the passage of Catholic emancipation. So Moore's county reform movement was gentry-led, having its genesis in ultra-Tory discontent.

Moore's 'other face of reform', based on a study of several counties, was labelled an hallucination by Davis, at least so far as Buckinghamshire was concerned. Davis found that in Buckinghamshire 'the reform movement was not primarily a movement of gentry, ultra or any other sort'.[12] In Aylesbury it was drawn from 'prominent members of the middling classes', some of whom opposed Catholic emancipation. The squires were nowhere to be found, and neither the currency issue nor protection ever aroused discussion. Moore's 'country party' was still-born in Buckinghamshire. Interestingly, developments in Cornwall between 1826 and 1832, when compared to the findings of both historians, reveal important similarities and differences. In fact Cornwall provides 'another face of reform' markedly different to that originally suggested by Professor Moore.

His case stands or falls on the existence of an identifiable group of ultra-Tories emerging after Catholic emancipation to press for parliamentary reform. Cornwall was satiated with aristocratic and gentry borough patrons, almost all of whom, together with their members, supported emancipation (Lord Falmouth was a notable exception). Therefore it may be readily – and correctly – assumed that it was this behaviour on the part of the Cornish patrons and their fellow borough-mongers elsewhere which upset many country squires. As well, most patrons faithfully toed the government line over emancipation, so they inevitably turned their backs on parliamentary reform after 1829. Thus Cornwall epitomised the circumstances which elsewhere produced Moore's ultra-Tory phenomenon.

However, there was also a visible clique of Tory extremists, if we judge membership of that group by their 'Protestantism' in particular. Among them were Lord Falmouth and Sir Richard Vyvyan, as well as Reginald Pole Carew and Earl Mount Edgcumbe's heir Viscount Valletort whose territorial bases lay in the south-eastern parishes. All four represented powerful families who might aptly be labelled 'oligarchical wielders of influence'. Among their allies were members of the lesser gentry, including Nicholas Kendall, Edward

---

12 Davis, *Political change*, 78.

Archer, Francis Rodd, John Coryton, Francis Glanville, various members of the Hext family and others. Most of them were eastern landowners of relatively minor social and political significance. By March 1829 these ultras, Falmouth, Vyvyan, Pole Carew and company, were extremely angry with the duke of Wellington's government.

Up to this point it is difficult to challenge the validity of Moore's model, but besides 'Catholics' some consideration must be given to 'corn' and 'cash' which, he alleged, also stirred ultra-Tory disenchantment. Neither issue was particularly significant in Cornwall. The reason was simple: besides the gentry it was yeomen and tenant farmers who were most directly affected by a deflated currency and a reduced scale of duties on imported corn. After 1832 Cornwall's rural middle classes maintained their alliance with the Whig reformers, being convinced that the best solution for their economic hardships lay in parliamentary reform – a more representative House of Commons. Throughout the later 1820s the farmers were in no mood to align themselves with the complaints of the ultra-Tories. Instead they preferred the reformer's analysis of the causes of the post-war slump, poor rates, tithes and taxes, and their solution to 'corn' and 'cash', parliamentary reform. In the spring of 1827 Carew, Glanville and Vyvyan promoted a petition among farmers in south-eastern Cornwall, complaining about the principle of the sliding scale on foreign corn imports. From Westminster Vyvyan explained to Carew that 'The Country Gentlemen are united to a certain degree, we have had some meetings but they all speak at once and without regarding the opinion of the predominant.'[13] In Cornwall they barely spoke at all, and when they did the evidence suggests they shared William Rashleigh's view. He observed to his steward Thomas Robins, 'Should the present alteration in the Corn Laws pass the House of Lords, I think they [sic] will prove beneficial to the Country.'[14] Until the beginning of 1830 when agricultural distress assumed worrying proportions in eastern Cornwall there were few public expressions of concern about 'corn' from ultras, Whig reformers or farmers.

The same conclusion can be reached on 'cash'. Proof that there was never a prolonged debate on this emerges from the activities of two ideological opposites, Vyvyan and Penhallow Peters, the prominent farmer–reformer. On 26 May 1828 Vyvyan wrote to all his Tory agents and others throughout Cornwall on the topic of promissory notes; he was 'convinced that nothing short of a continuance of one pound note circulation will save us from stagnation in our mines and agriculture, a depreciation of value in every article of produce and a melancholy want of employment'.[15] Vyvyan hoped that the response to his doleful predictions would be dozens of petitions and memorials. Instead he was rebuffed. Men were not interested, believing a gold and

---

13 Vyvyan to Carew, 9 Mar. 1827, MSS Carew Pole CC/N/60.
14 Rashleigh to Robins, 23 Mar. 1827, CRO, MSS Rashleigh R 5320.
15 Vyvyan to election agents, 26 May 1828, CRO, MSS Vyvyan V 36/47.

silver currency was a necessity. Never again did Vyvyan return to the currency question.

Several days before Vyvyan's letter Penhallow Peters proposed a meeting on the same subject. Through the *West Briton* he announced that: 'The dissatisfaction that everywhere exists in the County, among all classes of persons, at the prospect of the Act, for withdrawing LOCAL ONE POUND NOTES' induced him to test public opinion.[16] At a well-attended meeting at Truro on 21 May, letters mentioning stagnation of business and the growing difficulties of paying miners were read. Peters spoke with some feeling on monetary problems facing agriculture. Because he believed 'It was unfair of the landowners to leave their tenantry to grapple with their invoicing difficulties', he proposed a county meeting at which the principal gentlemen connected with agriculture, mining and trade could help the freeholders and others to arrive at well-reasoned protests.[17] Presumably Peters anticipated that Cornwall's leading Tories would help to pressure the government. Like Vyvyan he was to be sadly disillusioned. No support was forthcoming and thereafter Peters was more cautious. In fact during his speech at the Bodmin county meeting in 1830 he avoided currency, preferring to rail against one of his favourite aversions, the oppressive church tithes.[18]

While it might truthfully be said that 'corn' and 'cash' were questions on which ultra-Tories and Whigs shared roughly similar viewpoints (for example there was little difference between Vyvyan and Pendarves over protection in 1825-6), neither aroused much interest before March 1830. There is nothing whatsoever to suggest, as Professor Moore does, that they were instruments in pushing 'many influential Tories . . . into clear opposition'.[19] As we have already seen, Catholic emancipation was far more influential in arousing ultra passions against Wellington's government, but in mid 1829 when applied to Cornwall, Moore's model collapses. According to him:

> It was the passage of the Catholic Relief Act, and, even more, the manner in which it was passed, which prompted many of these latter [the oligarchical wielders of influence] first to appraise the political structure of the kingdom and then to add their more effective voices to the cry for reform.[20]

Almost without exception the Cornish ultras remained silent at this time, as they did in Buckinghamshire too. The question is why were they mute at a time when the 'cry for reform' was heard so clearly?

There appear to be several related explanations, the first of which is self-evident. Cornwall's ultra-Tories felt very strongly about Catholic emancipation, but this was not the climax to a series of grievances against various Tory

16 *West Briton*, 16 May 1828, 3.
17 Ibid. 23 May 1828, 2.
18 Ibid. 26 Mar. 1830, 2.
19 Moore, 'Other face of reform', 17.
20 Ibid. 18.

governments. Instead it was the single issue which prompted them to make a public declaration of principle and, by itself, it was insufficient to tempt them to turn on the Wellington government. Also, since 1825 Falmouth, Vyvyan, Pole Carew and other ultras had continually revealed uncompromising attitudes towards parliamentary reform. Because of Pendarves's prolonged campaign before his election in 1826 and his public involvement with the Cornwall reform movement since 1809, the ultras were drawn into making firm and repeated denials of the need for parliamentary reform which became a key issue in the county election. Under such circumstances Vyvyan, his chief supporter Lord Falmouth, and their hard-working band of ultra followers, having taken a public stand on reform before emancipation, would have been hard pressed to perform a credible *volte-face* after March 1829. Allied to this was the long-standing antipathy between Tories and reformers, a feature of the Cornish political landscape since 1809. For the ultras there was no chance whatsoever of even a fleeting 'country party' alliance of the type suggested elsewhere in England.

The breakdown of Moore's model is exemplified by a series of well-attended meetings held in eastern Cornwall during February–March 1830. Callington and Liskeard were the venues for hundred meetings, Bodmin the scene of a full-scale county meeting. None of the ultras already mentioned spoke at any of the gatherings. Nevertheless the drift of the arguments at Callington fits Moore's model, for the chairman Stephen Archer suggested that the current rural distress might have been caused by free trade policies or the change in currency.[21] This question and the overwhelming burden of taxation were taken up by a prominent Liskeard solicitor, Peter Glubb, who suggested at each of the hundred meetings that parliamentary reform was an urgent necessity. 'Ministers would not grant adequate relief until *compelled* to do so by an *honest* House of Commons, Constitutionally elected by the voice of the People.'[22] Before this Glubb had been a Tory; he now changed his political colours but he was not a member of the gentry and was politically insignificant by comparison with Vyvyan, Pole Carew and the rest.

As for the county meeting, the ultra-Tory sheriff Edward Collins tried to stop it. Currency and parliamentary reform were the central topics of discussion, but all the speakers belonged to the reform party which had been so active in the past. Moore's 'rural Whigs' – half of the 'country party' – completely dominated proceedings which reaffirmed the strength and unity of the farmer–reformer alliance.

It seems therefore that so far as the 'other face of reform' is concerned only fragments of it were present in Cornwall. As early as 1825 there was an identifiable ultra-Tory faction which was characterised more by Protestantism than a dislike of government economic or fiscal policy. That they were an

---

21 Archer admitted that he had little idea of the precise causes of distress: *West Briton*, 26 Feb. 1830, 2.
22 Ibid. 13 Mar. 1830, 2.

influential segment of county opinion was proved by their successful re-election of Sir Richard Vyvyan in 1826; however even Vyvyan, who was appalled by Wellington's apostasy over Catholic emancipation, would not flirt with reform in 1829–31. Such an action by him or the other ultras would have exposed them to public ridicule from the Whig reformers, and therefore weakened their political authority.

County meetings and reform

If the 'country party' composed of ultra-Tories and rural Whigs is at the centre of Professor Moore's model, it is 'prominent members of the middling classes, some of whom happen to have opposed Catholic emancipation' who headed the Buckinghamshire reform movement. Professor Davis added that, 'far from being dominated by "squires", ultras or any others, one of the prime motives behind the movement was an intense dislike of landed and all other sorts of exclusive influence'.[23] He also found that a reform meeting held in Aylesbury in February 1830, undoubtedly a part of Moore's 'county' reform movement, revealed that the 'other face of reform' in Buckinghamshire was 'an hallucination'. Anti-Liberals did not influence it, the deflated currency was not seriously discussed, and few of the requisitioners were ultra-Tories. Several of these conclusions are mirrored in Cornwall, where in March 1830 there was a well-attended county meeting at Bodmin having little resemblance to proceedings at Aylesbury.

When the meeting was held in the county town on 22 March the sheriff, Edward Collins, who was a notable ally of Lord Falmouth, should have been in attendance but was not. Though seven magistrates and several hundred freeholders had signed the requisition, Collins declared that too few of the clergy and 'principal freeholders' were on the list.[24] In effect he was attempting to ignore the very development which Cornwall's reformers had successfully sponsored – county meetings open to all, not merely substantial freeholders.

Collins believed a county meeting was unwarranted; he also felt unable to justify endangering the 'unanimity and peace of the county' in times of difficulty and distress. Consequently the authorisation was given by eight Whig magistrates, among them the Reverend Robert Walker, William Peter and David Howell, all prominent reformers. None of the magistrates can be identified as ultras; certainly none were anti-Catholics.

There are several interesting points arising from these preliminaries. Apparently the principal ultra-Tories totally disapproved of a meeting on parliamentary reform; otherwise, Collins's decision would have been very different. Also, county meetings may have been rare in Buckinghamshire, but after

23 Davis, *Political change*, 85.
24 *West Briton*, 12 Mar. 1830, 3.

1809 they were commonplace in Cornwall. Finally, when concluding his speech seconding the petition, the Reverend Robert Walker said to the yeomanry of the county:

> It has been our [the reformers] great ambition to instil into their minds a conviction of the necessity of a Reform in the Representation of the People, for the salvation of the county: and I think we have succeeded; for previous to this meeting being called, I was informed, that if we did not call the Yeomanry together, as we have been accustomed to do, they would assemble of themselves without us.[25]

This then was a meeting of the farmers, so it was the farmers' concerns to which speakers had to address themselves. Undoubtedly this was to be a public reaffirmation of the farmer–reformer alliance.

The proceedings were chaired by Richard Bennet, JP, a gentleman landowner who was regularly identified with Rashleigh's reformers in the 1820s. Colman Rashleigh could not attend as he was out of the county, but in his stead the Reverend Robert Walker, Penhallow Peters, William Peter, his brother Robert and John Rundle, a Devonshire reformer, were the principal speakers. Apart from Peters, the acknowledged leader of the yeomanry, all were minor country gentry and well-known reformers. Their speeches drew attention to the widespread distress endured by agriculture and trade, the cause of which was the accumulated debts and taxes plus the contracted currency. The petitioners agreed on the need for reductions in government expenditure and rigid economy, concluding their appeal with the statement that

> they cannot look at the present situation, or reflect on the past history of their country – its wars, its debts, and its taxes, – without ascribing the far greater portion of its calamities to the very defective and inadequate state of the Representation – to the want of a House of Commons created by – responsible to – and having no interest distinct from – the great body of the People.[26]

This had been the catch-cry of Colman Rashleigh and the Whig reformers for two decades, and was very familiar to the farmers. However Peter and Walker spent most of their time discussing the unfortunate outcomes of a deflated currency – a topic never before raised on such an occasion. What prompted this unusual emphasis?

Peter and Walker contended that the return to a gold-based currency and the suppression of small notes meant a call on the people 'to bear the burthens of 1830 with the means 1792 [sic] to compel them to pay in gold the interest of an enormous Debt contracted, for the most part, in depreciated

---

25 Ibid. 26 Mar. 1830, 2.
26 Ibid.

paper'.[27] Each argued that a reduction in the amount of circulating currency was a prime cause of depressed agricultural prices, the relatively low return to the producer then exacerbating their assorted financial difficulties. Could any government, they asked, act in this way without seriously considering a corresponding reduction in taxation? Other speakers also referred briefly to the currency issue, but it must be emphasised that all were Whig reformers – not ultra-Tories. All had publicly supported Catholic emancipation, all except Rundle had long been identified with the Cornwall reform movement, and all agreed that parliamentary reform would eventually curb the deflationary monetary policy.

It is apparent that Peter and Walker's opinions were directly influenced by the February 1830 Speech from the Throne, and the Amendment to the Address moved by Sir Edward Knatchbull and the marquess of Blandford. By suggesting that distress prevailed only 'in some parts of the Kingdom', the ministers provoked many agriculturists, particularly those in Cornwall. Both speakers at Bodmin carefully quoted the government's view-point, then drew a distinction between the relative prosperity in the western mining districts of the county and the near desperate plight of the farming regions farther east. They also adapted Knatchbull and Blandford's opinions– that a prime cause of the existing distress was a contracted currency. The solution offered was, as always, straightforward – parliamentary reform resulting in a more representative and responsive House of Commons. As they had done since 1815 the reformers gave their farmer allies the well-known 'cause and cure' analysis, substituting national for local causes of distress.

The evidence of the Bodmin meeting and political developments preceding it leave few doubts that Cornwall's Whig gentry, supported by many yeomen and tenant farmers, were at the centre of this county reform movement as they had been for years beforehand. Despite the speeches of Walker and Peter at Bodmin it would be true to say that the currency issue made little impact on this farmer–reformer alliance. Penhallow Peters's unhappy experience in 1828 proves that, nor did the government's tampering with the Corn Laws move them into action. These reactions underline an important similarity between Cornwall and Buckinghamshire; another is the total absence of embittered ultra-Tories (and therefore of anti-liberalism) at these meetings. In Cornwall the Whig gentry were pre-eminent at the Bodmin meeting while at Aylesbury their counterparts were farmers and the urban middling class. The major difference between the reform movements in the two counties was in their leadership, which in the case of Cornwall had long been publicly recognised. In neither county was there a country party alliance along the lines suggested by Moore.

Before leaving the concept of 'another face of reform' attention must be paid to two related developments in the Cornwall of 1829–32. One, men-

---

[27] Ibid. It was Peter who made this statement in the course of developing his currency arguments at great length.

tioned in the previous chapter, was the gradual appearance of a small town reform movement similar to that in Aylesbury, Truro and Liskeard being examples. Davis contended that, 'Reforming sentiment in Buckinghamshire, then, far from being a product of the discontents *of* the landed classes, was rather largely a product of discontent *with* the landed classes, springing from an intense resentment against landed influence.'[28] Truro and Liskeard certainly mirrored patterns of political development in Aylesbury, Buckingham and Marlow, the three towns demonstrating Davis's point.

The other was the outcome of growing popular support for reform. As early as February 1831 Thomas Coulson of Penzance explained to his son how he attended a 'rampant meeting' on the subject. 'It is impossible to conceive the strength of the feeling in the County about reform', he wrote, 'we shall have to our petition the names of nineteenth twentieths of the freeholders and substantial householders of the town.'[29] It was becoming obvious that most Tory borough patrons would be hard-pressed to retain their influence or control – if the boroughs survived disfranchisement. In this political climate several ultra-Tories who offered no support for reform in 1829-30, now endorsed a plan doomed to failure.

The author of the scheme was an anti-Catholic 'squarson', Francis Hext, rector of Helland, a sparsely populated moorland parish near Bodmin. His family were at best minor gentry, with some local influence as landowners and magistrates in the Bodmin–Lostwithiel area. Hext, just over fifty years of age in 1831, was related by marriage with the Kendalls of Pelyn. In fact Nicholas Kendall, one of Vyvyan's most outspoken and staunch supporters, was his nephew. The Hexts were on the fringes of county politics, at least until 1831 when Francis, through the columns of the *Gazette* and under the *nom de plume* 'YZ', addressed a letter to Vyvyan containing assorted proposals for reform. The proposals were expanded in successive letters, and before long they aroused considerable discussion among the Tories.[30]

When the House of Lords rejected the Reform Bill in October 1831, 'the opportunity was seized by the moderate section of the Cornish opposition to produce those concessions to reform which were considered safe and not an attack upon the constitution'.[31] That explanation is confusing and even misleading. Hext and all his supporters including Reginald Pole Carew, the chief among them, were dedicated ultra-Tories. On their past record this group could hardly be described as 'moderate' in any sense. As for 'concessions to reform', the plan was no more than a gesture. Unlike Professor Moore's ultras who apparently wished to purge the constitution, partly for revenge on Peel and Wellington, partly because even they could see some of the anomalies,

28 Davis, *Political change*, 87.
29 Thomas Coulson to Walter Coulson, 5 Feb. 1831, Coulson correspondence, CRO, X, 696/165.
30 Elvins, 'Reform movement', ch. vi, p. 1.
31 Ibid.

the Cornwall group offered a very different justification. Prompted early in 1831 by fear of far-reaching borough disfranchisement and the danger of mob rule, they drew up a chimerical plan designed to keep their party from an electoral abyss. Desperate and unprincipled, it was a last-ditch bid so blatant in its motivation that with one exception all Cornwall's principal Tories shied away. Even fears of disunity could not persuade them to make common cause with socially inferior gentry who were prepared to ignore principled opposition to reform. Rather than being fathered by moderate Tories, Hext's plan was a unique manifestation of ultra extremism.

The principal features were as follows: no existing boroughs would be disfranchised, the pecuniary qualifications of borough electors should vary according to local circumstances and the town or city's population, counties would not be split into divisions, and parliamentary candidates giving pledges to 'any specific measures of legislation' would be disqualified from taking their seats.[32] The plan attracted some support in April–May 1831, but then it was shelved as Cornwall's Tories became preoccupied with their attempts to return two ultras (Vyvyan and Valletort) for the county in the general election.

Afterwards, in November 1831, Hext decided on one last bid for approval of his plan. His aim was to resubmit it to the 'gentry and magistracy' for their approval before addressing the king; what he achieved was rather less, and, of great importance, the Tories again split, although not into ultras versus moderates as had occurred in 1829. Instead, with the exception of Reginald Pole Carew, they divided between greater and lesser gentry, Hext failing to win more than one of the former to his side. Lord Falmouth summed up the general feeling when he argued that the bill had to be opposed on principle as alternatives would only splinter the already 'reduced ranks' of the Tories.[33] The Hext plan finally came to an ignominious end in February 1832 when only 300 signed an address to the king.[34]

When compared with Buckinghamshire and Moore's more wide-ranging conclusions, Cornwall presents another, different face of reform. There was no 'country party' because the county's ultra-Tory faction knew an alliance would have been instantly repudiated by the well-established farmer–reformer alliance. Therefore they made no commitment, temporary or otherwise, to parliamentary reform following emancipation. Earlier the currency question had aroused little interest, alterations to the Corn Laws even less. Divided over emancipation, Cornwall's Tories at first maintained an uneasy unity against parliamentary reform, because unequivocal opposition was essential if the borough empires were not to be completely swept away. However, as revealed in 1825–6 and again in 1829, the Tory Party was prone to split between ultras and moderates, and in 1831–2 a new splintering

---

[32] Ibid. appendix 3.
[33] Falmouth to Pole Carew, 13 Jan. 1832, MSS Carew Pole CC/N/64.
[34] Hext to Carew, 8 Feb. 1832, ibid. CC/Q/5.

occurred, this time on social lines with the greater and lesser gentry being at loggerheads.

Cornwall also presents an important exception to Clark's views: Catholic and Protestant dissent counted for little, democracy for much.[35] Reform in this relatively isolated south-western county (yet one probably not dissimilar to others in England), was not 'a consequence of the shattering of the old order by Emancipation', but the outcome of very different pressures.[36]

Popular responses to Reform

No great public issue so convulsed the entire Cornish population as did parliamentary reform. From the time of the resignation of Wellington's ministry shortly after his ill-judged speech defending the existing constitution in November 1830, the political temperature climbed steadily higher, due in part to the untiring efforts of the *West Briton* and the gentry reformers. The initial stimulus came from the county meeting at Bodmin on 19 January 1831 which, according to the *West Briton*, was the largest and most respectable gathering ever to assemble to discuss reform. In the ensuing weeks many boroughs and unenfranchised towns followed this example, holding their own meetings at which there was little opposition. The Penzance meeting attended by Thomas Coulson, referred to earlier, was probably typical. Initially the mayor refused to convene a meeting for the purpose of sending a petition to Westminster, despite a requisition signed by 110 townspeople. Under pressure, he agreed to do so, when it was explained he was not being requested 'to mix himself up with the question, but merely to preside and use his option on the final issue'.[37] Later in the meeting the mayor was so moved by proceedings 'that he professed himself a reformer', then when the ballot was discussed he 'cried out I am for ballot too!'[38]

Many towns took to heart William Peter's January condemnation of the borough system, with its associated degradation:

> If, in their progress through the country, they [his audience] meet with a town more desolate, more dirty, more woe-begone, than another, – sterile in the midst of fertility, poor in the midst of plenty, – where industry pines, manufacturers languish, and commerce decays, – if they meet with such a place, in nine instances out of ten, they will, on enquiry, find it to be a borough town, returning Members to Parliament.[39]

35 Clark, *English society*, 409.
36 Ibid.
37 Coulson to Walter Coulson, 5 Feb. 1831, Coulson correspondence, CRO, X, 696/165.
38 Ibid.
39 *West Briton*, 21 Jan. 1831, 2.

Amid the cheers, interjectors were quick to point out that the audience would not need to leave Cornwall to see these.

In such an environment Pendarves and Vyvyan, having been re-elected in 1830 without serious threat of opposition, once again in May 1831 had to face the voters. Earlier, parliament had been dissolved by the king when the government had been defeated on Gascoyne's motion – that the number of MPs for England and Wales not be reduced. Furthermore local feelings had been aroused by the March county meeting, the occasion when Vyvyan refused to appear in person, preferring to write explaining he could 'never support a measure which if carried will in my opinion lead to anarchy and military despotism'.[40]

At the dinner customarily held after the meeting the Reformers requested Colman Rashleigh to contest Vyvyan's seat, then when he refused, asked William Peter. Despite his precarious financial state Peter agreed, on the understanding that he would retire if and when a suitable alternative could be found.[41] Vyvyan's response was contemptuous: 'An individual had come forward to oppose him for the County of Cornwall, who under normal circumstances would never have presented himself', he was reported as saying.[42] Privately he confessed to Reginald Pole Carew his amazement that Peter should seek such a prominent position, 'and that must open the eyes of all Tory freeholders who are not completely demented on this occasion'.[43] Meanwhile, after much procrastinating Sir Charles Lemon, whose social standing and wealth were far greater than Peter's, was persuaded to replace him, while the Tories partnered Vyvyan with Viscount Valletort. The first four-way contest since 1774 proved to be a debacle for the Tories, who trailed their opponents by almost 1,000 votes when they withdrew.

G. W. Gregor of Trewarthenick, a member of Vyvyan's committee, expressed strong views about the election: 'Indeed as far as my opinion goes it was useless to commence it, Sir R. V. and Lord V. never having had a shadow of a chance from the beginning.'[44] Several months later, amid wrangling among the Tories about payment of election expenses (their bill was £24,000, compared to the Reformers' £12,000 – for half the number of votes), Gregor shrewdly concluded that his party 'had been on the decline since the Election of 1826'.[45] However there were other reasons for the thrashing.

One was the unique strength of the farmer–reformer alliance, again evident as it had been in 1825–6. Rashleigh and the Whig lesser gentry finally reaped their reward for, as the *Gazette* put it, 'the spirit of reform has done its work. It mattered little who came forward at our election; the

---

[40] Ibid. 25 Mar. 1831, 3.
[41] Ibid.
[42] Ibid. 1 Apr. 1831, 3.
[43] Vyvyan to Pole Carew, 31 Mar. 1831, MSS Carew Pole CC/N/64.
[44] Diary entry, MSS Gregor G 1935/5.
[45] Elvins, 'Reform movement', ch. iv, p. 18.

Reform Question stood in the place of any merits in the candidate; against this magic word it was in vain to contend'.[46] The Whig–Liberals' victory was the climax not of a short-lived period of agitation but two decades of solid, unremitting effort. Lemon's victory was also due to another, equally powerful force – his family connections. Valletort had no illusions about this: 'With those who opposed him on political grounds he felt no cause of quarrel but there were some who were his opponents on other grounds, who approved of his principles whilst for personal family reasons they supported his opponent. To these he chiefly owed his defeat and he regarded them with very different feelings.'[47] Naturally Lemon and De Dunstanville ritualistically denied the accusations, which were to resurface continually until Lemon's final retirement from his West Cornwall seat in April 1857.

The last great Reformer-led county meeting at Bodmin was held on 26 October 1831, a little over two weeks after the government's bill was defeated by 199 votes to 158 on its second reading in the House of Lords. Again Cornwall's freeholders and inhabitants reaffirmed their commitment to parliamentary reform, in spite of open opposition at the meeting from Lord Valletort and Lord Eliot.[48] In the House of Lords the earl of Falmouth fought bitterly in opposition but by no stretch of the imagination could he be said to be representative of more than a tiny pocket of Cornish public opinion. For the great majority the quicker the excrescences of the old corrupt borough system were eliminated, the better. When the county constituency was finally divided in two after the passage of the bill, and four Whig–Liberals were elected in December 1832 – Pendarves and Lemon for West Cornwall, Sir William Molesworth and William Trelawny for the East – the reformers were entitled to feel elated. Together they and the farmers dominated county politics.

The impact of 1832 on county politics

Following the 1832 general election West and East Cornwall began to exhibit quite different political characteristics. The former became an uncontested Whig–Liberal bastion until the 1880s, the latter a constituency where more often than not representation was shared after contested elections. West Cornwall was unquestionably the home of Cornish Dissent, principally because of the mining concentration sprawling from St Agnes to Truro, westward through Gwennap, Illogan, Camborne and on to Cape Cornwall. Tin and copper mining, fishing and agriculture all coexisted. East of Truro where the peninsula thickened, life and economic patterns provided a contrast. Eastern Cornwall was pre-eminently agricultural, a region where arable and livestock farming were often practised side by side. Here, in the heartland of

46 Ibid. 19.
47 Ibid. 18.
48 *West Briton*, 28 Oct. 1831, 2.

the farmer–reformer alliance, the Church of England waged a more even battle with Dissent. Whereas the west witnessed the rise of powerful mining families such as the Williams of Scorrier and the Daveys, each on the brink of diversifying into landed acres and political life, eastern Cornwall remained a haven for gentry landowners and large farmers whose lifestyle was little different from that of the mid eighteenth century.

It has been suggested that after 1832 counties such as Cornwall exhibited 'close personal relationships' among the county gentry, who maintained a 'relative indifference to the feuds of reformers and anti-reformers that agitated the distant metropolis'.[49] As seen already this extrapolation of the traditional view of eighteenth-century county politics is quite misleading, something which may be demonstrated by scrutinising the activities of the gentry, the alleged 'managers' of county representation.

Table 5 reveals how county MPs continued to come from the ranks of the wealthier, more prestigious gentry, almost all of those listed probably enjoying landed incomes in excess of £5,000 *per annum*. At the top of the list were the Eliots of St Germans and the Boscawens of Tregothnan. In 1873 their gross estimated rentals *per annum* were £17,191 and £35,953 respectively.[50] On the other hand Nicholas Kendall, MP for East Cornwall from 1852 to 1868, had little more than £2,000 *per annum*. The table also highlights the absence of contested elections in West Cornwall, suggesting either gentry compromises or prolonged Conservative weakness.

The compromise explanation, Professor Gash's belief that until at least 1842 county electoral politics were the outcome of 'arrangements' among the gentry, only seems plausible if, as he assumes, they (the Cornish gentry) were not clearly divided by party or other differences. In fact feuds and party enmities had long been a feature of county politics. If the reverse had been true Lord Falmouth would not have been so worried by the ramifications of the 'Lemon connection' which ostensibly led to his son's withdrawal in 1835. Falmouth himself was determined to unseat one of the sitting members, preferably Pendarves, but with no local organisation and no attention being paid to the registers since 1832 such a goal was extremely difficult to achieve. His tactics appear to have been to isolate Pendarves, forcing his retirement by demonstrating that the influence of the Lemon connection was against him. Hence Falmouth's frustration with the Conservative opposition to his son's candidacy. Yet he exaggerated the electoral importance of the Lemon family network which so annoyed him.

Tremayne, a large landowner, had most of his property in the eastern division. So did the Bullers with whom the Lemons had intermarried half a century earlier. As for the dying De Dunstanville and his influential relative Canon Rogers of Penrose near Helston, they had supported Lemon in

[49] Gash, *Politics*, 190.
[50] *House of Commons, sessional papers: returns of owners of land in England and Wales* . . . 1872–3, PP 1874, lxxii.

Table 5
Representation, East and West Cornwall, 1832–52

East Cornwall			West Cornwall	
1832 Molesworth, Sir W., Bt			Pendarves, E. W. W.	L
Trelawny, W. L. S.			Lemon, Sir C., Bt	L
1835 Molesworth, Sir W., Bt	L		Pendarves, E. W. W.	L
Trelawny, Sir W. L. S., Bt	L		Lemon, Sir C., Bt	L
1837 Eliot, Lord	C	2,430	Pendarves, E. W. W.	L
Vivian, Sir R. H., Bt	L	2,294	Lemon, Sir C., Bt	L
Trelawny, Sir W. L. S., Bt	L	*2,250*		
1841 Eliot, Lord	C	3,008	Pendarves, E. W. W.	L
Rashleigh, W.	C	2,807	Boscawen Rose, Lord	C
Trelawny, John S.	L	*1,647*		
			1842 Boscawen Rose succeeded to	
1845 Eliot succeeded to peerage			peerage	
Carew, W. H. Pole	P		Lemon, Sir C., Bt	L
1847 Carew, W. H. Pole	P		Pendarves, E. W. W.	L
Robartes, T. J. Agar	L		Lemon, Sir C., Bt	L
1852 Robartes, T. J. Agar	L	2,609	Pendarves, E. W. W.	L
Kendall, Nicholas	P	1,996	Lemon, Sir C., Bt	L
Carew, W. H. Pole	C	*1,979*		

(names of unsuccessful candidates italicised)
Source: *McCalmont's parliamentary poll book: British election results, 1832–1918*, ed.
J. Vincent and M. Stenton, Brighton 1971.

previous elections and there was no good reason for them to change. When these points are considered, along with the undoubted voting strength of the Whig–Liberals, the strong bond between Pendarves and Lemon, and growing public interest in the tithes question, municipal incorporation and church rates, all more likely to be settled by a Whig–Liberal government, Boscawen Rose was attempting to swim against a very strong tide. Ultimately he and his father acknowledged this and saved their money.

Six years later, in 1841, Sir Charles Lemon unexpectedly retired a week or so before the election. Gash considered this to be a possible arrangement among the gentry, thereby creating the vacancy for Boscawen Rose. In fact it was nothing of the sort. At the preceding election Lemon had been embarrassed on the hustings by critical comments from several among the crowd over his attitude to Dissenters and their obligation to pay church rates. He went to great lengths to explain why he had opposed the government's plan to remove them, voting instead for a committee of enquiry.[51] As a sincere

[51] *West Briton*, 11 Aug. 1837, 2, 4.

supporter of the Church of England, with influential friends and relatives who were similarly disinclined to agree to any erosion of the Church's finances, Lemon faced a dilemma. Western Cornwall was rife with complaints about the rates in 1838–40, so in 1841 he was certain once again to be subjected to critical questioning. An additional complication was his unpopular support for the Melbourne government's proposed introduction of a low fixed duty on imported corn. Add to this his occasional votes with the Conservatives in 1840–1 and Lemon was in trouble.

Compounding his problems was the ultimatum from his 'connection'. According to a knowledgeable onlooker 'Lady Basset, J. H. Tremayne, Canon Rogers etc. intend to divide their influence between Lord Boscawen and Sir Charles Lemon, provided the latter does not coalesce with E. W. W. Pendarves.'[52] Lemon refused to desert Pendarves so his relatives redirected their influence and support to Boscawen Rose. Clearly this was another consideration in Lemon's retirement decision. But it was not the only one, for principles were also at stake.

Boscawen Rose was finally successful because for once the leading Conservative families were united, not in a compromise but in opposition to the Whig–Liberals. Being a protectionist obviously helped Boscawen Rose, both with the farmers and many of the miners who were dismayed by his prediction that free trade would bring cheaper bread and therefore lower wages. However his was a short-lived success for at the end of the year his father died and Boscawen Rose was elevated to the House of Lords. Overcoming his initial irresolution Lemon seized the chance. According to Gordon Gregor, a member of Boscawen Rose's election committee:

> Sir Richard Vyvyan who was applied to in the first instance, continues to adhere to his resolution of not giving up Helstone, and the very few gentlemen of our party in his Division, who could have the smallest chance of success, are deterred from coming forward, from various family and other reasons; – so that Sir Charles Lemon, who has thrown himself into the arms of the Radical Party, has every chance of walking over the course.[53]

By modifying his views on the low fixed duty on corn imports and avoiding the touchy church rates question, as well as receiving a petition signed by 1900 electors, Lemon knew his re-election was a certainty even without support from several of his relatives.

The suggestion that the feuds of reformers and anti-reformers were largely irrelevant in Cornwall, representation being decided by agreement among the gentry, is clearly wrong. Cornwall's gentry were divided on ideological grounds long before 1832 and remained so afterwards. In the west, as we shall see later, new middle-class men from commercial backgrounds, particularly

---

[52] A. Jenkin to T. J. Agar-Robartes, 24 May 1841, RIC, Jenkin letterbooks, HJ/1/19.
[53] Gregor to Sir Robert Peel, 29 Jan. 1842, BL, MS Add. 40451, fo. 130.

mining, worked cheek by jowl with the older reformers to keep Pendarves in the House of Commons and return Lemon. Their opponents were weak and sometimes so badly divided that they actually augmented Whig–Liberal support.

But the reformers and anti-reformers never sat down together to bargain over the representation of the county. Informally they agreed that between them West Cornwall MPs should represent the mining and agricultural interests, and they always combined forces when the well-being of the mining industry was endangered, as they thought it was in 1838–9. Although the tinners were determined to secure the abolition of the duchy coinage duty, ultimately they were also forced to agree to a relatively low protective duty on foreign ores to compensate the duchy. Cross-party agreement was always guaranteed when the port of Falmouth's mail packet station seemed likely to be shifted, but in obvious electoral matters there was no common view. As for East Cornwall, although the emerging pattern of electoral politics was in complete contrast to that in the West, there too ideological differences among the gentry over-rode more personal considerations.

Party organisation after 1832

One of the clearest contrasts between pre- and post-1832 electoral politics in Britain was the appearance of formal party organisation. Both Conservatives and Whig–Liberals bent their backs to this task, one party in an attempt to erase the debacle of the 1832 general election, the other as a reaction to this initiative and also, like the Conservatives, to take advantage of the voter registration provisions of the Reform Act. In the winter of 1834–5 Conservative and Constitutional Associations sprang up in many English counties and boroughs. Meanwhile the Carlton Club, founded in 1832, provided Francis Bonham and other Conservative party organisers with a headquarters. The Reform Association, organised by the Whig–Liberals in 1834 to attend to registrations, was reorganised the next year, with many constituency branches and a central registration office in London. The Reform Club (founded 1836) and the Westminster Club (1834) were the Whig–Liberal equivalents of the Carlton. Both parties had organisers who worked with a small coterie of MPs in order to keep their fingers on the electoral pulse. Thus, after the 1837 general election, 'Registration was now generally regarded by party leaders, election agents and journalists as the key to electoral success.'[54] In this context, from as early as 1835 it was the Conservatives who made by far the greater effort, and in doing so laid the foundation for their 1841 victory.

In Cornwall, no attention was paid by either party to the registrations of

[54] D. H. Close, 'The general elections of 1835 and 1837 in England and Wales', unpubl. DPhil. diss. Oxford 1967, 457.

1833 and 1834, but immediately after the sudden general election early in 1835 this began to change. In June a group of Pendarves's middle-class supporters, mostly connected with the mining industry, formed the Redruth Reform Association. Michael Williams (later a West Cornwall MP) and William Davey were among the committee members, and under the central committee were sub-committees in each of the nine parishes for which Redruth was the polling station – Gwennap, Camborne, Illogan, St Agnes, Phillack, Gwinnear, Gwithian, Stithians and Mabe.[55] The function of these sub-committees was to maintain parochial registers, draw up lists of claims and objections, then pass this information to the central committee.

Two weeks later the West Cornwall Reform Association came into existence, a divisional organisation embracing four district committees at Truro, Helston, Penzance and Redruth. Humphrey Willyams was chairman, Davey treasurer and William Ferris of Truro, Lemon's election agent, secretary.[56] Again the primary object was 'to watch over the registration' but the most striking feature of these associations was the men who controlled them. With the exception of the landowner-banker Willyams, who had been involved with the Truro reformers since 1818, they were socially mobile middle-class men of new wealth gained from mining or the professions. Most of them townsmen, their social and political networks were among people of similar background, while the gentry were less prominent. This was not the case in East Cornwall where, in the same year, a similar association initiated by the newly knighted Sir Colman Rashleigh included many well-known gentry reformers on the committee.[57] They and their colleagues belonged to a different social class, and appear to have been less diligent than their western counterparts, possibly because soon after the association's birth many of the members became embroiled in a divisive ideological conflict causing Sir William Molesworth's retirement from his seat.

Surprisingly, and contrary to the national trend, the Conservatives were much slower off the mark than their rivals. In fact in West Cornwall they barely made it to the starting line, the 1835 registration being attended to on an *ad hoc* basis by a number of solicitors retained by Lord Falmouth. At the beginning of 1836 two Protestant Conservative Associations were formed, ostensibly to defend the Church–State nexus but also to attend to registrations. Although the two later amalgamated, the outcome was not productive and the combined association soon became defunct, almost certainly because of the lack of interest shown by leading Conservatives.[58] Thereafter any effort was left to potential candidates and their supporters.

How successful were they? Newspaper evidence is no more than fragmentary, but it is enough to explain the pattern evident in table 6. Judging by the

55 Elvins, 'Reform movement', ch. vii, p. 17.
56 Ibid.
57 Ibid. 18.
58 *West Briton*, 29 Jan. 1836, 3; Elvins, 'Reform movement', ch. vii, p. 21.

Table 6
Registered county voters

	Registered voters				
	1832	1835	1837	1839–40	1841
West Cornwall	3,353	3,612	4,928	4,911	5,040
East Cornwall	4,462	4,392	5,469	5,957	6,076

Source: *House of Commons, sessional papers: number of electors*, PP 1833 xxvii. 21; 1834 ix. 604; 1836 xliii. 373, 421; 1837–8 xliv. 553; 1840 xxxix. 187; 1843 xliv.

silence of the *Royal Cornwall Gazette*, the West Cornwall registrations between 1835 and 1837 were almost entirely a Whig–Liberal affair, a fair reflection of the Reform Association's energy. In 1837, when for a short time a third Whig–Liberal, Cartaret Ellis, seemed likely to contest the division, it came out squarely in support of Sir Charles Lemon – whom Ellis unsuccessfully aimed to unseat.[59] After this the association's efforts died away, simultaneously motivating the Conservatives, and so in 1839 Lord Falmouth decided to renew his efforts on his son's behalf. The result was Conservative gains of seventy-nine and 163 in the Redruth and Truro districts (in the latter the party clearly held an advantage in objections, adding 169 new votes to the Liberals twenty-seven). Reviewing the division the *Gazette* claimed an increase of more than 500 votes, and the story was much the same in 1840, Conservative gains again being made in the same districts.[60] So even though the total number of voters increased by little more than 100 after 1837, the composition of the register swung in the Conservatives' favour. This achievement was due to solicitors hired by men such as Falmouth, rather than a divisional organisation.

The story was very different in East Cornwall: not until twelve months after Lord Eliot's success in the 1837 election did the Conservatives decide to go a step further by setting up a Registration Association. Their justification was straightforward: 'The Contests for the representation of this County have been very expensive to the Conservatives, arising from want of organised plans, the consequences of all arrangements being left until the verge of the election and of general want of attention to the Registration since the Reform Act.'[61] Like the western Liberals they chose a three-level structure – a central committee with at least one member representing each of the eight polling stations (St Austell, Bodmin, Callington, Camelford, St Columb, Launceston, Liskeard, Stratton), an agent to work in each district, and at the bottom of the pyramid, parish leaders. A resolution of an early meeting suggests how thorough the Conservatives were, for it was agreed:

59 Ibid. ch. vii, p. 31.
60 *Royal Cornwall Gazette*, 18 Oct. 1839, 2.
61 Elvins, 'Reform movement', ch. viii, p. 8.

in districts where necessary an additional agent shall be paid a small annual salary and that he be taken from that station and class of persons forming the largest body of electors in the District for which he acts and although he may be of humble station in society he must possess character and industry and such an influence over the minds of the Electors of his district as will serve the cause he espouses.[62]

The chairman was Francis Rodd, a well-known opponent of the Reformers, William Pole Carew (county MP 1845–52) treasurer, and Charles Gurney, a Launceston attorney with a long-standing involvement in electoral work, secretary. Most members of the central and district committees were lesser gentry or farmer freeholders, another sign of the gradual collapse of the farmer–reformer alliance. The association appears to have been well funded and at the registrations of 1838 and 1839 totally eclipsed the Whig–Liberals. It was this success together with John Trelawny's radicalism and his support for the low fixed duty on corn which in 1841 persuaded the Conservatives to run a second candidate, William Rashleigh, Jr.

Summing up the importance of party organisation and registrations, the over-riding impression in both divisions is of Conservative ascendancy after 1837. Even without a divisional body in West Cornwall Conservatives managed to outstrip their opponents to the point where the always cautious Lord Falmouth finally committed his son to a contest. As for East Cornwall, it accurately reflected a national trend in English counties: clear superiority by the Conservatives at the registrations, enabling them to make a realistic bid for both seats. The strength of the Registration Association proved that its members realised the old politics of arrangements and compromises were quite unsuited to the new political milieu. Helped by widespread disquiet resulting from the attack on agricultural protection, the Conservatives demonstrated their mastery of the new circumstances.

The impact of national issues on county politics

We have already seen how national issues and their local variations were conspicuous in Cornwall county politics before the conclusion of the Napoleonic Wars. They remained so throughout the 1820s due to the efforts of the gentry reformers. The decade following the Reform Act was no different, with the farmers channelling their activism into those issues which most directly affected them, for example the campaigns against tithes and the introduction of free trade. Because of the Melbourne government's sympathy for Dissenters' disabilities, coupled with its inability to settle the most contentious issue – payment of Church rates – a barrage of protests broke out in West Cornwall in the late 1830s. However, long before this parliamentary

---

[62] Copy of resolutions, meeting at Five Lanes, 27 Aug. 1838, MSS Kendall, KL.

candidates ignored the rates question at their peril. Nor, because of their popular support, did they neglect protection or other major issues which periodically enlivened county politics.

From the mid 1820s the Cornish farmers' vigorous campaign against tithes languished, as they were swept up in the parliamentary reform movement. Immediately after 1832 they quickly renewed their opposition, arguing that tithes were an iniquitous and outdated tax, deprived the poor of employment and posed a formidable obstacle to the improvement of waste land. Meetings early in 1833 in Veryan, Trigg and elsewhere agreed on proposing commutation to a money system of payment, and also demanded that the jurisdiction of ecclesiastical courts over farmers for tithe disputes should be abolished. As usual Penhallow Peters was in the thick of the campaign.[63] In 1834 he took a prominent part at meetings in East and West Cornwall, stating at the latter 'That the enormous injuries inflicted by the Tithe System have at length become insufferable'. He also pointed to the calamitous consequences for the Church if nothing was done.[64] Petitions for commutation were agreed to by both meetings, and in May 1834 Peters was chosen as delegate to join others in London working for changes to the government's bill for commutation. Most concern was focused on the method of determining the commuted payments and the amount, both of which were satisfactorily resolved in the 1836 act. Before then, at the 1835 general election, Cornwall's four county members had been drawn into the debate. Meanwhile, in the East other matters of longer-term significance were beginning to preoccupy the Whig–Liberal parliamentary representatives and their supporters.

The root of the problem was Sir William Molesworth's radicalism. Gradually it dawned on the old gentry reformers, most of whom like Sir Colman Rashleigh resided in the division, that Molesworth's 'extremism' went beyond their beliefs. Simultaneously many farmers became alarmed, presaging the disintegration of the long-standing farmer–reformer alliance. The first hint of a possible rupture between the allies came in 1833 when Sir William Molesworth was the only Cornish member in the House of Commons to support a proposed alteration to the Corn Laws. At a time of comparative prosperity for the farmers little attention was paid to his vote, but afterwards Molesworth never hid his opinions on the subject. Electors and non-electors began to appreciate that Molesworth was a thorough-going Radical, for he voted for secret ballot and shorter parliaments, and occasionally he also supported Daniel O'Connell on Irish questions. His fellow MP William Trelawny was much the same, although he was a protectionist and therefore seemed more sympathetic to the farmers who elected him.

Following his 1835 re-election Molesworth came into conflict with Rashleigh, the cause being an article in the short-lived *London Review* of which Molesworth was the proprietor. The contentious contribution argued for the

[63] See, for example, *West Briton*, 19 Apr. 1833, 2.
[64] Ibid. 24 Jan. 1834, 1, 4; 31 Jan. 1834, 3.

abolition of the hereditary principle in the House of Lords, a view Moles-worth endorsed. Obviously, Rashleigh pointed out, there was a wide ideologi-cal gulf between them, one that could never be bridged.[65] Despite assurances to the contrary, Rashleigh did not confine his thoughts to private correspon-dence, inevitably undermining the county member's position. Molesworth therefore took the initiative: in September 1836 he announced his retire-ment, criticising the Whigs for being 'timid and irresolute', acknowledging he belonged to the Westminster Radicals and no doubt inwardly realising that with signs of an agricultural downturn his re-election prospects were remote.[66] Encouraged by this public squabbling and the forthcoming vacancy for the division, the Conservatives enticed Edward Eliot, eldest son of the second earl of St Germans, to stand. A member of a highly respected family with the reputation for being generous landlords, Eliot was a strong candi-date. Moreover he favoured removal of Dissenters' disabilities, commutation of tithes and agricultural protection, and opposed the Radical programme so dear to Molesworth's heart. Not surprisingly he topped the poll in 1837 and 1841, for he was in total sympathy with the farmers, many of whom now pro-ceeded to walk away from their reformer allies.

Protection was the reason for the farmers' defection. Since 1828 a sliding scale of import duties on foreign corn meant that, as the domestic price rose above 66s. per quarter, for each 1s. increase in price the duty fell by the corre-sponding amount. When the domestic price reached 73s. only a 1s. nominal duty remained. At the other end of the scale, as the domestic price sank below 66s. so the duty increased. Until the end of the 1830s protection remained the official policy of Whig–Liberals and Conservatives, but in the final years of Lord Melbourne's government this began to change. Charles Villiers was responsible for an annual repeal motion in the House of Commons and in 1839 the government allowed a free vote on the issue. As more and more Whig–Liberals agreed that cheaper bread was desirable, pro-tectionists dug in to preserve the agricultural interests from possible ruin. After 1837, as protectionist sentiment rose in the countryside, the Conserva-tives realised this was a potent issue to use against the Whig–Liberals; thus in Lincolnshire, Buckinghamshire and Essex, Tory–farmer alliances appeared – as they did in East Cornwall.

There the farmers gradually took up the pivotal role they were to play in electoral politics until the 1870s, swinging between supporting Liberals or Conservatives according to their circumstances and concerns. Beginning in the mid 1830s when agriculture was enduring yet another depression their concern was entirely selfish – to block imports of foreign corn. Consequently Edward Eliot attracted some of their support in 1837, he and William Rash-leigh, the second protectionist, even more in 1841. Both were firmly opposed to the government's low fixed duty proposal. By their actions their supporters,

---

[65] Elvins, 'Reform movement', ch. vii, pp. 18–24.
[66] Ibid.

the protectionist farmers, were reaffirming their political independence; that is, their votes would go to whichever party showed greatest sympathy for their plight. As we shall see this was one of the recurring themes of East Cornwall politics in the mid Victorian years.

Nevertheless it would be wrong to oversimplify the farmers' independence: they too were divided, and by January 1839 battle lines between protectionists and free traders were clearly drawn. The *West Briton* advocated free trade, the *Gazette* naturally opposed it, saying it would ruin agriculture. At Launceston, Penryn and St Columb, meetings condemned the free trade movement.[67] Meanwhile opponents at these meetings were heartened by the response to the Anti-Corn Law League's Richard Acland as he progressed through the county: in May–June 1839 he drew large audiences in the Methodist chapel at Stratton, at Launceston, Callington, Liskeard and Camelford in the East, Truro and Redruth in the West.[68] Thenceforth, from 1841 the League's activity was minimal.

Even in 1839 during a spate of protectionist meetings there was no shortage of articulate opponents ready to challenge the predominant view-point. Later the same year free trade views even infiltrated the ostensibly non-political Cornwall Agricultural Association. So threatened did some members feel by Acland's tour and the growing sympathy for free trade, that they took the opportunity to give vent to their feelings at the annual meeting in Truro.[69] This was too much for many members: toasts were rowdily refused; Penhallow Peters and Mr Rickerby, editor of the *Falmouth Packet* and a vocal supporter of the local Chartists, launched devastating counter-attacks on several of the more diehard Conservatives. Although in later years the association returned to its usual non-political somnolence, Peters did not, continuing to attack the Corn Laws up to the 1841 general election. Despite his and others' efforts protection carried the day.[70] As Brian Elvins pointed out in 1841 'protection proved to be the unifying factor for the Conservatives which Reform had been for the Liberals up to 1832'.[71]

Support for protection also played a part in Boscawen Rose's victory in West Cornwall. Pendarves was understood to represent the mining interest, Lemon agriculture, yet Lemon was opposed to the existing sliding scale of duties. Local landlords and farmers took the opposite view, being notably unenthusiastic about the Melbourne government's last ditch stand in its budget. So the agriculturists whom Lemon represented quickly made him aware of the condition for their support, opposition to a low fixed duty, a position he refused to adopt.

---

[67] *West Briton*, 11 Jan. 1839, 2 (Launceston); 25 Jan. 1839, 2 (Penryn); 1 Mar. 1839, 2 (St Columb).
[68] Ibid. 31 May 1839, 2.
[69] Ibid. 7 June 1839, 2.
[70] Elvins, 'Reform movement', ch. viii, p. 23.
[71] Ibid. 24.

If protection overshadowed all other issues in East Cornwall, the vexed question of church rates played an analogous part in the West. Much more will be said about the political importance of Dissent, particularly Wesley-anism, in the next chapter; however despite the lack of pollbooks and accurate statistical evidence it is still possible to draw several conclusions about Dissent's contribution to county politics. The 1851 religious census confirmed Dissent's grip on West Cornwall: in 1827 a contemporary had observed of two typical West Cornwall towns that they contained no household without a Methodist. Several years later the Reverend Mr Grylls, vicar of Crowan, during his annual visitation sermon at Penzance, declared that the battle against Methodism was lost. As early as 1824 it was estimated that one in nineteen of the county's inhabitants was a Methodist member, a higher proportion than in any other English county.[72] Despite this the stark fact of life for them and for Baptists, Independents, Quakers and other nonconformists was that even after repeal in 1828 they remained second-class citizens.

Amid the mass of grievances – including prohibition on marriage in their own chapels and burial by their ministers in the parish churchyard, and being forced to officiate as churchwardens – the greatest source of anger was Dissenters' obligation to pay rates for the upkeep of the church building and grounds. Increasingly in the 1830s and despite successful legislation overcoming several disabilities, church rates roused continual public discussion in West Cornwall. So intense was the debate that no parliamentary member or candidate could afford to ignore it, and as Sir Charles Lemon found to his embarrassment in 1837, members' votes at Westminster were carefully watched. One year later the infamous church rates riot occurred in Truro, resulting in short-term imprisonment for five Dissenters whose goods were distrained upon their refusal to pay rates. This was no isolated outburst of anger; from Zennor to Helston it repeatedly flared up. Hence, after 1835, the determination of every county candidate, Whig–Liberal or Conservative, was to be publicly identified with the drive for abolition of the hated rate. Sir Charles Lemon was the single exception: prior to the 1837 election he was one of four Cornish members (the others represented boroughs) to oppose Spring Rice's abolition motion, preferring the establishment of a committee to investigate alternative sources of church revenue. Afterwards, in his published election addresses or on the hustings where he faced persistent questioning over his reasons for ignoring the beliefs of his many Dissenter constituents, Lemon was always on the defensive. Ultimately this became an important reason for his brief retirement in 1841.

---

[72] D. H. Luker, 'Cornish Methodism, revivalism and popular belief, c. 1780–1870', unpubl. DPhil. diss. Oxford 1987, 79, 147.

Table 7
General election results, 1832–41

(Cornwall totals in brackets)

National	1832	1835	1837	1841
Whig-Libs	473 (10)	379 (9)	344 (7)	291 (6)
Cons	185 (4)	279 (5)	314 (7)	367 (8)
Counties				
Whig-Libs	102 (4)	71 (4)	45 (3)	20 (1)
Cons	42 (–)	73 (–)	99 (1)	124 (3)

Source: *McCalmont's parliamentary poll book.*

Conservative revival in the 1830s

Summing up, to what extent did Cornwall county politics between 1832 and 1841 mirror developments elsewhere in England – most obviously in the gradual swing to the Conservatives?

The general election results detailed in table 7, especially those in the counties, show that Cornwall was similar to others, for example Norfolk, Sussex, Devon, Northamptonshire, Nottinghamshire, where the Conservatives turned near or total defeat in 1832 to Conservative control by 1841.[73] The party gained twenty-five English county seats in 1841, two of them in Cornwall, giving local Conservatives a three-to-one majority for the first and only time between 1832 and 1885.

Explanations for the Cornish trend are roughly congruent with those for other counties and nationally. In Buckinghamshire, for example, county electoral politics polarised around the party of Dissent (Whig–Liberals) and the party of the Corn Laws (Conservatives) and well before 1841, aided by several highly politicised agricultural societies, the agriculturists gained the ascendancy. Similarly in agricultural Lincolnshire, where four Whig–Liberals were elected in 1832, but only one nine years later, government members found great difficulty convincing farmers of their sympathy for their difficulties during the mid 1830s depression.[74] Advocacy of a low fixed duty seemed like more of the same, although in an exception to the general rule the Conservative, Lord Worsley, retained his seat despite supporting the government's proposal.

In 1837 Cornwall diverged from much of the rest of England insofar as the new Poor Law was at best a minor issue. Four years later in the county, as elsewhere, the election was fought primarily on the Corn Laws and protection.

---

[73] E. Jaggard, 'The 1841 general election in England and Wales', unpubl. MA diss. Western Australia 1977, 176.
[74] Davis, *Political change*, ch. vii; Olney, *Lincolnshire politics*, ch. ix.

Samples of Conservatives and Whig–Liberal election addresses from candidates throughout England show that these questions far outweighed the defence of Church and State, the Poor Law, redress for Dissenters and other questions.[75] Within three days of the budget's unveiling in May the *Morning Chronicle* reported that 'The sensation produced by the government notice of Friday night on the Corn Laws is rapidly extending through the country. Everywhere it is the signal for excitement and determination.'[76] The proposal allowed Whig–Liberals in the large cities to pose as the advocates of cheap bread. Conversely rural Conservatives had little difficulty in reconciling themselves to the role of protectors of the agricultural interest and/or prophets of lower wages, an argument used by Boscawen Rose.

There are parallels between Cornwall and elsewhere on the introduction of registration committees. Nationally, after the 1835 general election when the Whig-Liberals were surprised by the extent of their reduced majority and aware of the likelihood of another election in the near future, they were motivated to pay much greater attention to locally based organisations. Reform associations were established to counter the Conservatives, and increasingly there were attempts to control the registrations. As early as 1836 the *Leeds Mercury* quite rightly recognised,

> The time has been when a grand excitement at an Election would do all that was needful by putting Reformers on their mettle. It is quite otherwise now. The system of registration has changed all that. Regular persevering systematic effort is the thing wanted under the Reform Act. A plodding shopkeeper on a committee who sees that the Registration is attended to does more good than a dozen wealthy squires who reserve all their energy for the Election itself.[77]

This certainly applied to the Whig–Liberals in West Cornwall and the Conservatives in the East, although the latter were slower to follow the national trend. In the aftermath of the 1837 election, when Whig–Liberals nationally failed to check the electoral tide running against them, their efforts slackened, whereupon the Conservatives seized the initiative. The degree to which they did so was reflected in the 1838, 1839 and 1840 registrations, nationally and in Cornwall.

Reviewing county politics in Cornwall in the decade after 1832 emphasis must be given to two well-defined strands of development. On the one hand the farmer–reformer alliance, which had in the 1820s successfully forced issues to the forefront of political debate, continued to do so until it fractured in the mid 1830s, resulting in the farmers realigning themselves with the protectionist Conservatives. On the other there was the post-reform necessity for the two major parties to impose a degree of organisation on themselves

---

75 Jaggard, '1841 general election', 86–7.
76 *Morning Chronicle*, 3 May 1841, 2.
77 *Leeds Mercury*, 26 Nov. 1836, 4.

and their supporters in order to enjoy electoral success. In the process various gentry families who had once been their chief political 'managers' found themselves being elbowed aside by attornies, farmers, 'plodding shopkeepers' and others eager to assist their party by serving on central or local committees.

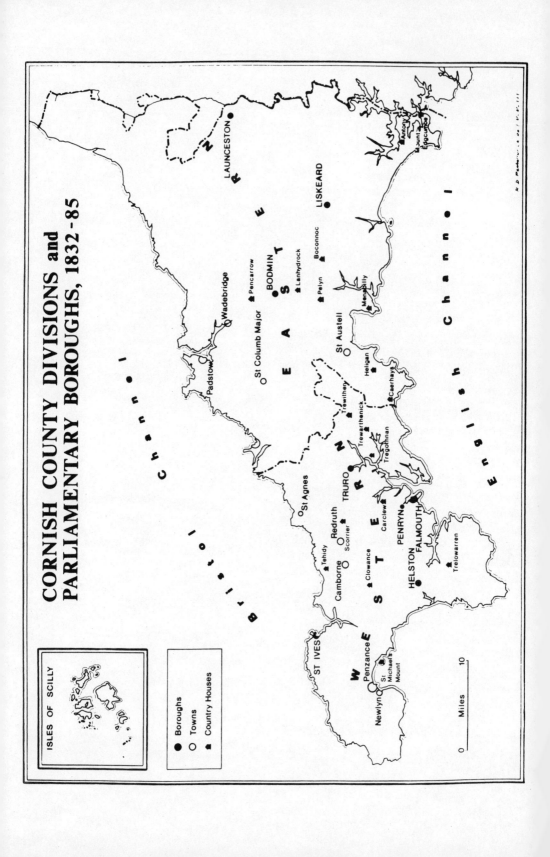

CORNISH COUNTY DIVISIONS and
PARLIAMENTARY BOROUGHS, 1832-85

ISLES OF SCILLY

● Boroughs
○ Towns
▲ Country Houses

Bristol Channel

English Channel

LAUNCESTON

LISKEARD

Wadebridge

Pencarrow
BODMIN
Lanhydrock

Boconnoc
Pelyn
Mevagissey

St Columb Major

EAST

St Austell

Padstow

Heligan

Trewithen
Trewarthenick
Caerhays

Tregothnan

St Agnes

NORTH

TRURO

Redruth
Scorrier
Carclew

PENRYN

Tehidy
Camborne
Clowance

FALMOUTH

Trelowarren

HELSTON

WEST

ST IVES

Penzance
St Michael's Mount

Newlyn

Antony
Mount
Edgcumbe

0   10
Miles

5

Reform and Dissent, 1830–1841

Small town dissenters and electoral politics

In November 1830, on the eve of the drawn-out crisis sparked by parliamentary reform, electoral politics in Cornwall's smallest, most corrupt boroughs were little different to what they had been fifty years earlier. In contrast to this, in their larger counterparts debate and discussion about national and local issues had now become commonplace, a process further stimulated by the arguments over reform. After 1832 Bodmin, Helston, Liskeard, Truro, Launceston, Helston, St Ives, Penryn and Falmouth, the survivors of the Reform Act, exhibited even greater political vitality, especially the first four. Together, the seven boroughs, none of which had more than 900 voters in December 1832, typified the heightened intensity of party rivalries occurring in most of England. What was distinctive about Cornwall was the social and local political context in which it occurred. On the one hand was the growing strength of Dissent, especially Wesleyan Methodism; on the other were enduring electoral influences originating in the unreformed era. Together each had a profound impact on those who represented the boroughs and the foundations of their popular support.

Gradually after 1830 Whig–Liberals and Dissenters found they shared common view-points on several major issues, becoming allies again as they sometimes had been beforehand. What also emerged was the political importance of this link, arising from Dissent's undoubted numerical strength. One way to understand this is to study the comparative weakness of the Established Church, for it was one of the major reasons for the growth of Wesleyan Methodism. The weakness was partially revealed in 1779 when the Diocese of Exeter's Visitation showed that only 41 per cent of more than 200 Cornish parishes had resident clergy.[1] The story was much the same in the 1821 Replies to Bishop Carey's Queries: the figure had risen to a little more than 50 per cent.[2] According to David Luker, the roots of the problem lay in the foundation of Christianity in Cornwall and the subsequent isolation of many parish churches from major centres of settlement.[3] The Church's local remoteness, the distance of Cornwall from the diocesan seat at Exeter, plus the obvious geographic separation from England's power centre in the south-

---

[1] Luker, 'Cornish Methodism', 58.
[2] Ibid. 60–1.
[3] Ibid.

east, contributed to the high incidence of non-residence and pluralism. Accentuating the Church's weakness was the Cornish population's post seventeenth-century geographic mobility as the western mining districts expanded, chiefly by attracting families from eastern areas. Consequently, 'Industrialisation in its socially disintegrative effects, loosened many of the remaining traditional bonds that tied parishioners to the Church.'[4]

By the 1820s the Cornish parochial system was strained to breaking point, helped no doubt by the back-sliding and laziness of those clergy who found ingenious excuses to avoid their duties. Correspondingly, Wesleyan Methodism, with its more flexible organisational structure and its popularity in the mining districts and fishing villages, flourished in places beyond the withered tentacular grasp of the Church. Side by side with old Dissent it attracted strong followings in the bigger towns too. For example the curate of Penzance reported in 1821, 'I do not know of any Papists, but Dissenters are numerous – Baptists, Methodists and Independents and Quakers.'[5] At St Austell, a town of more than 1,000 families, there were seven Methodist chapels and a Bryanite (Bible Christian) meeting room; it was much the same in Truro (ten licensed meeting houses in the parishes of Kenwyn and Kea), and Falmouth, where 'we have a few Papists and numerous Dissenters; viz Independents, Baptists, Unitarians and Quakers'.[6]

By 1824 Methodism was believed to be strong throughout the county, and three years later it could be argued of two typical west Cornwall towns that they contained no household without at least one Methodist. The Anglican clergyman Richard Tyacke offered a unique explanation for this popularity: on a rainy day in April 1829, when his church was 'but thinly attended', he wistfully noticed how

> the roads that led to the Methodist chapel were thronged in every direction. My religious sentiments are not uncharitable, but Methodism I am convinced is not the only notice that calls them to this conventicle. The greater portion are the young of both sexes, the time is at night most suited to assignations and the secrets of love. These are causes that will attract members, and if religion has a share, there is a secondary object that claims a share also.[7]

Soon afterwards the Reverend Mr Grylls, vicar of Crowan, declared, 'we have lost the people. The religion of the mass is become Wesleyan Methodist', an observation overwhelmingly confirmed by the 1851 census.[8]

The information collected so assiduously at that time publicised trends developing over previous decades. At the most basic level it is obvious that

---

4 Ibid. 75.
5 *The diocese of Exeter in 1821: Bishop Carey's replies to queries before visitation*, ed. Michael Cook (Devon & Cornwall Record Society n.s. iii, 1954), 65.
6 Ibid. 21–2.
7 Diary of Richard Tyacke 1826–9, entry for 5 Apr. 1829.
8 Luker, 'Cornish Methodism', 147.

Table 8
Percentage of population present at most numerously attended services, 30 March 1851

	Pop.	C of E	Dissent	others	Total
England and Wales	17,927,609	16.6	17.4	1.5	35.5
South West	1,803,291	22.6	21.2	0.4	44.1
Cornwall	356,641	12.6	32.5	0.2	45.3
Devon	572,330	22.6	17.2	0.3	40.2

Source: Hayden, 'Culture, creed and conflict', 55.

Table 9
Religious attendance, south-west counties, 1851

	Anglican		Methodist	
	*IA	PS*	IA	PS
Berkshire	40.1	60.8	12.8	19.4
Wiltshire	44.7	52.2	16.0	18.7
Dorset	48.2	62.2	13.7	17.7
Devon	40.1	56.9	13.2	18.7
Cornwall	19.2	28.2	43.8	64.5
Somerset	43.3	61.6	12.5	17.8

Source: Coleman, 'Southern England', 171.

* Index of attendance is produced by aggregating the morning, afternoon and evening attendances and presenting the total as a percentage of the population of the area in question. Percentage Share is the share of total attendance gained by a denominational group.

Cornwall's church-going public was far more numerous than the national average and, predictably, the largest component in this was the Dissenters.

The same point can be made in a more localised and slightly different way by considering index of attendance (IA) and percentage share (PS) figures for the south-west counties (see table 9). Once more Anglican weakness and the remarkable strength of Cornish Methodism are obvious.

Whatever form the statistics take, the result is the same. In Bruce Coleman's view, Cornwall was *sui generis* – elsewhere in southern England there was nothing like this strength of Nonconformity in the context of very weak Anglicanism.[9] Even outside the region it was unusual. Only seven registration counties, all of them Welsh and/or heavily industrialised, had lower Anglican indices.

[9] B. I. Coleman, 'Southern England in the census of religious worship, 1851', *Southern History* v (1983), 172.

Cornish Methodism was strongest in the west, especially in Truro, Redruth, Helston and Penzance, each the centre of thriving mining districts. Even so, in thirteen of the county's fourteen divisions (St Germans was the exception), Methodism's index of attendance and percentage share far outstripped the Church of England.[10] The Wesleyan Connexion was the most significant force within West Cornwall's Nonconformity, while farther east Bible Christians and the Wesleyan Association predominated. Interestingly, Methodism was stronger than 'old Dissent' in every district, and, 'In nine of the fourteen districts a Methodist denomination was the largest single denomination, the Church of England included.'[11] Analysing this in terms of the social pyramid, Methodism's membership clustered mainly at the bottom, a phenomenon noted by the Richard Tyacke: 'the Methodist meetings however in this neighbourhood are far more frequented by the lower class than the established church'.[12] In the larger parliamentary boroughs the situation was different: many Methodists belonged to the middle classes, the same stratum of society from which old Dissent drew much of its strength. Under those circumstances it was a foolhardy parliamentary candidate who ignored such a reality, particularly if Dissenters were numerous among a town's reformers, as they were in Truro.

This explains why the Truro Whig–Liberal candidate, William Tooke, was so pleased several days before the 1832 general election: 'I am to hear Mr Moore who is a most agreeable man', he wrote, 'as also is Mr Clarke with whom I drink tea on Monday to meet Mr Moore, the Reverend Mr Steadman and the two Wesleyan Ministers Mr Martin and Mr Boot. They and all their congregations support one most strenuously.'[13] Thomas Martin, Richard Boot, William Moore (Congregationalist) and the Baptist Minister Edmund Clarke all duly voted for Tooke. Presumably many of their congregations did the same, giving him a crucial margin over his Conservative opponent.

Dissent's acknowledged strength meant that, more than any issue in the 1830s, the campaign to abolish church rates dominated Cornish borough politics. Over the decade it is easy to distinguish a sequence of other issues moving in and out of public focus. For example renewed opposition to colonial slavery, commutation of tithes, municipal reform and changes to the Irish Church overlapped one another early in the thirties, before Dissenters stepped up the pressure, winning concessions over London University's right to grant degrees and a civil registry of births, deaths and marriages. Later, public attention swung to the merits of free trade and protection, but these issues waxed and waned in conjunction with one constant: at each general election no question intruded more frequently into parliamentary candidates' published addresses and speeches, or was the catalyst for more public meet-

10 Ibid. 187.
11 Ibid. 172.
12 Diary of Richard Tyacke 1826–9, entry for 17 May 1829.
13 William Tooke to Amelia Tooke, 13 Dec. 1832, CRO, FS/3/1289/5.

ings, than the complaints of Dissenters, especially the legal compulsion to provide financial support for the Church of England.

That this issue should have been so prominent long before the establishment of the British Anti-State Church Association is understandable, and events in Truro illustrate how popular feelings could be aroused. Long before the Primitive Methodist carpenter Richard Spurr and four companions had their goods distrained in 1838 for failing to pay the rate, trouble had been brewing in the town. At a well-attended public meeting in March 1834 Dissenters and moderate reformers urged change, and thereafter the agitation never slackened.[14] In 1835 almost all county and borough parliamentary candidates gave some degree of support. One year later, with feelings rising, a Truro meeting, disturbed that the liberal policies adopted by the government on other matters were not being followed on Church rates, pledged itself 'to employ every constitutional means for obtaining speedy and entire relief from that burden'.[15] Reformers such as John Benallack, Edmund Turner (the chairman) and Robert Michell took a very active part in proceedings, which were almost the last display of unity between radical Dissenter and reformers.

When Truro's Dissenters protested to the House of Commons in February 1837, 'That it is in the judgement of your petitioners alike unchristian, unreasonable and unjust, to compel persons to support Religious Institutions from which they conscientiously Dissent', – adding that the levying of the rates was detrimental to the character of the Established Church – the action was the outcome of a meeting of William Tooke's lower middle-class supporters.[16] Samuel Randall iron-monger, Jacob Edwards pipe-maker, Martin Magor and Thomas Barlow were among them – very likely Spurr was there too, and it was plain that Tooke was still their champion. Immediately afterwards Truro's Tories launched a counter petition, while Dissenters in Helston, Penzance, Penryn, Falmouth, St Columb and Launceston joined in the fight.[17] By now, in some parishes, packed vestries were refusing to strike a rate for the forthcoming year, so it was inevitable that the issue should blow up into one of major importance at the 1837 general election. The injustice of payments was freely admitted by the candidates of all parties, in almost every constituency, yet with the government stonewalling tempers became frayed, and there were many sharp exchanges between Dissenters and those soliciting their votes.

This, and Tooke's 1837 defeat when many moderate reformers deserted him, splitting their votes between a second Liberal and a Conservative, was the backdrop against which the Spurr upheaval was played out. Confronted by a government intent upon ignoring their demands, plus the unseating of their local hero and Sir Charles Lemon's equivocations, in May 1838 Truro's

14 *West Briton*, 21 Mar. 1834, 2.
15 Ibid. 24 June 1836, 4.
16 Ibid. 3 Feb. 1837, 3.
17 Ibid. 7, 14, 21 Apr. 1837, 2.

Dissenters took action. Spurr, Jacob Edwards pipe-maker and Bible Christian preacher, Samuel Randall iron-monger, Richard Barrett draper and William Ball watch-maker, provoked what has been dubbed the 'Truro Church Rate Riot'.[18] All five had refused to pay rates for the previous two years; their distrained goods were to be auctioned by William Oke, who, like them, had voted for Tooke in 1832. When the sale commenced Spurr, together with William Rowe who was to be his Chartist ally the following year, publicly accused Oke of lying over money, whereupon the crowd began wrecking Oke's premises. Before the day was over Barrett and Edwards attempted to break into Oke's now locked shop, while a mob of 600 had to be restrained by the mayor and town constables.[19] From this time Spurr and Rowe became the town's popular agitators, repeatedly interjecting at public meetings and later joining the Chartist movement, as well as demanding the repeal of the Corn Laws. The 'Church Rate Riot' illustrated the strength of popular feeling against the government. More particularly, it suggests why the compulsion to pay the rate was addressed by almost every Cornish parliamentary candidate in the 1830s and 1840s. Given the high proportion of Dissenters in the population, to have ignored this would have been an act of foolishness.

Side by side with such upswellings of Dissenting opinion, borough politics were also moulded by lingering influences from the unreformed electoral system. Although the seven Cornish boroughs were uniformly small, and it might therefore be assumed that their patterns of political behaviour were similar, nothing could be further from the truth. Launceston and Helston remained pocket boroughs, although of very different types. St Ives and Penryn & Falmouth typified the manipulation and corruption characteristic of an earlier period, while Liskeard, Bodmin and Truro, with greatly enlarged electorates, became comparatively open boroughs where the Conservatives never regained complete control. The change in the latter three was partly due to their being corporation boroughs prior to 1832, a circumstance generating continuous animosity between ambitious townspeople and the exclusive governing bodies who chose the town's MPs.

In Liskeard, Bodmin and Truro before the Reform Act, parliamentary representation was determined by the town's patron whose wishes were enacted by hand-picked, compliant corporation members, or, as in the case of Liskeard, in conjunction with freemen selected by the same unrepresentative body. Truro's corporation comprised twenty-four members, Bodmin's thirty-six, while at Liskeard nine plus forty-eight freemen enjoyed the right to vote. Helston may also be placed in this category – a corporation of five, plus seventy-four freemen – although as we shall see, the town's reformers lacked the numerical strength of their counterparts elsewhere. Evidence published by the Commission on Municipal Corporations of England and Wales (1835)

---

[18] John Rule, 'Richard Spurr of Truro: small town radical', *Cornish Studies* iv/v (1976/7), 50–5.
[19] Ibid. 51.

pinpoints why these patron-dominated bodies were highly unpopular with many townspeople before 1832, producing a powerful backlash which afterwards overflowed into parliamentary and municipal politics.[20]

This unpopularity had several causes. A narrow exclusivity of voting privileges meant many prosperous and ambitious townsmen were blocked from direct participation in the electoral system. In return for their privileges, and because the patron or his agents selected them in the first place, corporation members slavishly carried out his wishes. There were exceptions to this, one being Truro at the beginning of the 1820s, when Lord Falmouth temporarily lost control after being deceived by so-called 'loyal' nominees to the corporation. Equally abhorrent, but a natural corollary of this 'loyalty', was what the commissioners noted in Liskeard: 'Whilst many respectable persons have been resident in Liskeard, the corporation has been chosen only out of members of a certain political party; and this circumstance has occasioned much ill-feeling.'[21] Indeed, as the commissioners suggested, this and most other corporations existed principally for political purposes (the furtherance of Tory interests), not for the welfare of the town; they therefore enjoyed neither the confidence nor respect of the community.

The corporations were also notorious for membership being confined to a small number of families. According to the commissioners, 'The Corporation of Helston is of a more than ordinarily exclusive character. The influence is chiefly vested in one family, connected in various ways with many of the other members of the body.'[22] Similarly at Truro, 'Many of the aldermen and capital burgesses are related to one another', for example Daubuz father and son, and Messrs James and Nankivell who were first cousins.[23] This meant the economic interests of other rival families were deliberately overlooked. The commissioners heard how in Truro, 'The negligence of the corporation in respect to the channel of the port is also matter of well founded complaint on the part of the merchants and traders of Truro.'[24] Liskeard was no different, with the welfare of the town being neglected in favour of narrow, selfish interests.

The outcome was as the commissioners described it in Truro: 'Many persons of respectability openly expressed the utmost dissatisfaction with the corporation, and earnestly endeavoured to impress upon our minds the necessity for a change in the system upon which the corporation are at present elected.' The commissioners added: 'We have not visited any town in which so much difference of opinion exists between the inhabitants and the

---

[20] *First report of the Commissioners on the Municipal Corporations of England and Wales*, PP 1835, xxiii/2.
[21] Ibid. 529–30.
[22] Ibid. 154. The Grylls family dominated the corporation.
[23] Ibid. 656.
[24] Ibid. 662.

Table 10
Borough voters

	Voters pre-1832	Voters 1832–3
Bodmin	36	252
Helston	5 + 74	341
Liskeard	9 + 48	218
Truro	24	392

Sources: Thorne, *House of Commons*, ii; *Number of electors*, PP 1833 xxvii. 21.

corporation as in the town of Truro.'[25] Liskeard and Bodmin were the same – 'boroughs which have been mainly sustained for the purpose of political corruption'.[26] These circumstances encouraged each town's reformers well before the euphoria of the early 1830s gained hold. They anticipated that reform would be accompanied by much more widely-based voting rights, and therefore that it would be possible for them and their friends to break the Tory hegemony.

No wonder the passing of the Reform Act was greeted with such enthusiasm, for the probable outcome in several towns was the demise of those patrons whose power reformers had long objected to. We have already seen this movement in action in Truro and Liskeard before 1820 and it slowly became more widespread in the years that followed. From the antipathy towards the old corporations emerged parties of reformers eager to demonstrate their independence in electoral politics, and for whom municipal reform was also high on their agenda.

The change in voter numbers in these former corporation boroughs was dramatic, as can be seen from table 10. Obviously a high proportion of new voters had never possessed the franchise beforehand, nor been subject to direct patronal influence at general elections, yet this does not explain why in three instances, but not the fourth, the patrons were peremptorily tossed aside. The common factor at Bodmin, Liskeard and Truro, was widespread dislike of the patron's grip, but more significantly the limits of their political control were far too narrow to survive. At Bodmin the marquis of Hertford and Davies Gilbert presumably divided between them the £500 annually spent on 'public purposes', most of which did not impinge on everyday life in the town. For many years the Eliot family had paid Liskeard's corporation 'whatever sums of money they expended beyond the ordinary income', but this was rarely great. Lord Falmouth's Truro interest was 'supported by gifts of places in the customs house', plus the occasional gift or loan to the corpora-

[25] Ibid. 661.
[26] Ibid. 450.

tion, but he, like the others, had no need to splurge too much money because the self-perpetuating corporation was firmly controlled.

A different set of circumstances prevailed in Helston, where successive dukes of Leeds (all Tories), provided cash for major improvements in public buildings such as the church and the market house. They also paid the borough poor rate, removing a significant impost from many people who were non-voters before 1832, and thereby earning their gratitude.[27] This meant that they enjoyed support beyond the seventy-nine voters (corporation and freemen), who made up just under one-quarter of the enlarged electorate. Furthermore, there was a strong financial inducement for the duke's agents, members of the Grylls and Borlase families, to continue in his service. They were paid large retainers to prevent opposition to the duke's nominees, and in 1832 they confidently assured him that they could continue to do so, proving their point until 1837. Under these circumstances Helston's reformers, no matter how well organised, struggled in vain to overturn their opponents.

The first elections for the reformed corporations, held on 26 December 1835, demonstrated the depth of feeling against the former governing bodies: the Whig–Liberals did best in the old corporation boroughs with their previously exclusive voting rights. Nowhere did town reformers achieve a more startling result than at Liskeard, 'where', as the *West Briton* explained, 'they have nobly done their duty by returning to the Town-Council twelve excellent men of their own principles'.[28] Six weeks beforehand the Conservatives had decided theirs was a lost cause. None of the old corporation bothered to stand, or even vote, knowing that 'every one from the mayor to the scavenger is to be turned out'.[29] The Bodmin result was identical – all the new council being reformers – and at Truro it was almost as decisive, fourteen of the eighteen being reformers opposed to the old interests. The six aldermen elected by the councillors were reformers too, in a town where the 'acrimony of party feeling' was allegedly endemic.

Helston, naturally, was different. The Grylls and Borlase families working on the duke of Leeds's behalf still held the upper hand, but it is easy to see why in 1837 the Whig–Liberals were eager to invite Arthur Buller, brother of Liskeard's Radical MP, to contest the general election. The *West Briton* gleefully announced after the first municipal elections that 'The Reformers have triumphed here, having a majority in the Council.'[30] At least six of the twelve can be identified as Whig–Liberals, including the outspoken Baptist solicitor Thomas Rogers, so the town had a nucleus of anti-Tory voters who could probably be relied upon to support a Whig–Liberal parliamentary candidate.

After 1832 then, the former Corporation boroughs of Liskeard, Truro and

---

27 Thorne, *House of Commons*, ii. 62–5 (Helston).
28 *West Briton*, 1 Jan. 1836, 2.
29 Ibid.
30 Ibid.

Bodmin became the most open constituencies, where the Whig–Liberals enjoyed consistent success; the Conservatives were strongest in Launceston, St Ives and until the 1850s, Helston, towns where there was not the same natural focal point for reformer discontent. One result was that these three were slow to change from their old ways. What now needs to be explained, in the context of this and the strength of religious dissent, is the place of principles, national issues and party organisations in post-reform Cornish borough politics.

Cornwall's boroughs and political modernisation

Recently, samples of voting behaviour from various constituencies in the decades after the Reform Act have been carefully analysed by John Phillips and Charles Wetherell – not the large villages and small towns typical of counties such as Cornwall, but the bigger centres and growing industrial cities where the enfranchised numbered thousands.[31] Exhaustive computer analysis of pollbooks recording voters' preferences at a succession of general and by-elections post-1832 reveals how they began to support consistently one or other of the major parties. Hence, according to Phillips and Wetherell, 'Voters before 1832 simply did not persist in their voting habits; voters after 1832 did.'[32] Moreover they highlight what they argue was one of the central features of England's political modernisation: 'Reform quickly destroyed the political system that had prevailed during the long reign of George III and replaced it with an essentially modern electoral system based on rigid partisanship and clearly articulated political principle.'[33] In this context 'modern' political behaviour was characterised by allegiance to parties, attention to local and national issues, and national debate. Some powerful influence must have been operating if electoral behaviour changed radically in the early and middle decades of the nineteenth century, while the rituals of electoral politics were largely unaltered. 'That influence', Phillips and Wetherell believe, 'seems to have been the new view of principle and principled behaviour that the parties in Westminster imposed on local politics after 1832.'[34]

Other historians have reached different conclusions about the behaviour of the electorate after 1832. For example James Vernon found from a sample of five constituencies, ranging in size from 900 to 10,000 voters, that national influence tended to be overwhelmed by local considerations and identities: 'Party politics was perceived to be socially and politically disruptive.'[35]

---

31 John A. Phillips and Charles Wetherell, 'The Great Reform Act of 1832 and the political modernisation of England', *American Historical Review* c (1995), 411–36.
32 Ibid. 432.
33 Ibid. 412.
34 Ibid. 425.
35 Vernon, *Politics and the people*, 163.

Another divergent view arising from constituency studies concluded that 'in each constituency there was [in 1857 and 1859] a constant molecular movement of agents, money, influence, argument, persuasion, personalities and gossip going on which could exercise an influence as vital if not more vital, than the political issues over the campaigns and their results'.[36] This contrasts strongly with the judgements of Phillips and Wetherell about the primacy of policy and principle.

So clear a portrait of the post-Reform electoral system, constructed mainly from voting patterns in medium-sized and large boroughs, obscures important elements of the electoral scene which emerge in Cornwall's seven boroughs, and elsewhere. Was the uniformity of voter behaviour, and the causes of such behaviour, observable in all boroughs, large and small? As we shall see there were constituencies where patrons, electioneering traditions and localism remained formidable if diminishing forces until late in the nineteenth century, especially in the small boroughs that outnumbered all other constituency categories in England and Wales. Launceston in Cornwall, Richmond in Yorkshire, both acknowledged pocket boroughs, suggest how the dominant Conservative and Liberal partisans in the respective towns showed exemplary party loyalty, but it had relatively little to do with principles. The story was similar in Marlow in Buckinghamshire, Woodstock in Oxfordshire, and many other 'closed' boroughs.

The Cornish seven, plus the Marlows, Woodstocks and others, bring to our attention two significant points. Firstly, conclusions about the political modernisation of England have been based upon samples of boroughs where pollbooks are available for several or more elections. Pollbooks were generated by contested elections, which were not always the norm. No contest, no pollbooks, no pollbooks, no analysis. No 'runs' of pollbooks for consecutive elections, again no analysis, and, no conclusions about partisanship. For these reasons probably more boroughs are excluded from the process than included, but what was happening in them? Secondly, much of Phillips and Wetherell's pioneering work derives from polling in boroughs with more than 1,000 voters, those which may be classified as larger boroughs. How relevant are their conclusions to the smaller boroughs with less than 1,000 voters, the most numerous category of constituencies in England and Wales. These related questions, which will be tested against Cornish evidence, deserve an answer.

In table 11 the broken line divides the seventy-two larger boroughs electing 140 members to the House of Commons, and the 131 smaller boroughs electing 201 members. Given this imbalance between the categories it seems reasonable to argue that the typical English/Welsh borough was one with less than 1,000 voters, electing one or two members. All seven Cornish boroughs are included in this category. Also, it is worthwhile noting that among the

---

[36] Caroline Harvey, 'The British general elections of 1857 and 1859', unpubl. DPhil. diss. Oxford 1980, 396. The constituencies were Bury, Gloucester, Leicester and West Kent.

Table 11
English and Welsh boroughs, 1832–67

2,000+	voters	28 boroughs	58 members
1,000–1,999	voters	44 boroughs	82 members
500–999	voters	57 boroughs	94 members
0–499	voters	74 boroughs	107 member

Source: *McCalmont's parliamentary poll book*.

smaller boroughs were constituencies most often controlled by a family, or patron or some other traditional influence. Thus of the 131 smaller boroughs listed in table 11 Gash calculated that thirty-three of the seventy-four boroughs with less than 500 voters could be classified as proprietary or family boroughs, and twenty of those with 500–999 voters.[37] So approximately 40 per cent (53 of 131) of smaller boroughs were subject to a degree of influence, control or coercion, and they elected eighty-two members to the House of Commons. Then there were the corrupt or venal boroughs with less than 1,000 voters (Penryn & Falmouth is a good example), and the number of members rises to more than 100.[38] Therefore between 1832 and 1867 in a substantial number of smaller boroughs, which as a category comprised well over half of all the English and Welsh boroughs (131 of 203), voters were probably more susceptible to various forms of influence than in bigger towns. The political and economic impact of influential landed families was more readily felt. Electoral traditions survived more easily from one generation to the next, and often local circumstance outweighed national issues during elections.

The Cornwall seven span the extremes from 'closed' to 'open' boroughs, besides including one venal constituency where government influence also intruded. With the exception of Launceston and St Ives general elections in each were characterised by lively exchanges between candidates, who paid attention to national as well as local issues. But these did not necessarily sway the townspeople to cast their votes for either Conservatives or Liberals. Local forces blunted partisanship's sharp edges: patronage, influence and pre-reform electoral traditions also shaped the voters' choices, the outcome being a slower pace of political modernisation in a significant category of constituencies.

[37] Gash, *Politics in the age of Peel*, appendix D.
[38] Ibid. ch. vii.

Remnants of patronage and influence

Preparation began as early as July 1832 for the ensuing December general election. As candidates announced their intentions in the various boroughs the reformers confidently predicted how the Cornish political world would be turned upside down. Everywhere there was renewed energy as Tories and Whig–Liberals competed with each other to gain a decisive advantage within the context of lingering influences from the unreformed system. In 1831 the county's total parliamentary membership comprised thirty-four Tories and eight Whig–Liberals. The reversal in the first post-Reform general election was dramatic: ten Whig–Liberals, four Tories and five of the seven boroughs being contested. As for the pre-1832 trend towards partisanship in several of the larger towns, it intensified early in the 1830s, but did it continue?

The impact of issues and principles was least likely to be felt in towns where patronage, influence and control predominated. Often contests were rare and voters' preferences were therefore unknown; nevertheless we must assume the majority's acquiescence in whatever forces were at work meant that these boroughs were leftovers from a much earlier period of electoral politics. Launceston, Helston, St Ives and, to a lesser degree, Bodmin fitted this category after 1832. Measuring the degree of partisanship in each borough is impossible because of the scarcity of pollbooks. Still, on the basis of electioneering and election results, some judgements may be offered about the progress of partisanship and political modernisation.

In the case of Launceston, the duke of Northumberland's pocket borough until the 1860s, progress was minimal; contests were rare, the townspeople apparently being in no haste to throw off the shackles of patronage. Sir Henry Hardinge, the duke's nominee at the neighbouring borough of Newport before 1832, switched across the Tamar with the patron's approval, continuing as MP for Launceston until 1841 when he was appointed governor-general of India. The patron immediately replaced him with Admiral William Bowles, who was re-elected unopposed until he retired from parliament. Yet even in Launceston this succession of Conservative nominees did not smother political debate or opposition to the *status quo*.

We have already seen how the first tentative signs of independent political activism surfaced in the 1820s, stimulated by Dissenters' very strong concern to see the end of colonial slavery. David Howell of Trebursye was one of the first county reformers to become involved in the affairs of a pocket borough, and in January 1829 he and his friends took a strong stand at an anti-Catholic meeting, criticising the lack of free and open discussion on both sides of the question.[39] Although Howell was absent, two years later as popular feeling intensified in favour of parliamentary reform, 'The inhabitants of Launceston having been at length roused to a due sense of the degradation they have so

---

[39] 'An appeal to the freeholders. . . .', 7 Jan. 1829, CRO, MSS Howell HL (2)/236.

Table 12
Parliamentary representation, 1832–41: Truro, Helston, Launceston, Liskeard

Elect.	Truro (2 members)	Helston 1 member	Launceston 1 member	Liskeard 1 member
1832	Vivian, Sir R.H. L – 291 Tooke, William L – 203 *Vivian, John E.* C – 196	Fox, Sackville Lane C	Hardinge, Sir H. C – 115 *Howell, D.* L – 103	Buller, C. L
1835	Vivian, John E. C – 316 Tooke, William L – 270 *Vivian, Sir R. H.* L – 174	Townshend, Lord C	Hardinge, Sir H. C – 103 *Howell, D.* L – 84	Buller, C. L – 114 *Kekewich, S.* C – 64
1837	Turner, Edmund L – 393 Vivian, John E. C – 254 *Tooke, William* L – 226	Cantelupe, Visc C – 160 *Buller, Arthur* L – 125	Hardinge, Sir H. C	Buller, C. L – 113 *Kekewich, S.* C – 95
1840		Basset, J. C		
1841	Turner, Edmund L Vivian, John E. C	Vyvyan, Sir R. C – 159 *Vigors, W. R.* L – 133	Hardinge, Sir H. C	Buller, C. L

(Names of unsuccessful candidates italicised)

Source: *McCalmont's parliamentary poll book.*

long suffered, as well as the evils inflicted on the County at large', decided to meet to discuss 'the present state of representation'.[40] It was a boisterous, well-attended affair, at which the Wesleyan William Pearse, his brother Thomas, T. S. Eyre a druggist, and the MP for Tavistock, John Rundle, all spoke out forcefully, as they continued to do in public in the 1830s.

Because of his political credentials Howell was pressed in 1832 to make an assault on Northumberland's control. However, even beforehand the reformers found how hard their task would be, for the initial registrations in November became a nine-day test of stamina. Every claim they made was strongly contested by the duke's solicitors. Simultaneously, many of his Newport tenants successfully applied for inclusion:

> a large number of these voters were registered as occupiers of Houses and Lands to the amount of Ten Pounds a Year and upwards, although only rated in many cases to the value of and rented at Two Pounds per annum, the difference between the actual value and the Rent paid being a retainer for their votes.[41]

In Launceston, a former freeman borough, the duke controlled corporation members by sinecures, grants of land at nominal rents, 'and by pensions for nominal services to the members of it and to the different branches of their families'.[42] Of course the corporation in turn influenced many of the innkeepers, who regularly applied for the renewal of licences; when the corporation's control of constables, town sergeants, mace bearers and other retainers is remembered, it is surprising that Howell managed as many as 108 votes, only seven less than Hardinge.

The reformers, as may have been expected, were heartened by this result. Throughout the 1830s each wave of public issues sweeping the county also washed over Launceston. No matter how assiduously the Tories attended to the registrations and pressured the duke's tenants to support Hardinge, opposition continued to surface. Firstly the anti-slavery association became revitalised. Soon afterwards reformers and Tories clashed heatedly at a large meeting to petition for municipal reform. There was far less opposition when 400 Dissenters gathered in February 1834 to petition over 'the grievances attached to the various denominations of Protestant Dissenters'.[43] With the Wesleyan William Pearse chairing the meeting and Eyre, Howell's ally, a leading speaker, Dissenting anger was unleashed in a wide-ranging protest against their exclusion from universities, the prevention of their ministers from performing burial rites in parochial cemeteries, the compulsory payment of church rates, and other forms of discrimination. It was a powerful expression of the popular mood, repeated three years later at an even larger meeting

40 *West Briton*, 4 Feb. 1831, 2.
41 'Draft petition from electors', MSS Howell HL (2)/247.
42 Ibid.
43 *West Briton*, 21 Feb. 1834, 2.

when the Methodists agreed to petition again for the abolition of church rates, this coming at a time when the question was being vigorously debated in many other towns.[44]

In the interim Howell contested the borough once more in 1835, but, owing to the suddenness of the election, his absence in France meant Eyre controlled his campaign and spoke on the hustings. Hardinge, probably chastened by his previous narrow victory, made a serious attempt to address two topics of concern in and around the town, commutation of tithes and 'the renewal of grievances of Dissenters', a turnaround from the generalities he espoused three years earlier.[45] Eyre argued that if the Tories continued in office they would be incapable of carrying meaningful measures of reform, provoking the solicitor Charles Gurney, Northumberland's agent, to launch an attack on Eyre, Howell and all the reformers.[46] This time the margin of Howell's defeat was greater. Nevertheless the duke could not afford to be sanguine. Following his nominee's re-election in 1837 (there was no opposition), the *West Briton*, commenting on the endemic drunkenness, sarcastically observed 'The streets of the town were like the field of battle; and N. H. Hardinge may be said to have slain as many by the juice of the grape at this election as he ever did by the prowess of his arm, notwithstanding his acknowledged bravery.'[47]

In spite of their understandable frustration the two Pearses, Eyre and other independent-minded men refused to be silenced. As the Corn Law controversy gathered momentum, temporarily superseding church rates in importance, they challenged the Northumberland–Hardinge position which was preservation of the existing law. Subsequently, in May 1839, they welcomed the Anti-Corn Law-League's touring lecturer to two meetings in the town.[48] Combined with his own wishful thinking such enthusiasm persuaded R. P. Collier to canvass the borough in June 1841. Being a free trader, a friend to civil and religious liberty and a critic of compulsory church rates, Collier felt confident enough to appear before 500 people, many of them electors, to explain his opinions.[49] Yet a week later he retired. 'I cannot help saying that I have met with some things in Launceston which surprise me', namely electors who approved Collier's sentiments but, as he put it, were obliged to oppose him.[50]

This didn't prevent a post-election reformers' dinner, chaired by the indefatigable Thomas Pearse, at which many criticisms were voiced about Hardinge's off-handed treatment of the borough. No doubt the duke of

---

44 Ibid. 21 Apr. 1837, 2.
45 Ibid. 9 Jan. 1835, 2.
46 Ibid.
47 Ibid. 28 July 1837, 3.
48 Ibid. 11 Jan. 1839, 2; 31 May 1839, 2.
49 Ibid. 25 June 1841, 2.
50 Ibid. 2 July 1841, 3.

Northumberland was suitably grateful for the way in which his agent Charles Gurney so adroitly combated the Whig–Liberal opposition over several decades.

Helston exhibited several similarities with Launceston, one illustration of this being the continuity of Tory MPs after 1832. Several were nominees of the duke of Leeds. As with reformers elsewhere in Cornwall, those at Helston were itching to challenge the patron, who had a predilection for returning undistinguished relatives. It was this, combined with perpetual dissatisfaction with the corporation, plus the presence of a former 'Hawkins' party, which caused the fragmentation of interests in the town. Nevertheless, the same broad trends of public debate and activism appeared here as elsewhere in the county in the 1830s, beginning with support for the abolition of colonial slavery and concluding with intense debate about the possible effects of the government's projected free trade policies. As the 1837 election revealed, another common feature was the fact that leading those who attacked the electoral *status quo* were the Dissenters. Their annoyance at the Melbourne government's inability to press on with solutions to their problems, and their natural alliance with the town reformers, was a constant source of political tension.

The town's Dissenters were among the first in Cornwall to petition for the repeal of the Test and Corporation Acts, and anti-slavery meetings drew packed audiences. In an area where in the 1830s Wesleyan Methodism and other Dissenting churches probably provided double the number of sittings for the population as the Church of England, this activism was natural. Leading the Dissenters were Thomas Rogers the Baptist solicitor, and Philip Robinson, relative of the ultra-Tory Sir Richard Vyvyan, but those who represented the *status quo* were more than a match for them. This is confirmed by their speedy response to an anti-church rates meeting held in March 1837: next day a meeting expressed support for the rates.[51] Held in the middle of the day, possibly to reduce opposition attendance, it was the corporation – Leeds's solicitors clique of the Grylls family, James Plomer and Christopher Popham, together with at least five local clergymen – who deprecated the government's short-lived plan to abolish the rates. Action and reaction were always paramount in Helston's tangled skeins of political life, and never more so than during the fifteen years after the Reform Act. Two examples demonstrate the point.

In 1837, heartened by their success in the municipal elections, Helston's reformers (including many Dissenters), sought and found an appropriate candidate. Sir Arthur Buller, brother of Liskeard's Radical member, agreed to test the turbid waters. Thomas Rogers was the driving force behind a candidate with several obvious strengths: Buller's Cornish origins (Viscount Cantelupe, his opponent, was an outsider), the Radicalism he shared with his brother,

51 Ibid. 17 Mar. 1837, 2.

and the well-known links between the Tories and the old, corrupt, pre-reform corporation. On the hustings Rogers and Buller ensured that their audience and potential supporters knew that the Conservative candidate was no friend to Dissenters.[52] This was a serious sequel to an amusing *faux-pas* by Buller's opponent, who inadvertently began his speech by announcing his opposition to the abolition of church rates. Immediately his backers seized him, and the crowd enjoyed a series of violent gesticulations and whispered exhortations from the coterie surrounding the Tories' man. When he was allowed to resume, having been primed, Cantelupe said he would look carefully at the question![53] Even though several large landlords allegedly allowed their tenantry within the borough a 'free' vote, there were still too many timid men who worried about the opinions of their superiors. Cantelupe's six attornies, 'Who are all day scampering about the county, bullying, misrepresenting, and entrapping', finally swung the vote, his expenses allegedly being £8,000 to Buller's £150.[54] After the election many of Buller's supporters among the tradesmen and small businessmen were threatened with loss of custom. Was the Tory victory then a triumph of old methods over reformist aspirations?

Two pollbooks, one printed, the other handwritten, provide inconclusive answers. They do reveal, as we would expect, that the duke's nominee had far greater professional help – two solicitors for each of the three parishes, challenging voters and generally looking after their candidate's interests.[55] Buller's helpers, fewer in number, were loyal middle-class supporters, and no match for their adversaries. Among those who voted for him were men of the same background as those on whom Tooke depended in Truro: Richard Woolcock bookseller, Henry Pascoe tailor, Thomas Edwards auctioneer, William Tressider wheelwright, Isaiah James draper, and John Menadue iron-monger.

The pro-reform credentials of these men were impeccable, for ten years later when Sir Richard Vyvyan (Conservative MP for Helston 1841–57), announced his intention of re-standing, they disputed his decision, calling a public meeting at the Guildhall. They believed 'That the steps taken by Sir Richard R. Vyvyan to engross the patronage of this Borough as well as the attempt of certain parties in the town to dispose of the Franchises in a private manner to him have created general dissatisfaction'.[56] The reformers bluntly informed Vyvyan that he had lost their confidence, then in a manner reminiscent of Truro's free burgesses in 1830 signed their names. The similarity did not end with the method. Once again it was a collection of auctioneers, drapers, tailors, blacksmiths, wheelwrights, bootmakers, carpenters and iron-mongers – small business or tradesmen – who were most conspicuous. Only

52 Ibid. 28 July 1837, 2.
53 Ibid.
54 Ibid. 21 July 1837, 2.
55 CRO, MSS Rogers RO 8377; B/Helston 104.
56 John Plomer to Vyvyan, 26 July 1847, MSS Vyvyan V 36/45.

one was listed in an 1837 pollbook as a Cantelupe supporter. The remainder of those who were on the register had all voted for Buller.

The second episode – in 1841 – originated in Cantelupe's resignation at the beginning of 1840 and his short term replacement by John Basset, nephew of the late Lord De Dunstanville. Basset was ostensibly a Tory although at various times he professed to being a 'free and independent' member. Certainly Helston's Tories regarded him as 'their man'. However he satisfied no-one by voting with the Conservatives on Lord Sandon's motion for reducing duties on slave grown sugar, then abstaining from the vital no-confidence motion in early June.[57] Dissatisfied with this shuffling and the duke's manipulations, elements of all forces in the town – Tories – Reformers – Dissenters – Corporation, combined to bring in Sir Richard Vyvyan. Prominent among his allies was none other than Thomas Rogers, the solicitor responsible for Buller's unsuccessful attempt four years earlier.[58] Once again the audience was treated to some none too subtle by-play on the hustings for W. R. Vigors, the Whig–Liberal candidate, openly accused Rogers of apostasy. Some obdurate Helston Liberals were not snared in the 'unholy alliance', but as Christopher Popham later wrote to Vyvyan: 'I am positive the Helston party never would have dared to face a Committee of the House of Commons knowing as they did that we were in possession of such facts as must have astonished a Committee and drawn some of their best friends into terrible scrapes.'[59] Vyvyan's correspondence reveals that both sides spent lavishly, but the critical element to emerge from the contest was that Rogers, for more than fifteen years a wily Whig–Liberal, had been bought off by Sir Richard Vyvyan and continued to be employed by him for several years.[60]

Unlike Helston, St Ives could never be labelled a pocket borough because it was a question of whose pocket. Contests were frequent (eight between 1832 and 1868), but five were between rival Conservatives. In 1865 Edward Vivian, a vice-president of the United Kingdom Alliance, unsuccessfully challenged the sitting Conservative Henry Paull. The alliance's executive later reported how Vivian, 'in the face of a considerable territorial interest, succeeded in evoking the goodwill of the inhabitants of the borough'.[61] Gash explains this fragmented territorial interest: the Stephens and Praed families had been contestants well before 1832, along with the notorious borough-monger Sir Christopher Hawkins. The Wellesleys also possessed property in the town, but all these interests were temporarily usurped by the wealthy local miner James Halse, MP for St Ives 1826–30, and again from 1832 until

[57] Basset's explanation for his voting difficulties was published in his 'Address', *Royal Cornwall Gazette*, 18 June 1841, 3.

[58] For Roger's later explanation of his about-face see *West Briton*, 6 Aug. 1847, 4.

[59] C. W. Popham to Vyvyan, 14 Sept. 1841, MSS Vyvyan V 36/45.

[60] Vyvyan and Rogers remained in an uneasy alliance until the mid 1850s, when the latter returned to the Liberals.

[61] Alliance House, Westminster, 13th Report of the Executive Committee of the United Kingdom Alliance, 1864–5.

his death in 1838.[62] His heir, Edwin Ley, continued the family's involvement in the complicated rivalries which meant that almost always local issues (town water supply, roads, mining concerns), took precedence over weightier matters. In 1852 Charles Dod believed influence was 'Chiefly possessed by the Praeds of Trevethow, but mining property of the late Mr Halse gave him weight here; and at Towednack [a parish inside the borough boundaries] the Gilberts of Tredrea have influence'.[63] Seven years later Sir William Jolliffe, the Conservative party's Chief Whip regarded St Ives as a safe Conservative seat, because almost always a combination of powerful landlords would agree on who should be elected.[64] Whenever they failed to do so, a second and sometimes a third Conservative candidate appeared. Finally, in 1868 when a Liberal won the seat without a contest, the victory was due to the pressure exerted to ensure non-interference of a solicitor representing the principal landlords.

Unusual local circumstances in Launceston, Helston and St Ives produced a decisive Conservative majority among registered voters. But it was a deformed partisanship that manifested itself; in each instance the majority was swayed more by local pressures and circumstances and less by the relatively new concepts of party or national policies. The small core of opponents experienced varied fortunes. By the 1850s in Launceston they had been reduced from a near majority of voters (many of whom lived in the rural parishes adjoining the town), to a handful of vocal opponents of the *status quo*. Helston's Liberals, motivated as much by opposition to Leeds and Vyvyan as by ideology, were finally successful in 1857. But by then the ideological passion evident in the 1830s and early 1840s had been diverted into factional feuds and manipulation. The difference between these two and St Ives was that there the Liberal leaders never lost their zeal for Liberalism and teetotalism.[65] What these three boroughs revealed was a partisanship having relatively little to do with national issues and principles. In them, development of political modernisation was painfully slow.

Bodmin was different. Prior to 1859 when Thomas Robartes successfully nominated the Liberal Leveson Gower, and continued to do so for more than two decades afterwards, it is not clear how much influence was possessed by him, the Molesworths and the Vivians, all large land-owning families ringing the town. According to Jolliffe in 1859 'Bodmin is anyone's borough', but another source (Sir Philip Rose) said the Vivian interest was 'always likely to secure one seat'.[66] A decade or so earlier Thomas Robins, a shrewd and

62 Gash, *Politics in the age of Peel*, 264–6

63 Charles R. Dod, *Electoral facts from 1832 to 1853 impartially stated, constituting a complete political gazetteer*, ed. H. J. Hanham, Brighton 1972, 272.

64 Jolliffe's election notebook, 1859, p. 1. Jolliffe's notebooks are in the Somerset Record Office, MSS Hylton DD/HY/24/23

65 *Royal Cornwall Gazette*, 26 Sept. 1867, 5; Hayden, 'Culture, creed and conflict', ch. iv.

66 Sir Philip Rose's election notebook, 1859. This is in the Bodleian Library, Oxford, MSS Eng. list C. 343.

analytical observer of the local political scene, wrote, 'Nothing but money will do for Bodmin – there is scarcely any political feeling there.'[67] Throughout the 1830s there were repeated allegations of intimidation of Bodmin's voters, as well as various forms of manipulation and bribery. Venality may still have been part of Bodmin politics in 1859, because after Dr Mitchell (Conservative) was elected – resuming a career interrupted in 1857 – he quickly accepted the Chiltern Hundreds when his Liberal rival petitioned against him.[68]

Growing importance of issues and principles

Elections in the 1830s and 1840s usually revolved around a combination of national and local issues: even where ideology predominated its form reflected variations arising from constituency view-points. Importantly too, local issues were not the same as local circumstances, one of which could be a preference for men directly associated with, or resident in a borough, rather than outsiders. In some instances this could over-ride party preferences and, therefore, the partisanship discussed by Phillips and Wetherell. Local circumstances and the survival of pre-1832 electoral traditions were particularly evident in Liskeard, Truro, Bodmin and, in a rather different way, in Penryn & Falmouth.

Liskeard managed to survive the ravages of the Reform Act by sacrificing one member. Therefore in the new, geographically expanded constituency (the borough increased in size from 3.7 to 12.7 square miles), contests were greatly simplified. There was also a powerful reforming sentiment dating back to the beginning of the century, partly aimed at the Eliot family's control, and partly a genuine expression of belief in the need for constitutional change. These view-points were elaborated upon in some detail in the town's petition to parliament in December 1830, a document which suggested the reasons for the later weaknesses of the Conservatives. By and large the capital burgesses and freemen were not representative of the town's population. Twenty of the thirty-eight freemen had never resided in Liskeard nor paid parochial rates, and among them were a privy councillor, a chancellor of the diocese of Exeter, three clergymen, an admiral and a clerk in the Treasury.[69] The townspeople strenuously opposed this Eliot-organised charade, as Ben Lyne, chairman of the 1830 meeting explained, adding that he, his father and grandfather had all been reformers.[70] They were not alone. The town, having chafed for so long under the Eliots' control, was genuinely Liberal and whole-

---

67 Thomas Robins to William Rashleigh, 10 Oct. 1842, CRO, MSS Rashleigh R 5545.
68 Insights into venal behaviour may be found in P. P. Smith to Col. Carlyon, 12 Feb. 1843, MSS Carlyon CN 3229/1.
69 Ibid. 31 Dec. 1830, 1.
70 Ibid.

heartedly supported the government which gave many townspeople the opportunity to overturn the family's dominance.

The inhabitants of Liskeard therefore sought a candidate who would genuinely represent their interests and opinions. Charles Buller, Jr, Radical member of the nearby borough-mongering family, who was forced from his West Looe seat in 1831, was privileged to accept the honour. To the mutual satisfaction of both parties the situation remained that way until Buller's death in 1848 (see table 12). Challenged three times, but never closely, his supremacy was exaggerated by the Tories' weakness within the town itself. When the first reformed municipal elections were held they did not nominate a single candidate, nor did most members of the old corporation even bother to vote![71]

Because the old guard Tories were so devastated by reform they left their successors without a nucleus upon which to build, forcing the latter to look outside the town to the neighbouring parishes for support. Yet no matter how hard they tried the Tories could make little headway. Two pollbooks for 1835 and 1837 (see table 13) illustrate their dilemma.[72] Even though they are riddled with discrepancies they nevertheless pinpoint reasons for the comparative weakness of the Whig–Liberals' opponents. Presumably it was they who were most active in the registrations of 1835 and 1836 when thirty-nine voters were added to the registers: a majority were yeomen from the outparishes which must have been scoured by Kekewich's friends. In fact when we compare the place of abode of the voters in 1837 we find that eighty of Buller's total came from within the town, and only forty of Kekewich's supporters. The latter's relative strength among the yeomen could not offset this, nor Kekewich's other great liability. Although he owned property in and around the town he lived in neighbouring Devon, so as an outsider he endured the sometimes latent, sometimes overt hostility experienced by many such candidates in Cornwall.

Of course the explanation for Buller's successes does not lie solely in the mechanistic town/rural parishes divide. As he proved repeatedly at Westminster, he was a full-blown Radical: the ballot, free trade, the eradication of all disabilities applying to Dissenters, municipal reform, were policies upon which he and his supporters were in total harmony. Like William Tooke at Truro and various Whig–Liberal candidates at Bodmin, he had the backing of the shopkeepers, small tradesmen – the *West Briton*'s 'middle and industrious classes' – who were grateful for being allowed to participate more directly in the reformed electoral system. Some of the prominent Buller supporters were Wesleyan Methodists, for example Richard Retallick, clock-maker and ironmonger, John Bowden and Samuel Hender, grocers, William Boase, bookseller and printer. The town's principal Quaker, John Allen, was another. The Methodists Retallick, Bowden, Boase and William Langford, also a loyal

[71] Ibid. 1 Jan. 1836, 2.
[72] CRO, B/Lisk. 349–50.

Table 13
Liskeard elections, 1835, 1837

| | Buller (Whig) | | Kekewich (Tory) | |
	1835	1837	1835	1837
Esquires	2	1	4	5
Gentlemen	4	5	5	3
Clerks	2	–	2	4
Yeomen	36	33	21	44
Masons	6	6	–	1
Innkeepers	5	5	6	4
Grocers	3	1	1	–
Tanners	2	2	2	2
Tailors	5	2	–	–
Attorneys	–	2	–	3
Shoemakers	4	4	–	–
Butchers	2	2	1	2
+ others	43	50	21	27
Totals	114	113	64	95

1835 – 211 on register – 178 voted (57 yeomen)
1837 – 250 on register – 208 voted (77 yeomen)

Buller man, were among the twelve members of the first reformed corporation;[73] Ben Lyne, the solicitor who chaired the 1830 Reform meeting, was the first mayor, with Boase his successor.

Therefore in Liskeard the Dissenting–middle-class element seems to have been solidly united in its Liberalism. Much of this strength arose from the town's former pocket borough status, engendering a determination among the more well-to-do inhabitants to send the Eliots packing. Afterwards they were more than happy with their Radical member, so Buller had few worries about rivals like Samuel Kekewich, who proudly proclaimed in 1837 that he was an 'independent country gentlemen', terminology reminiscent of an earlier era now shunned by the voters.[74]

In an obvious parallel with Liskeard, Truro's reformers quickly asserted themselves in 1832; for the next two decades they always elected at least one MP, and sometimes both. There were other similarities too. Truro had been under the thumb of its patron for centuries, it was a one-time corporation borough and after 1832 it was middle-class Dissenters who provided the core

73 The first reformed corporation was listed in the *West Briton*, 1 Jan. 1836, 2.
74 *Royal Cornwall Gazette*, 28 July 1837, 2.

of William Tooke's support, if not that of Sir Hussey Vivian. Yet there were subtle differences between the electoral politics of the two, in Truro's case originating with highly visible middle-class activism beginning in 1818–20. When the climax came at the 1830 general election, those men readily identifiable with a variety of popular causes and sharing a common opposition to the Falmouth-controlled corporation, unsuccessfully supported two reform candidates, Lubbock and Tooke. Heading the list of 179 'free burgesses' were many mentioned previously, Willyams, Milford, Major, Blee, Cuming, Randall – as well as Silvanus James a teetotal grocer and the more radical Richard Spurr, Thomas Barlow, William Rowe and William Tealor, all of whom later broke away from the Whig–Liberals following Tooke's surprising defeat in the 1837 general election.[75] James, Rowe, Barlow, Magor and Spurr were all Methodists of various sorts. So were many others on the list.

Truro's reformers were fortunate in having Tooke take up their fight. He unsuccessfully contested the borough again in 1831, then when reform became a reality, lost no time in announcing he would renew his candidacy. He knew his prospects of success were excellent, for the old county reformers such as William and Robert Peter and Penhallow Peters gave their support, as did some of Truro's professional middle class, the solicitors J. F. Bennallack and Henry Stokes being two examples. Tooke was proved right. In 1832, after a struggle lasting almost three years, he and his partner Sir Hussey Vivian were finally successful, completely vanquishing the Tories. And, 82 of the 179 'free burgesses' from 1830 were among his votes.[76]

In the euphoria following the victory (Tooke wrote of 'a roaring and happy party of sixty friends'), there were several signs suggesting that Whig–Liberal control of both seats would be short-lived.[77] Like Kekewich at Liskeard, Tooke was an outsider. Although he had taken up the reformers' cause in 1830 and made prodigious efforts on their behalf, he always suffered from that drawback. For example on the hustings in December 1832 much was made of local ties which the respective candidates did or did not have. Humphrey Willyams, in nominating Tooke, pointed out to his listeners that his friend was no carpetbagger – 'am I to be told that all these merits are to be smothered by the false argument that he is a stranger?' To be told this by men who in the past had themselves brought upon Truro 'the disgrace of being always misrepresented by strangers!' was too much.[78] Tooke countered the same criticism by pointing out that he had been invited to stand by a requisition of 200 householders. Even so nothing could douse this flame of discontent.

Another potential problem was that Tooke, like Buller at Liskeard, was a Radical. In 1832 he told his audiences he favoured vote by secret ballot, the emancipation of slaves, reduction of taxes, triennial parliaments and

75 RIC, *Truro: further account of election proceedings*, 26–7.
76 Ibid. 65–9.
77 Tooke to Amelia Tooke, 16 Dec. 1832, CRO, FS/3/1289/7.
78 *West Briton*, 14 Dec. 1832, 2.

reformed corporations.[79] Although such a platform had the complete approval of Willyams, Bennallack, Milford, Blee, Randall and many other reformers, it was a far cry from the moderation of Tooke's running mate Sir Hussey Vivian, and in 1837, another Whig–Liberal, Edmund Turner. They had very strong reservations about the ballot and triennial parliaments, both of which frightened those Conservatives who were prepared to split their votes with moderate reformers.[80] Tooke's extremism was certainly popular with many voters in a centre of Dissent but the narrowness of his margin over Ennis Vivian (Conservative) in 1832 – 203 votes to 196 – plus the decisive margin (more than eighty votes) Hussey Vivian had over both, suggests the moderate reformers outnumbered their radical brethren.

Lurking in the background – at least until 1836 – was Edmund Turner, an ambitious merchant and banker. Before 1832 he was less forthright about reform than many others, but in that year he voted for Tooke and presumably Hussey Vivian. Soon after he surreptitiously began laying the foundations for his eventual election. Town properties were bought, enabling him to influence the occupant-voters, alliances were formed with moderate Conservatives, and in 1836 he boosted his public profile by being elected mayor. A year beforehand, when the sudden general election took everyone by surprise and Hussey Vivian was in Ireland, Turner became his spokesperson – unsuccessfully, as Vivian was defeated. Few people had any doubt that Turner would now run at the first opportunity.[81]

Finally, and unhappily for Tooke, Truro's Conservatives did not collapse after 1832. Fifteen new capital burgesses had been appointed to the old Tory Corporation after 1823 and they became the nucleus of the revived party. In fact in 1832 it was suggested that Ennis Vivian was 'their candidate', and there was also a hint of Boscawen involvement. The party soon made its presence felt at the annual registrations, so Tooke ran the risk of falling victim to moderate Whig–Liberals of the Turner type, and moderate Conservatives like Vivian who were prepared to support Dissenters' claims. Any agreement by the two groups about split votes would be fatal. Nevertheless, Tooke's defeat in 1837 was a surprise to many.

What were the immediate reasons for his rejection? Clearly it was a case of Turner appealing to those interests who favoured a local commercial man (one of their own), and scrupulously avoiding any mention of the ballot, or shorter parliaments. Turner in fact committed himself to very little, apart from advancing Truro's commerce. He was conspicuously absent from a January 1837 meeting in the town to protest about church rates, a meeting at which Stokes, Milford, Magor, Randall, Baynard, Jacob Edwards and many

[79] Ibid.
[80] Ibid. and 9 Jan. 1835, 2. In 1835 Turner proposed the absent Vivian and took the opportunity to explain his own views.
[81] James Borlase to Matthew Moyle, 25 Jan. 1835, CRO, AD 801/2; A. Jenkin to A. M. Agar, 22 Sept. 1834, Jenkin letterbooks, HJ/1/16.

other more radical reformers took the lead.[82] It might be argued that Turner's absence meant little – after all Humphrey Willyams was another absentee. But Willyams's principles were never in doubt – they had been heard by his audiences at each general election from 1830, for he was Tooke's perpetual proposer and shared his radicalism. On the other hand Turner was constantly linked with Hussey Vivian, who until 1835 had been reluctant to make a definite commitment to anything except the abolition of slavery and municipal reform.

Another problem arose from Truro's radical Dissenters and their supporters, the core of Tooke's support. By their comparative extremism they weakened his position. Everything suggests they became steadily more determined to press for solutions to such questions as the ballot and the liability of Dissenters for payment of church rates. The 1836 Dissenting Marriage Act failed to satisfy them and the government's dropping of an 1837 bill to abolish church rates sparked new tensions. Wesleyan Methodists, Bible Christians, Primitive Methodists, Baptists and Independents agreed in their opposition to the rates, expressing it in a series of well-attended public meetings. Meanwhile their moderate Whig–Liberal allies paid lip service to Dissenters' demands, busied themselves in the affairs of the Truro Reform Association (created in 1836), and became deeply involved in the annual registrations.[83] Ultimately Turner was the beneficiary of this split within Truro's reformers.

Judging by the acrimony which burst forth after Tooke's defeat, the *West Briton* may have accurately summed up the situation:

> While the Tory party is made up of a portion of the Aristocracy of the place, a few of the respectable tradesmen, and the most dependent and corrupt of the electors, the Liberal party embodies a considerable number of the most wealthy and influential merchants and tradesmen, and the great bulk of the middle and industrious classes – men who are capable of forming sound opinions.[84]

Obviously many of the second category of Liberals were Dissenters. They were left out in the cold while the remnants of the unreformed corporation, Tories such as the Nankivell, Paul, Carlyon and Daubuz families – with their allies – struck a bargain with the moderate reformers. 196 Tories split with Turner, only twenty with Tooke.[85] Tooke was furious at this duplicitous campaign to dump him, because during recent sessions of parliament Turner had sent him a stream of personal applications recommended by him (Turner), for Tooke's patronage. The purpose, according to Tooke, was '*Strengthening my interests*' with the electors of Truro. Instead his position had been under-

[82] *West Briton*, 3 Feb. 1837, 3.
[83] The Truro Reform Association was founded on 15 Feb. 1836. More than 600 people attended, having been given only two days notice: *West Briton*, 19 Feb. 1836, 2.
[84] Ibid. 28 July 1837, 2.
[85] Ibid. 18 Aug. 1837, 3.

mined.[86] Turner's success led to a prolongation of the bargain between the two parties, representation being shared for another twenty years.

The mixture of pre-reform traditions and local forces was far more overt at Bodmin. After 1836 remnants of the unreformed corporation kept one tradition alive – always promoting a contest in order to line their pockets. There were the two parliamentary parties, the influence of powerful landlords, and this shadowy fourth party – usually on the Conservative side. The leaders were Mr Belling an iron-monger, James Eleson a wine and spirit merchant, Nicholas Stephens a horse dealer, the Grose family, and one or two other allies.[87] Their influence meant they could always command a high price, but they were always likely to over-reach themselves. They did so in 1841 when they withdrew their support from Sir Samuel Spry (MP 1832–41), preferring the free spending of his fellow Conservative J. Dunn Gardner. Consequently, when the sitting Liberal retired in 1843, Spry's presence in the by-election field, together with the Liberal Charles Graves-Sawle, left them in an awkward position.

Spry scrupulously avoided the corrupt faction perhaps because he was anxious to improve his reputation with Sir Robert Peel, from whom he had recently requested a peerage. The rest of the story is best told by P. P. Smith, a Truro solicitor employed by Spry:

> The Houses of Lanhydrock [Robartes] Glynn [Vivian] and Pencarrow [Molesworth] not satisfied with their own strength, and that of the Liberal party, on Sunday week formed an alliance with Messrs Belling Nic Stevens [sic] & Co who had before been holding out for a third man. On the following day Mr Robartes took the field in person, and canvassed for his friend Mr Sawle, and the same evening Mr Belling began his canvass for Mr Sawle.[88]

Spry's victory by four votes prompted universal amazement, for he resisted all overtures to pay for support as he had done in the past. The 'fourth party' continued to interfere until at least 1852 when Dod explained, 'of late years little *personal* influence has prevailed'. Hanham inferred from the italics that Dod 'intended to convey the impression that Bodmin could be bought'.[89] Here was a tradition linking Bodmin and some of its Conservative MPs with behaviour redolent of the eighteenth century. Despite the parliamentary candidates' party rhetoric at every contested general election, the results often reflected a balance between very different forces.

Penryn's well-observed notoriety for bribery has been referred to previously. The correspondent who wrote of the 1761 election in the town, "tis said the money is drove abt in wheelbarrows' (Penryn was a scot and lot

---

86 Ibid. 4 Aug. 1837, 1.
87 Edward Geach to William Rashleigh, 11 Feb. 1843, CRO, MSS Rashleigh R 5545.
88 P. P. Smith to Col. Carlyon, 12 Feb. 1843, MSS Carlyo CN 3229/1.
89 H. J. Hanham, *Elections and party management: politics in the time of Disraeli and Gladstone*, Hassocks 1978, 28.

borough) referred to a practice that, although the form changed, was still common in the next century.[90] When Penryn was linked to its neighbour, Falmouth, the venal voters soon passed on the tricks of their trade.

Eventually, in a burst of political self-righteousness the Liberals agreed to take action. During a meeting at the Royal Hotel, Falmouth, in May 1852, the election committee decided the time had come to wean the voters from their traditional electioneering pleasures. Elimination of bribery and other illegal practices, and the signing of a pledge by committee members were the principal objects. Members had to promise not to pay money for votes, or as compensation for any services, 'or to, or for any Inn Keeper, Victualler, Tavern keeper, Coffee house keeper, or other person for any Victuals, Drinks or Refreshments supplied for or on account of such Elections'.[91] Naturally the first Liberal candidate subject to these conditions was unsuccessful, but from 1857 onwards the party won both seats until the 1868 general election. According to the Conservatives, 1857 was a victory for the 'lavish distribution of patronage and promises', which 'induced two influential Cons[ervatives] to Rat' so that they and their relatives could share the Liberals' rewards.[92]

Electoral politics in Penryn & Falmouth were not for the scrupulous, at least until the end of the 1850s. Another complication was that neither of the parties remained united for long, dockyard issues were always prominent, and government influence could never be ignored. Amid this medley of factors plus the difficulty of luring candidates to the ports, interest in national issues was not always obvious, especially in Penryn.

Post-reform political modernisation in Cornwall

In 1865 all Cornwall's seven boroughs had less than 900 voters, as they had had in 1832, so in thirty-three years the overall growth in the electorate, apart from the two county divisions, was minimal. Like many of their small counterparts throughout England they exhibited diverse forms of electoral behaviour, this being the product of the interplay of principles and issues, together with various forms of influence and control, long-established traditions and local circumstances. What remains is the relative weighting to be given to these factors.

The general impression of mid-Victorian Cornwall politics is that because of the overwhelming dominance of Dissent, particularly Wesleyan Methodism, the Liberal party enjoyed widespread support. But general election results between 1832 and 1868 reveal a different picture. What cannot be overlooked is the obvious tendency for a greater percentage of Methodists to

90 William Roberts, Jr, to Thomas Hawkins, 30 Mar. 1761, RIC, MSS Hawkins HH/13/76.
91 CRO, X (Penryn & Falmouth), 394/32, 33.
92 Jolliffe's election notebook, 1859, pt 1.

vote Conservative than their Baptist and other Dissenting counterparts.[93] So, twice in the period when protection was an important election issue, 1841 and 1852, this too may have helped the Conservatives win a majority of the fourteen seats. If county divisions are excluded, in only four of the general elections did the Liberals capture more than half of the ten borough seats. Prior to 1857 the Conservatives more than held their own: afterwards the general trend of results clearly favoured their opponents. Such a pattern of Liberal successes in the 1830s, followed by a swing to the Conservatives in the 1840s and early 1850s, then back to the Liberals again, was not confined to Cornwall's small boroughs. It was replicated elsewhere in England, probably reflecting the rise and fall of the debate about the Corn Laws.

In the decade after the First Reform Act Cornwall was no different from the remainder of England in several additional respects. Liberal and Conservative Associations appeared in most boroughs, party contests were very evident in municipal elections and at the registration courts, and post-reform Liberal enthusiasm ended the Tories' supremacy in several boroughs. Predictably, the latter did not concede without a struggle, short-lived in Liskeard, more prolonged and ultimately successful in Truro. Both towns exhibited a lively political vitality before 1832, this being generated by opposition to the patrons and an attachment among voters and non voters to either of the political parties. The vitality intensified in the 1830s, suggesting that the type of partisanship characteristic of political modernisation flourished.

Where partisanship was far weaker was in Launceston, St Ives and Helston. If, as Phillips and Wetherell suggest, 'Reform infused elections with a new sense of principle and the electorate responded with a new degree of inter-election partisan loyalty, most voters following one party vote with another at successive elections', evidence of this is lacking in these Conservative strongholds.[94] Influence, intimidation and coercion were much more apparent, but there were opponents of the *status quo*. For example, leading the small reform party in St Ives was the teetotal tailor William Docton (a Wesleyan), who in 1852 travelled to London with a requisition for the Liberal Hussey Vivian, Jr.[95] He was responsible for organising other contests in the 1850s and 1860s, and he had his counterparts elsewhere in Cornwall's boroughs.

The clear trend towards the Liberals after 1857 suggests several conclusions about partisanship in small boroughs. Firstly, continuing from developments in the 1820s, vigorous party activity appeared in all towns, even Launceston, between 1832 and 1841. These were years of lively political debate with national issues such as parliamentary and municipal reform, the payment of church rates, the future of the Irish Church, and the Corn Laws

---

[93] Further information on this point may be found in Phillips, *Great Reform Bill*, ch. viii.
[94] Phillips and Wetherell, 'Great Reform Act', 426.
[95] See, for example, *West Briton*, 14 May 1852, 4; *Royal Cornwall Gazette*, 6 May 1859, 1.

helping to delineate the two opposing parties. Organisationally, the Cornish boroughs were the scene of party activity at the annual registrations too, until the early 1840s. By then, however, electoral traditions, local circumstance and various forms of influence were once again visible – 'the constant molecular movement of agents, money, influence, argument persuasion, personalities and gossip'.[96] Especially among the Conservatives they remained ascendant until the end of the 1850s. Then, despite the exceptions of Bodmin, Launceston and St Ives a more permanent partisanship slowly began to re-emerge. Secondly, even in smaller boroughs where influence and control were minimal, other powerful factors – one referred to earlier being political memory, the traditions of the unreformed system – remained healthily alive. Bribery at Penryn, the activities of the 'fourth party' at Bodmin, Truro's preference for local men, all slowed the modernisation process.

Thirdly, if we reconsider table 11, listing 131 smaller boroughs, in the light of Gash's estimate that post-1832 there were as many as sixty-two proprietary and family boroughs (of which fifty-three had less than 1,000 voters), on the basis of Cornwall that estimate may be too low. Only Launceston was listed – Helston, Bodmin (after 1857) and St Ives could have been, and Penryn & Falmouth defied political modernisation for different reasons. So, in five of the seven boroughs voting at times seems to have been a direct reflection of personal and/or economic relationships, rather than principles and issues. Progress towards political modernisation was therefore spasmodic. Overall, the evidence from Cornwall and elsewhere suggests that among smaller boroughs after 1832 degrees of influence and local factors cannot be discounted, and their declining importance may date from the 1850s rather than the 1830s.

[96] Harvey, 'British general elections', 396.

6

Landlords, Farmers and Influence, 1841–1868

Mid century tensions

On 19 January 1845 and after a long illness William Eliot, second earl of St Germans died at the age of seventy-eight. His heir was his eldest son Edward Granville Eliot, who had been a Conservative MP for East Cornwall since 1837. At the resulting by-election caused by Edward Eliot's shift to the House of Lords, Cornwall's Liberals were totally unprepared, so William Pole Carew, the Conservative replacement, was unopposed. Furious at the Liberals, whose cause it had championed for almost forty years, the *West Briton* declared:

> Let them take a lesson from their opponents, and observe with what patient, unwearied perseverance they have gone on year after year, banding themselves together, always at work, watching the registration with the most careful scrutiny – adopting every means to consolidate and strengthen their own power, and to undermine that of their opponents. Let them observe, too, the activity and energy displayed by the whole race of Tory squires, from the veteran Tremayne down to the last newly fledged squireling, whenever the time for action is come; and let them imitate this activity and energy.[1]

The annual registration of voters, the paper suggested, was, and had long been the key to Conservative success, but the Liberals seemed unaware of this reality. The vacuum left by Sir Colman Rashleigh's withdrawal from political life, plus bitter ideological arguments among the Liberals, had played into their opponent's hands. Helped by the threat to agricultural protection the Conservatives were the beneficiaries of the break-up of the long-standing farmer–reformer alliance, at least in the short term. As the *West Briton* lamented, an efficient organisational structure and detailed attention to the registers meant that by 1845 the East Cornwall Conservatives were impregnable.

Eight years later they were in a state of near terminal weakness, disorganised and debilitated by a feud lasting for almost a generation. The cause was the 1852 general election. At the centre of the controversy were two well-known Conservatives, both prominent in the 1845 by-election: one, Pole Carew was an East Cornwall MP from 1845 to 1852. The other was Nicholas

---

[1] *West Briton*, 14 Feb. 1845, 2.

Kendall, the man who eventually unseated him with the help of the farmers. It would be a simple task to argue that the two fell out because in 1852 the Conservatives made an error in believing they could win both seats, or, as in several other English counties the protectionist, the farmers' candidate, was the beneficiary of a combination of local and national circumstances. Unfortunately, neither explanation reveals the complexities of the situation.

In some agricultural constituencies, among them East Cornwall, the 1852 general election mirrored the divergent opinions between Lord Derby and his Chancellor of the Exchequer, Benjamin Disraeli, over the plight of British agriculturalists. Disraeli, convinced of the electoral liability of a return to protection, favoured a package of measures to alleviate the farmers' financial burdens. Conversely, Derby preferred raising tariffs which in theory would result in higher prices for farmers.[2] From 1849 onwards, as earlier in the decade, both view-points had their adherents in East Cornwall. The debate was complicated by a succession of religious questions, which as we have seen previously, frequently stimulated Cornwall's remarkable political vitality. The Maynooth Grant, Puseyism, 'papal aggression', and the impact of the British Anti-State Church Association, were contentious and stirred passionately held beliefs. It was the intersection of the debate about protection and these religious questions which widened the differences between Conservative aristocracy and gentry on the one hand, the yeomen and tenant farmers on the others. Eventually the outcome was disastrous for the party in both county divisions.

The focus of this chapter is county politics in the mid century years, 1841–68, a period notable for three developments. First, the farmers consolidated their electoral importance, especially in East Cornwall where Nicholas Kendall was their candidate in 1851–2, and remained so until 1868 when his former supporters ruthlessly dumped him. Second, the importance of Dissent and religious questions repeatedly intruded into political debate, almost always to the Conservatives' discomfiture. Third, there was the continuing eclipse of such landed families as the Boscawens, Tremaynes, Bassets and Carews, whose ability to affect the fortunes of the local Conservative party was almost negligible. 'There is no aristocratic influence here', Sir Richard Vyvyan observed of West Cornwall in 1864, 'on the contrary the prevalence of dissent and of an independence of character which is almost republican (although there is a universal attachment to the Queen) suggests no attempt to strain the landlords [sic] power.'[3] Vyvyan's comments were equally applicable to the East, where the decline of the county Conservatives gathered pace after the 1840s.

---

2 Robert Stewart, *The politics of protection: Lord Derby and the protectionist party, 1841–1852*, Cambridge 1971, 195–7.
3 Vyvyan to William Williams, 6 Jan. 1864, MSS Vyvyan V 22M/80/36/46.

Decline of the county Conservatives

The seeds of their slow demise were sown soon after the 1841 general election. In 1842 Sir Robert Peel's government altered the sliding scale of import duties, reducing the level of protection to the farmers. A further step one year later, favouring Canadian wheat imports, worried Cornish farmers even more, especially as their MPs seemed prepared to support Peel rather than listen to the complaints of constituents. Compared with Lincolnshire, Essex and Buckinghamshire, where farmers expressed great dissatisfaction with these actions, Cornwall was quieter.[4] Nevertheless there were signs that prominent members of the Conservative aristocracy and their gentry allies were not willing to openly champion the complaints of a group (the farmers), who became increasingly vocal. This gradual divergence of opinion became more apparent in 1845 at the East Cornwall by-election.

Pole Carew appears to have been the Conservatives' only choice to replace Eliot, and it was his friend Nicholas Kendall who travelled to Berkshire to persuade him to stand.[5] It was not the first time Kendall had acted in this way; in 1841 he was responsible for William Rashleigh's successful candidacy, and he had been actively involved in party affairs for many years. Before the 1845 by-election there was some thought of Liberal opposition, but the canvassing results caused a hasty reappraisal.[6] They showed the Conservatives to be even stronger than in 1841 when they won both seats, hence the *West Briton's* chagrin mentioned earlier. On the hustings Carew explained to his listeners – many of them yeomen and tenant farmers – that he would pledge himself to oppose any proposals for reduced duties. Kendall, seconding his nomination, reinforced the message: 'as an individual, exceedingly anxious at this moment, when the cry of free trade is so rife, and the clamour of the league so excessively strong, it becomes me to contend that we ought to choose a man to represent us who is wedded to our interests by every tie'.[7] Kendall thought Carew fitted the bill – a dedicated protectionist – even though the latter announced he was 'no party man'.

Afterwards, at the post-election dinner, the former county member John Tremayne referred to the growing disquiet in the county over Peel's increasingly obvious ideological conversion to free trade, then expressed the hope that Carew would not desert the prime minister.[8] Thomas Liddell, a tenant farmer, voiced very different views: 'he and his brother farmers did not feel that confidence in Sir R. Peel which Mr Tremayne and other gentlemen entertained', justifying desertion from the Conservatives, because 'they [the farmers] considered their interests had been betrayed by the Parliament

---

4 Davis, *Political change*, 151–2; Olney, *Lincolnshire politics*, 115–21.
5 Copy of enclosure from Kendall to earl of Derby, 1867 (?), MSS Kendall KL.
6 *West Briton*, 14 Feb. 1845, 2.
7 Ibid. 21 Feb. 1845, 2.
8 Ibid.

which was returned in 1841'.[9] Still, Carew at this point enjoyed the farmers' support.

The onset of the potato blight increased rural tensions (reports of its disastrous progress in the county began in August 1845), and helped to clarify the arguments about the merits of protection and free trade. There were at least four view-points; firstly, those typical of members of the Wadebridge Farmers' Club who sensed that the loss of protection would mean ruin for tenant farmers; secondly, the free-traders led by such Radicals as John Trelawny and Sir William Molesworth who encouraged petitions in support of Peel's free trade proposals; thirdly, the optimists who, although opposed to free trade, were convinced it would be better to have it immediately and get on with high farming, rather than wait for two or three years; and lastly the landowner-miners who appreciated how free trade would produce cheaper bread and therefore allow them to pay lower wages.

As Elvins noted, 'The County's large Conservative landowners were split completely over free trade and there was nothing like the unanimity which one would have expected from their previous protestations against free trade.'[10] Lord St Germans, Lord Mt Edgcumbe and G. M. Fortescue were some of those in favour; opposed were Pole Carew, Lord Falmouth, Sir Richard Vyvyan and John Tremayne. Perhaps the most interesting aspect of the controversy was the virtually silent opposition of men like Tremayne and most notably Pole Carew, who frowned on the farmers' public meetings of protest.[11] From their respective attitudes to these developments of 1845–7, Kendall's unequivocal opposition to free trade, Carew's rather different stance, emerged the first signs of a later polarisation. Kendall's sympathies lay with the protectionist farmers, Carew's with the more ambivalent large landowners.

William Rashleigh, Jr, retired in 1847, despite Kendall's urgings to continue. Pushed into parliament in 1841, he had later endured a series of scathing attacks by the *West Briton* for his lack of ability and ideological inflexibility, then in 1846 at a meeting at Bodmin was publicly humiliated by free trade farmers who ridiculed his protectionist views.[12] With the eastern Conservatives arguing among themselves, and troubled over registrations, Rashleigh informed his father that 'I told Kendall for my part if an honest Whig like Robartes stood I would sooner vote for such a man than I would for a dishonest Peelite, or in other words, a would-be-Farmers-Friend in the shape of a Conservative, – & in this he quite agreed with me!'[13] Robartes did stand successfully as a Liberal, along with his brother-in-law Carew, who was questioned intently by several electors on such diverse subjects as protection,

9   Ibid.
10 Elvins, 'Reform movement', ch. ix, p. 12.
11 Ibid. 12–13.
12 *West Briton*, 13 Feb. 1846, 2, 4.
13 W. Rashleigh, Jr, to his father, 16 June 1846, CRO, MSS Rashleigh R 5339.

the ballot and restriction of liquor sales on the sabbath. Tremayne repeatedly referred to divided opinions among local farmers while another landowner, Edward Archer, thought the best solution to their difficulties was to emancipate them, 'from both the fixed duty and the sliding scale'.[14] Interestingly, Carew made it clear that he now 'would not support protection against the opinions of the legislature at large'. Such flexibility was completely at variance with Kendall's dogmatism.

After 1847 rising grain prices stifled the farmers' grumblings. It was generally admitted that Cornish wheat growers could pay their way if wheat was no lower than 56s. per quarter, close to the price paid in 1846. Shortages in 1847 pushed the price well beyond that level, keeping the agriculturists happy, but precipitating some of the most frightening mob violence in nineteenth-century Cornwall.

At Wadebridge, Callington, Camborne–Redruth, Helston and especially St Austell the authorities, led by Kendall in his role as sheriff, struggled desperately to quell food riots. Fortunately, with no cohesion between miners, clay workers or quarrymen a general uprising was impossible.[15] Soon afterwards wheat prices began to fall again, and consequently disjointed lower-class agitation gave way to renewed farmer militancy.

Primarily confined to eastern Cornwall, the unrest originated with farmers' meetings in the hundred of East – at Callington, Liskeard and elsewhere – in spring 1849. However it was a bi-partite movement, occasionally misinterpreted in earlier accounts of farmer activism. Several writers have suggested that a member of the lesser gentry, Edward Archer, was the leader of the die-hard protectionists, overlooking the various solutions to the farmers' problems.[16] In fact Archer was prominent not because he was a protectionist (for him the policy was dead in 1847), but from his sharing the farmers' desire for local tax relief. Although he found himself at the head of the resurgent farmers' movement in its early stages, this was only because they were seeking relief from the financial burdens on land, and a reimposition of protective duties. While the outcry for the equalisation of county rates and taxes was hopelessly entangled with protectionist arguments, the yeomen and tenant farmers followed Archer's lead; once the differences were ironed out after a county meeting in February 1850, he was discarded. The meeting, attended by more than 2,000 people was one of the high points of farmer activism.[17] Falmouth, Tremayne and Carew sent letters of apology, expressing their doubts about the expediency of urging a restoration of protection at the present time. Liberals such as the West Cornwall MPs Lemon and Pendarves firmly refused to support the outcry, lining up with Robartes in believing the solution to the farmers' problems lay in rent adjustment and more efficient

14 *West Briton*, 13 Aug. 1847, 4.
15 Rowe, *Cornwall in the age of industrial revolution*, 161–2.
16 For example, ibid. 251; Elvins, 'Reform movement', ch. ix, pp. 14–22.
17 *West Briton*, 15 Feb. 1850, 2.

farming. On this occasion the major speeches were made by tenant farmers: one of them, William Snell, who expressed the antipathy aroused by Robartes's free trade votes in parliament, said 'I have been endeavouring to organise a society to extend through East Cornwall and whenever the time shall come he [Robartes] will be ousted by a tremendous majority.'[18] One month later Snell was as good as his word – the East Cornwall Society for the Protection of Native Industry (ECSPNI) was formed in March 1850.

Snell and his friends may have been influenced by the earlier creation of the National Association for the Protection of British Industry and Capital. Many Cornish farmers were aware that their concerns were shared by others elsewhere in England. The diarist Charles Greville wrote that 'the farmers have been so terrified and excited by their leaders and orators that there is good reason to fear, . . . that they will . . . break through all the old patriarchal ties, and go to any lengths which they may fancy they can make instrumental for their relief'.[19] With farmers' meetings in Devon, Norfolk, Lincolnshire, Staffordshire, Berkshire, and talk of running farmers' candidates at the next general election, his observations were portentous.

Meanwhile, within a month of its formation the ECSPNI carried out a perfunctory canvass of the division. A member of the society reported to Kendall that, 'it appeared that there is a majority of Protectionists over Free Traders, Neutrals & Doubtfuls together in every one of the Districts from which returns have been received'.[20] Emboldened by this the society therefore decided to select a parliamentary candidate to represent their interests. Not surprisingly, given his past record, the choice was the former county member William Rashleigh, 'a firm consistent friend of the farmers'.[21] Kendall was the alternative, so when Rashleigh declined, he was the next to feel the farmers' pressure. Kendall's opinion was that the offer should go to a man of property and great standing (implying that he did not satisfy these criteria), but in an emergency he would, reluctantly, stand with Carew.[22] His proviso was expenses – he could afford to pay no more than the statutory legal costs. Kendall must also have known how complex the whole question of protection was at this time. While many tenant farmers were out-and-out protectionists, numerous small landowners supported the society only because a reimposition of import duties would allow them to maintain their rents at the current high levels, rather than reducing them as some large landowners were doing. Other farmers were as much concerned about the equalisation of county rates and taxes ('a reduction of the burdens on land'), as they were about protection. No wonder Kendall was cautious about becoming a candidate for East Cornwall.

18 Ibid.
19 Quoted in T. L. Crosby, English farmers and the politics of protection, 1815–1852, Hassocks 1977, 163.
20 William Geach to Kendall, 25 May 1850, MSS Kendall KL.
21 Ibid.
22 Printed brochure in the Kendall papers, undated, ibid.

Religion and politics in East Cornwall, 1845–51

By June 1850 the outwardly cordial relations between Carew and Kendall could not disguise the fact that the former was at best a reluctant protectionist, by comparison with Kendall's strident advocacy. Meanwhile there were other forces at work in the relationship, notably their different attitudes to religious questions.[23] The crux of the problem lay in Kendall's ultra-Toryism. He was a close friend of Sir Richard Vyvyan, and had opposed Catholic emancipation and parliamentary reform. In most respects he was an old-fashioned rural Conservative, and he reacted like one in April 1845 when Peel decided to assist the process of Irish reconciliation to British rule. The prime minister's startling proposal was to increase the annual grant to the Catholic seminary at Maynooth, as well as providing a one-off grant for a new building. Many Conservatives in and outside parliament were appalled. Besides reminding them of Peel's 1829 apostasy, the proposals hit one of the rawest nerves in his party, the supremacy of the Church of England in Ireland. In the four months between February and May 1845 more than a million people petitioned against the bill, fewer than 18,000 for it. The majority was made up of several components: those whose rabid anti-popish fervour resurfaced, others who argued on more cerebral grounds about the preservation of the Anglican supremacy and the hegemony of the Irish Church, and Dissenters, many of whom as in Cornwall, believed 'the state ought to endow no religion whatever'.[24] Kendall, of course, was among the first group, and in opposing the grant he was, for once, in tune with both county newspapers and general public opinion. Carew, on the other hand, voted for the bill's second and third readings, justifying his vote on the same grounds as Peel when he put forward the proposition. Naturally Carew's opinions antagonised many of his Anglican, Wesleyan and Bible Christian constituents, but the anger apparently subsided before the 1847 election.

Towards the end of the 1840s the constant undercurrent of religious tensions reappeared in a different form. Cornwall's Dissenters again moved into the spotlight when the 1848 annual meeting of the British Anti-State Church Association resolved to send deputations to South Wales, Devon and Cornwall.[25] The two emissaries to Cornwall hammered away at the need to separate the government of the country from the Church of England, the unfairness of university restrictions and the principle, state endowment of a Church, underlying the Maynooth grant.[26] Their proselytising aroused plenty of enthusiasm among many Dissenting farmers in the eastern districts,

---

[23] *West Briton*, 9 Apr. 1852, 5. Several letters in the Kendall–Carew correspondence were reprinted in this issue.
[24] Ibid. 2 May 1845, 1: speech by Revd William Moore at Truro meeting several days earlier.
[25] Ibid. 13 Oct. 1848, 2.
[26] See, for example, ibid. 16 June 1848, 2.

particularly in Bible Christian strongholds such as St Columb where strong protectionist sentiments were also surfacing. Added to this were more frequent complaints of 'Puseyism' in the county press, so it was a time of heated debates on religious and economic topics. Pole Carew, meanwhile, was about to make an unfortunate contribution to the situation.

In June 1845 Carew, the patron, had presented his brother-in-law J. Somers Cocks to the living of Sheviock in south-eastern Cornwall. Whether he knew of his relative's Tractarian predilections is uncertain, however in later years the appointment became a millstone around his neck. Early in 1850 Somers Cocks presided over the dedication of the restored Sheviock church chapel, in a service notable for its elaborate rituals.[27] Several months later the *West Briton* published a lengthy report under the eye-catching heading, 'Puseyism at Sheviock', including a litany of complaints about Cocks, forwarded by the churchwardens and parishioners to the bishop of Exeter. Chanting of psalms, changes in the position of the reading desk, frequent bowing by the rector, removal of the rails around the communion table, created growing consternation.[28] The bishop responded quickly and with firmness; after meeting the churchwardens the changes were reversed. This widely publicised episode meant Pole Carew's religious opinions again came under critical scrutiny by East Cornwall farmers, many of whom remembered his votes on Maynooth.

Pole Carew added to his difficulties in 1850–1 when the prime minister, Lord John Russell, took his notorious stand against the reintroduction by the pope of a diocesan system and a Catholic hierarchy in England, labelled by its many critics 'papal aggression'. Helped by Russell's open letter of protest to the bishop of Durham the episode fanned the no-popery flames into another explosion of anti-Catholic feeling.[29] Once more crude religious animosities became the bedfellow of concern about Puseyism within the Church of England. In North Lincolnshire strong Protestant anti-Catholic feelings surfaced alongside opposition to Puseyites and ritualists, although Wesleyans were less prominent than they had been in 1845.[30] Further south in Buckinghamshire Aylesbury Liberals greeted 'papal aggression' with 'scorn and derision' but other towns such as Buckingham and Marlow were far less dismissive, petitioning for the outlawing of the new hierarchy.[31] As for Cornwall, in a now familiar pattern, meetings erupted from Launceston in the east to Penzance in the west.[32]

Throughout the county ministers of all denominations announced their

27 H. Miles Brown, *The Catholic revival in Cornish Anglicanism: a study of the Tractarians of Cornwall, 1833–1906*, St Winnow 1980, 39.
28 *West Briton*, 18 Oct. 1850, 4.
29 Norman Gash, *Aristocracy and people: Britain, 1815–1865*, London 1979, 252.
30 Olney, *Lincolnshire politics*, 57, 61.
31 Davis, *Political change*, 185, 226.
32 *West Briton*, 22, 29 Nov. and 6 Dec. 1850, contains reports of these meetings.

resistance to this 'outside' interference. Additionally, Dissenters seized the chance to denounce 'the conduct of those Bishops and Clergy of the Established Church, who by their tractarian tendencies have been promoting the objects of the Papacy'.[33] They also criticised those rabid anti-papists who were eager to push all Catholics into the Irish Sea. The occasion seemed to be an opportunity for at least some of Cornwall's principal Conservatives to rehabilitate themselves by defending the Protestant cause. But they were beyond the unity necessary for such action. Divided over this, as well as the merits of reintroducing protection, and more importantly, leaderless, they surrendered the initiative to Nicholas Kendall whose extremism many of them loathed. Not for the first time he organised a county meeting, but the requisition attracted fewer than 500 signatures. By the time of the meeting, in January 1851, the movement had lost most of its sting, allowing squabbling gentry to employ the occasion to reveal their divergent opinions.[34] At the centre of the row were Kendall and Carew.

Logically and clearly Carew explained in a letter to Kendall why he refused to attend. Besides refusing to view with alarm the establishment of a Catholic hierarchy, he was certain there were several precedents for the pope's actions.[35] He recognised the influence of Tractarians, but, convinced they were thin on the ground in Cornwall, thought a county meeting was no place to discuss the topic. Overall, Carew's letter was one of Christian toleration. In his reply Kendall left no doubt that they were in complete disagreement on the matter. Equally significant, however, was his earlier promise to Carew to confine the meeting simply to 'papal aggression', Kendall claiming no desire to enter the Tractarian controversy.[36] Carew must then have read with bewilderment the address (presumably approved by Kendall, as he was the initiator), presented to the meeting:

> It is with great pain that we record our belief that one of the causes of these aggressive movements of the papacy, has been the dissemination, in our own Established Church of opinions and practices, alien to her spirit and formularies, assimilating both to Romanism, and leading to the secession of many of her Clergy.[37]

Kendall's about-face was probably dictated, not for the last time in his career, by popular mood. Anti-Tractarianism was in the air. Kendall sensed this, and he was proven right when the meeting was dominated by that question. This, however, was not the only outcome. Many leading Conservatives who sympathised with part of the meeting's objectives were absent, allowing the three Liberal county MPs, Lemon, Robartes and Pendarves, to capitalise on what-

---

[33] Ibid. 22 Nov. 1850, 2.
[34] Ibid. 10 Jan. 1851, 4–5.
[35] Ibid. 6.
[36] Ibid.
[37] Ibid. 4.

ever was left of popular feelings.[38] The old Cornish Conservative families, the party's one-time wire-pullers, were giving up without a struggle, and Kendall knew this better than anyone.

Protection and electoral politics

Despite Kendall's efforts 'papal aggression' was no more than a four-month wonder in Cornwall. What it did manage to do, however, was draw attention once again to the ideological gulf between Carew and many of his constituents. Soon afterwards Kendall became temporarily immersed in West Cornwall affairs, the reason being the Liberal Pendarves's poor health (he was now seventy-six) and the necessity for the Conservatives to agree upon a suitable candidate when he died. Having discovered that the only possibility was John Tremayne (son of the former county MP), who could not oppose his uncle Sir Charles Lemon if there were a three-way contest in the West, Kendall refocused on the Eastern division.[39] Aware of the very successful canvass by the ECSPNI the previous year, in mid 1851 he finally succumbed to temptation, agreeing to stand with Carew as the second protectionist.[40]

The decision was a fateful one because the two men represented different 'constituencies' within the division and shared little common ground on vital political issues. No one doubted that Carew was the aristocracy and wealthy gentry's man, as he had been since 1845. Social and political status were important in choosing knights of the shire and this was why he, William Rashleigh and Edward Eliot were successful: they were judged to be men of sufficient rank to occupy the position. Consequently Carew could be sure that the landed interest, especially the Conservative section, would be behind him. Kendall's position was different. The ECSPNI was established by the yeoman and tenant farmers together with several of the lesser gentry, so he was the farmers' candidate. Since 1845 the wealthy gentry and the farmers had drifted apart because of their respective views on protection and religious questions, and the rift was widening in 1851. As for opinions, Kendall saw what he conceived as true Conservative principles – protection, maintaining the primacy of the Established Church and the Church–State relationship – all endangered (although publicly he said little on the latter), and Carew was unlikely to spring to their defence.

However protection was the key to their relationship. By the end of 1851 the large landlords and farmers were further apart than ever. Most of the former (Liberals and Conservatives), believed protection could never be revived, so a practical solution to farmers' problems was to reduce artificially

38 Ibid.
39 Viscount Falmouth to Kendall, 15 May 1851; C. Carlyon to Kendall, 18 Mar., 7 Apr. 1851; and Kendall to Carlyon (copy) 5 Apr. 1851, MSS Kendall KL.
40 Elvins, 'Reform movement', ch. ix, pp. 20–2.

high rent levels. Even though they embarked on this course many farmers, facing plummeting wheat prices, refused to be mollified. In December 1851 the ECSPNI's William Snell announced that 'the tenant farmers were resolved to act together and if the landed proprietors did not put themselves in their proper position at the head of the farmers, the latter would choose their own leaders'.[41] Fortified by this knowledge Kendall apparently began planning to somehow extricate himself from his pledge to Carew that he would be the *second* protectionist, and do nothing to endanger the incumbent Conservative's seat.[42]

The split between the two came at a March 1852 meeting of the ECSPNI at Liskeard, when both men were invited to present their views. Unfortunately, at the last minute Carew was prevented from attending: in a letter to Kendall explaining this he expressed his views on protection, agreeing that while his own views on the general question were very different to Kendall's, the two of them shared similar opinions about corn. Carew also conceded that Kendall was probably closer to the society's view-point than he, so, 'now that you have expressed your willingness to stand I think that I ought, if there is a doubt as to both of us being able to be returned, to give way'.[43] Not content with this concession from Carew, Kendall proceeded to strengthen his own position by arguing in correspondence with the society after the meeting, that Carew's opinions on protection were similar to those of his free trader brother-in-law, East Cornwall's Liberal MP, Thomas Agar Robartes.[44] Carew resented such misrepresentation, but the damage was done. Kendall felt justified in breaking his earlier promise to stand as the second protectionist, placing Carew in serious danger of losing his seat. Henceforth Kendall was prepared to seek the support of the rural middle classes, leaving the aristocracy and wealthy gentry to their factional intrigues.

Meanwhile, at Westminster Lord Derby's ostensibly protectionist government had taken office on 21 February 1852. Almost immediately it became clear that protection was lost, for when announcing the imminent dissolution of parliament the prime minister made it clear that the general election would not be fought on the merits of free trade or protection. Instead the battleground would be the defence of Protestant institutions. Agricultural prices were now showing signs of improvement and in April Disraeli, in the course of presenting the government's provisional financial statement, expressed the wish for free trade to continue. Far from stifling farmers' discontent in many English counties, including Cornwall, this made them more determined than ever to express their opinions. By then Kendall was no longer obliged to play second fiddle to Carew.

41 Quoted ibid. 21.
42 *West Briton*, 9 Apr. 1852, 5.
43 Pole Carew to Kendall, 4 Mar. 1852, MSS Kendall KL.
44 For the exchange of letters between the two candidates and with the secretary of the ECSPNI see *West Briton*, 9 Apr. 1852, 5.

Towards the end of May 1852, after an attempted reconciliation on the grounds that Carew's seat should be 'safe', he and Kendall were in an uneasy canvassing coalition. At the same time there was a torrent of accusations from both sides that the other was seeking plumpers, rather than split votes.[45] In addition, several leading Conservatives such as Lord St Germans and G. M. Fortescue temporarily switched parties, becoming Robartes supporters to avoid being forced to aid Kendall, and it was believed that many of Fortescue's tenants would do the same.[46] Lord Falmouth also refused to countenance Kendall's activities, actively helping Carew and giving 'passive' support to Robartes.[47] Sir Thomas Acland and John Tremayne, also Conservatives, took a similar line, Tremayne undoubtedly expressing a common view-point when he explained to Robartes that

> I should support Carew and have nothing to do with Kendall not being able to identify the political connexion between them. All that I know of Kendall is that he is put forward as the delegate of a party by no means the most influential in the County and is bound by this party to promote as far as lies in his power the immediate return to protection, a measure which I am not prepared to think advisable at present. I shall withhold all opposition to you except as Carew's antagonist but I could not give you my actual support.[48]

Kendall's principal supporters were Sir Richard Vyvyan, Lord Mt Edgcumbe and his steward Deeble Boger, the farmers, and a swarm of solicitors headed by Edward Coode and Charles Gurney. They had the numbers, they believed, and they extracted a promise of co-operation from Carew's friends.[49] Meanwhile Kendall stayed aloof and independent, believing he was under no obligation to assist Carew.

The poll was, as expected, a cliff-hanger, although Robartes was never in any danger. At the end of the first day Kendall narrowly led Carew, and he maintained his lead to the end. Table 14, showing the breakdown of votes by polling districts, helps to explain the outcome.[50] Several features stand out. The first is that Robartes's canvassing report was remarkably accurate – a discrepancy of only ten votes in an electorate of almost 5,700. Secondly, the ECSPNI's canvass was either incomplete or carried out in the most cursory manner, and it was on the basis of this report that the Conservatives attempted to win both seats. Thirdly, those such as Fortescue who wrote of Kendall, 'He is a good electioneer & even if he is – his friends are not over scrupulous in their promises or threats. The contest therefore will be between

---

45 Deeble Boger, Charles Prideaux Brune and Edward Coode to Kendall, 21–9 May 1852, MSS Kendall KL.

46 Ibid.

47 Elvins, 'Reform movement', ch. ix, p. 24.

48 Ibid.

49 Fortescue to Acland, 10 July 1852, and Francis Glanville to Acland, 21 May 1852, Devon Record Office, MSS Acland 1148M/8/4.

50 Undated memorandum, election results, MSS Kendall KL.

Table 14
General election results, East Cornwall, 1852

Polling District	Day 1			Day 2			Totals			Rob's Cnvs
	Rob.	Kend.	Car.	Rob.	Kend.	Car.	Rob.	Kend.	Car.	
St Austell	373	150	147	37	20	25	410	170	172	400
Bodmin	402	120	110	45	14	16	447	134	126	432
Callington	241	250	250	28	29	9	269	279	259	270
St Columb	251	218	203	28	22	18	279	240	221	284
Launceston	163	182	185	10	13	19	173	195	204	174
Liskeard	320	279	336	27	3	21	347	282	357	369
Lostwithiel	307	252	208	19	19	12	326	271	220	346
Stratton	99	254	255	23	20	26	122	274	281	125
Camelford	218	127	122	17	15	14	235	142	136	218
Totals	2,374	1,832	1,816	234	155	160	2,608	1,987	1,976	2,618

The results of the 1850 canvass by the ECSPNI were:

Robartes – 1,700
Kendall – 1,990
Carew – 2,360

Carew & Robartes', completely misjudged Robartes's ability to head the poll.[51] Fourthly, in the 1845 canvass undertaken by Carew, the Liberals showed a majority in only one division. Now they dominated in five, St Austell, Bodmin, St Columb, Camelford and Lostwithiel, while it was line-ball in Liskeard and Callington. Obviously Robartes had taken the Liberal organisation firmly in hand, particularly at the annual registration courts.[52] Fifthly, judging by the wide discrepancies in their totals at Liskeard and Lost-withiel, the respective districts of Carew and Kendall, the coalition broke down so badly that each side's plumpers were used to secure a possible winning advantage.

Such an analysis conveys nothing of the bitterness which now broke out among the Conservatives. Suddenly Carew's friends, the one-time Conservative wire-pullers, realised they had not only been outwitted but made fools of by Kendall and the farmers, whose collective political influence they totally underestimated. For example Fortescue explained to a friend:

[51] Fortescue to Acland, 10 July 1852, MSS Acland 1148M/8/4.
[52] Evidently most of this activity was concerned with having bad votes removed from the register. In 1845–6 the electorate was 6,197; in 1852, 5,694.

I can't tell you the pain or disgust with which I witnessed the close of our contest. Robartes [sic] victory was an easy one, tho the absolute confidence with which his opponents asserted their certainty of success made it impossible for me, pledged as I was – to move a finger in behalf of Carew till the morning of Wed. when it was intimated that the coalition was only on one side – that Kendall instead of withdrawing, as I considered he ought to have done, intended to continue the Poll, as he had not been a party to the compact![53]

Apparently after a 'reconciliation' between the two parties on 17 May 1852, Carew's supporters believed Kendall was no longer an 'independent' candidate, that is, the coalition was firm. As Kendall explained, he had always believed he was independent and therefore had no intention of helping Carew. Unhappily Carew heard nothing of this until long after the election.[54] Yet this could in no way alter the fact that Cornwall's principal Conservative families had reached the end of a long road stretching back for centuries. Never again would they be allowed to play their formerly self-appointed role in county politics, for it was the yeomen and tenant farmers who now controlled the division.

Elsewhere in England in 1852 there were equally notable farmers' victories, a result of more than a dozen protectionists standing for election. In South Nottinghamshire, for example, W. H. Barrow was re-elected after having won his seat at a well-publicised by-election one year earlier when he defeated Lord Newark. Barrow, a solicitor, was a firm protectionist who had, like Kendall, spoken out against the actions of the Catholic Church in 1850–1.[55] Other farmers' candidates were J. B. Stanhope (Lincolnshire North), Edward Ball (Cambridgeshire) and G. H. Vansittart (Berkshire), all of whom won seats in the House of Commons.[56]

Discussing Barrow's 1851 victory John Fisher wrote, 'With the traditional hierarchy being perceived as unwilling or unable to protect community interests effectively, they were potentially vulnerable to challenge from alternative leaders in local politics.'[57] In many cases these leaders were not necessarily those elected; rather they were the moving forces in protectionist societies or similar bodies, men who could see that Fisher's 'traditional hierarchy' was failing the farmers, and who took action in 1851–2. They had no intention of upsetting the existing social order – they simply wished their

53 Fortescue to Acland, 24 July 1852, MSS Acland 1148M/8/4. Fortescue went on 'but the soreness that is left behind will I fear long remain and the County will not forget the discreditable exhibition of two gentlemen nominally coalesced contending against each other with greater abandonment. . . . than was exhibited against their opponent!'
54 *Royal Cornwall Gazette*, 10 Apr. 1857, 5, 7.
55 J. R. Fisher, 'Issues and influence: two by-elections in south Nottinghamshire in the mid nineteenth century', *Historical Journal* xxiv (1981), 155–65.
56 See Crosby, *English farmers*, 173–4, and *McCalmont's parliamentary poll book*.
57 J. R. Fisher, 'The limits of deference: agricultural communities in a mid nineteenth-century election campaign', *Journal of British Studies* xxi (Fall, 1981), 99; Crosby, *English farmers*, 173–7.

usual leaders to reflect their strongly held opinions. Similarly, after examining farmer behaviour in several English counties Travis Crosby found a general disinclination by the rural middle classes to overturn traditional county leadership, suggesting that in times of rural stress agriculturists 'wanted merely to spur on those whom they considered their natural leaders'.[58] Fisher found greater intransigence among some farmers, but both he and Crosby agreed that yeomen and tenant farmers were usually content to allow the aristocracy and wealthy gentry to act as their spokespersons.[59]

The farmers' ascendancy in East Cornwall

The East Cornwall election was a watershed in county politics because its outcomes were so far-reaching. Much to the dismay of leading Conservatives it confirmed the electoral significance of the farmers. As G. M. Fortescue put it, Kendall was a candidate 'after having been put forward by the Tenant Farmers, some Protectionist Attorneys and only one or two Gent[n] of the County, the main body of the Conservative Gentry not only holding aloof but discountenancing the agitation'.[60] Five years later in 1857 the farmers again humiliated 'the main body of the Conservative Gentry'. Not only did Kendall stand for re-election but Carew, still simmering over the loss of his seat, also decided to run. The latter again enjoyed the support of the principal landowners, but close to polling day he withdrew. On the hustings Richard Pollard, a farmer, explained why there would not be a repetition of the 1852 controversy: 'With a very few and honourable exceptions that I see around me, the contest has been entirely between the yeomen of the county and the gentlemen of the county.'[61] There had been a trial of strength, Pollard observed, forcing the gentlemen to withdraw their nominee (Carew) and allowing the yeomen to enjoy another triumph, even though 'they have had the principal part of the landed gentlemen of the county opposed to them'. Unfortunately, the union of interest binding the wealthy Conservatives and the farmers together between 1837 and 1847 was a distant memory. In fact the role of the farmers in 1852 and 1857 resembled that in 1825–6 when the Whig reformer Edward Pendarves enjoyed their support.

Soon after his 1857 victory Kendall temporarily deserted Conservatism as a protest against his party's attitude to Palmerston, but this made no difference to his popularity.[62] The farmers supported him when he was re-elected in 1859 and 1865, because they appreciated his blunt honesty, and hard work on behalf of local interests. Nevertheless, Kendall was particularly firm about

---

[58] Ibid. 2.
[59] Fisher, 'Issues and influence', 104.
[60] Fortescue to Sir Thomas Acland, 10 July 1852, MSS Acland 1148M/8/4.
[61] *Royal Cornwall Gazette*, 10 Apr. 1857, 6.
[62] Robert Stewart, *The foundation of the Conservative party, 1830–1867*, London 1978, 316.

the temperance cause (with which he had little sympathy), and Noncon-formist demands, notably church disestablishment (with which he had none), so his relationship with farmer Dissenters was not one of total harmony.

In 1868 the farmers once more demonstrated their pivotal role in county politics, this time by forcing Kendall to retire. For many years he had will-ingly served as chairman of the County Gaol Committee. However, during his absence at Westminster in 1867 the committee decided to recommend to the justices at the Michaelmas Quarter Sessions that the annual salary of the gaol's governor, Captain Colvill, be increased from £300 to £400. This took place against a backdrop of growing unrest among the farmers, who besides bearing the losses from the recent cattle plague, were particularly disgruntled about the burden of county rates, and sensitive about a likely increase.[63] Although he privately disagreed with the committee's decision, publicly Kendall had to support it. In fact as chairman he believed he should give the proposed increase his unreserved backing, and after some indecision the rec-ommendation was approved at the Epiphany Sessions in January 1868. Because of his position as chairman of the Gaol Committee Kendall was identified in the popular mind as the villain, and now he had to face the consequences.

Throughout his life, and especially after the 1840s, Kendall prided himself on being the friend of the small farmers. He appeared regularly at meetings of their clubs and agricultural societies, and it was at the annual meeting of the Wadebridge Farmers' Club in 1868 that he was first made aware of the extent to which he had offended his usual supporters.[64] Normally the meeting was a quiet affair with plenty of good fellowship. This time the Molesworth Arms was packed with more than 150 angry farmers who gave Kendall a very mixed reception when he took his place as chairman. From that point proceedings became rowdier by the minute. A mixture of cheers and hisses greeted the toast to the county members; later Kendall strongly defended the Colvill decision and his reluctant support of Disraeli's Reform Act. He also admitted that he favoured county financial boards, which it was popularly believed would bring a reduction in the rates. But none of these topics deflected his opponents from continually returning to harangue him over Colvill. All his arguments were ridiculed. In terms of Kendall's re-election prospects the affair was a total disaster, and from it came the 'Colvill Cry' which was to haunt him for the next ten months.

The irony of his re-election campaign was the reversal of support for him; this time 'the principal part of the landed gentlemen of the county' were on Kendall's side, the farmers his opponents. The Tremayne family and Fortes-

63 *Royal Cornwall Gazette*, 17 Oct. 1867, 8. The episode is discussed in detail in E. Jaggard, 'Patrons, principles and parties: Cornwall politics, 1760–1910', unpubl. PhD diss. St Louis 1980, 355–6.
64 *Royal Cornwall Gazette*, 16 Jan. 1868, 8.

cue of Bocconoc were some of those who changed their previous stance, believing the 'Colvill Cry' was unfair and knowing there was no alternative candidate apart from the still angry Carew.[65] While Kendall accepted this support his attitude to his farmer friends was curious. In mid July he explained to one of his confidants:

> The last three or four days I have had much information from various quarters, & tho' I think I see my way pretty clearly to the Discomfiture of the enemy, still it must be by a hard fight, much expenditure of money, if not by coercion, at least by votes unwillingly given, under the present Colvill excitement.[66]

Kendall emphasised that he had little desire to be re-elected against the feelings of his usual supporters, but at the same time he persuaded himself that with the financial backing of the principal eastern landlords, plus judicious use of 'the screw' on members of the rural middle classes, he stood a fair chance of success.[67] Soon afterwards his long time friend Deeble Boger, Lord Mt Edgcumbe's steward, injected a note of reality into Kendall's thoughts. He explained how 'the old traditional notions of the weight of large "landowners" in Elections require great modification in the present day when Tenants follow the leaders of their own class – both from inclination and from Class pressure'.[68] Boger could have added that the farmers did so in 1852, to Kendall's benefit and against landlord influence, so it would be foolish to expect a reversal in 1868.

The retirement of the one time 'farmers' candidate' only one week before the poll demonstrated how East Cornwall's farmers were far from being passive participants in electoral politics. If we study farmer behaviour from the days of the farmer–reformer alliance to Kendall's retirement in 1868, it reveals a single-mindedness of purpose – self-interest – which frequently left them at loggerheads with 'the traditional county leadership' mentioned by Fisher and Crosby. The obvious exception was the period 1837–45, when the threat to protection brought a fragile unity. Thereafter, as before 1837, Cornwall's farmers revealed a consistent independence in their actions.

Of course the concept of 'traditional county leadership' raises another question – could the leading Conservatives provide this? The 1852 general election suggested they could not. When De Dunstanville and the first earl of Falmouth died (in 1835 and 1841 respectively), Cornwall's Conservatives began to falter. Neither Basset's wife nor his heirs revealed the same zest for political life, while the second earl of Falmouth, the former Boscawen Rose, rarely appeared in the political limelight and allowed others to act for him. Nor did the 'eastern aristocracy', the earls of St Germans and Mt Edgcumbe,

---

65 Deeble Boger to Kendall, 5 Aug. 1868; John Tremayne to Kendall, 4 Sept. 1868; and G. M. Fortescue to Kendall, 10 Sept. 1868, MSS Kendall KL.
66 R. Taylor to Kendall, 12 July 1868, ibid.
67 Kendall to D. Horndon, 12 July 1868, ibid.
68 Boger to Kendall, 5 Aug. 1868, ibid.

thrust themselves forward. This explains why the Conservative revival between 1837 and 1847 was so short-lived – the hard, grinding work of constantly watching over the registrations was left to men such as Kendall, lesser gentry who lacked the status to lead the party. Linked to this was a lack of money to maintain the party's position. Most of the aristocracy and wealthy gentry were loath to commit themselves to heavy expenditure, a reluctance exposed in 1851 when there were rumours of a possible vacancy for West Cornwall. 'The idea of young Tremayne's coming forward', Kendall wrote, 'is very rife and the enemy are furious but doing nothing – Robartes 30,000 to be spent in Eastern Division & Michael Williams 10,000 in the West are the present Bug-bears.'[69] Even when many of the wealthiest Conservatives united they were ineffectual.

Accentuating this innocuity were two other factors, the divisions produced by Carew's 1852 defeat and the 'Lemon connection'. Sir Richard Vyvyan was among Kendall's wealthiest supporters in 1852. His estates were spread across both county divisions, he was an important mine-owner, and he was a Conservative renegade in the sense that he was rarely in agreement with others in the party. The general Cornish view was that Vyvyan's influence was considerable, and in the feuding among the gentry over Carew's defeat he remained one of Kendall's staunchest allies. Despite living at Trelowarren near Helston in West Cornwall, Vyvyan manipulated the Conservative fortunes in both divisions. A long letter to Kendall in 1857 (just before the general election) explained how: John Tremayne, Jr, was a candidate for West Cornwall, but also acted as the chairman of Carew's committee in the East. So Vyvyan wrote to Gregor, the chairman of Tremayne's committee, 'calling on Tremayne for neutrality in the East, where Carew's interest was opposed to that on which he stood in the West – foretelling the advent of a new govt candidate here [West Cornwall], if he openly opposed you [Kendall] the govt candidate there [East Cornwall]'.[70] Tremayne's response was to declare his undivided support for Carew (ignoring Kendall) whereupon Vyvyan suggested his undivided support would be given to Michael Williams, the West Cornwall Liberal candidate, if Tremayne refused to be neutral in the East! Soon afterwards Tremayne retired, complaining how 'some of those who still call themselves Conservatives have withdrawn from me their support in the Western Division'.[71]

The bitterness of the feud between Carew, Kendall and their respective supporters was also referred to in Vyvyan's letter. Tremayne had recently visited Trelowarren; the two men agreed they were 'anti Puseyite', anti-Gladstone, anti-centralisation, and were in harmony on all points of policy. Despite this Tremayne considered Vyvyan to be an enemy because he was Kendall's friend. 'The extent to which he [Tremayne] entertained this

69 Kendall to Dr C. Carlyon, 5 Apr. 1851, ibid.
70 Vyvyan to Kendall, 31 Mar. 1857, ibid.
71 *Royal Cornwall Gazette*, 27 Mar. 1857, 5.

personal feeling must have been a sort of mania.'[72] Such a scenario must have been played out repeatedly in the 1850s and 1860s. There is no reason to disbelieve Carew's claim when he made his abortive attempt in 1857, that he came forward with the support of the 'great landed proprietors'.

They, in turn, refused to forgive Kendall or the farmers, but what they overlooked was their candidate's weaknesses. As long as Carew challenged (and there was no-one else willing to do so), divisive religious issues would be raised. Carew himself foolishly did so in 1857: in his published address he said that in 1852 a cry had been set up against his religious opinions, therefore he repeated that he opposed extreme views and ultra ceremonial observances in the Church of England.[73] The outcome was that in 1857, and two years later when he contested Liskeard, the cries 'Puseyism', 'Maynooth' and 'Sheviock' were raised, criticisms repeated much later in his life. Even after protection faded away, Carew had an Achilles heel which left him and his party politically impotent.

As for the 'Lemon connection' it has been mentioned previously in the context of West Cornwall elections; Sir Charles Lemon's impact on the Cornish Conservatives continued until his death in 1868. With his family links to the Bullers, Bassets, Aclands and Tremaynes he was in a position in the 1850s and 1860s to prevent one of the most eligible Conservatives, John Tremayne, from ever making a serious challenge for a seat during Lemon's own lifetime. The same was true of John's younger brother Arthur, Lemon's heir, who was occasionally spoken of by Conservatives as a possibility. He too did not take the electoral plunge until after his uncle's death. Lemon's influence over his relatives therefore meant that Cornish Conservatives were split into three – Carew supporters, Kendall's friends including Vyvyan, and those attached to Lemon. The last-named ensured there was no wholehearted Conservative opposition to the Liberals in West Cornwall, and because of Lemon's ties to the Tremaynes, forced the Conservatives to rely on Carew in the East. No wonder they achieved little, preferring as they did, faith in the 'politics of influence' to voters on registers.

Landlord influence and deference

The complete ineffectiveness of Conservative landed influence after 1841 is one of the most remarkable features of county politics. Referring to West Cornwall in 1864, Sir Richard Vyvyan wrote that 'There is no aristocratic influence here.'[74] In fact by then this was true of both county divisions. Given that such influence was almost extinguished by the 1860s, and the electoral repercussions following this, an effort should be made to explain how it arose.

---

[72] Vyvyan to Kendall, 31 Mar. 1857, MSS Kendall KL.
[73] *Royal Cornwall Gazette*, 13 Mar. 1857, 4.
[74] Vyvyan to Sir William Williams, 4 Jan. 1864, MSS Vyvyan V 22M/60/36/46.

Certainly there was a lack of will on the part of many Conservative landlords to consistently employ their influence, but allied to this was the longer term independence and assertiveness of the farmers. Without pollbooks any conclusions must be tentative. Even so, alternative sources do suggest why landlords' influence was relatively unimportant.

William Rashleigh, Sr, of Menabilly was one of Cornwall's largest, wealthiest and most respected landowners. In the aftermath of the passing of the First Reform Act he issued the following instructions to his steward, Thomas Robins:

> I certainly should wish my Tenantry to be empowered to exercise their Franchise by having their votes registered, to enable me to exercise the influence my property may give me, in the Event of any person coming forward for the representation, whom I should <u>decidedly</u> wish to befriend, & therefore will thank you to employ some person to get it done, though I should have thought they wo^d all have themselves taken care to do so. . . . I think it is right to be prepared to throw weight into the scale (if obliged to do so) in defence of those principles I wish to advocate.[75]

Four days earlier Rashleigh had informed Charles Buller that with respect to Liskeard, 'if I had a Vote, [there] it wo^d not be given to an <u>Ultra Reformer</u> – & so I shall tell my Tenants if they apply to me'.[76] Rashleigh had no opportunity to exercise his influence, for Buller's election was unopposed.

Throughout the papers of the leading Cornish families there are scattered references to influence of the kind to which Rashleigh referred. Tradition and courtesy dictated that landlords were consulted before parliamentary candidates (or their agents) canvassed their tenants. There were very good social reasons for this – landlord and farming tenants were bound in a unique relationship of inter-dependence, characterised by respect for, and attention to, each individual's view-point. It was essentially a two-way relationship, giving rural areas their special cohesion. In this respect Cornwall may have been different from other English counties, for one crucial difference was the widely scattered landholdings making up many estates. There were few parishes where one or two landowners predominated. Added to this was the traditionally independent outlook of the Cornish, an attitude nurtured by the knowledge that family prestige and influence ultimately sprang from some form of wealth. Opportunities flowing from tin and copper mining, and the fortunes to be made in trade, banking, shipping or victualling, gave every chance – and incentive – for upward mobility. The Williamses, for example, who were mine-owners, bankers, smelters and landowners, were an excellent illustration of the wealth which could be amassed within two generations. Under these circumstances there is a suspicion that many men, aware of the evolutionary patterns of some prominent nineteenth-century Cornish

---

[75] William Rashleigh to Robins, 15 Aug. 1832, CRO, MSS Rashleigh R 5325.
[76] Rashleigh to Buller, 11 Aug. 1832, ibid.

families, respected their political preferences and view-points, but by no means felt compelled to obey them with a forelock-touching loyalty.

Clearly this was the root of the problem between Reginald Pole Carew (father of William) and one of his tenants, Charles Jefferey, in August 1832. Pole Carew wrote:

> As I set some Value on your Vote & much more on your good opinion, I am desirous of knowing, what you have seen in my character, which makes you suppose that I am capable of recommending you to Vote for a Person for whom your conscience tells you ought not to vote, or what it is, that you have heard of the Character of that Individual which you can have had no Personal Opportunity of knowing, which has impressed you, with the idea, that you could not conscientiously give Him your Vote.[77]

Lord Valletort was the candidate being referred to; Pole Carew believed he was a just, honourable and patriotic man, and what further qualifications were needed for membership of the House of Commons? Despite the brow-beating and moralising, Jefferey and his brother were adamant: they opposed Valletort because he would not agree to the abolition of slavery in British colonies. Carew's arguments about the injustice of pledges, etc. were to no avail, for Jefferey retained his independence of mind on that issue, and proposed alterations to the Corn Laws, on which they also differed.[78] Pole Carew was an elderly and highly respected Tory, one of the most powerful of that group, yet it is clear that landlord and tenant could still be separated by questions of political principle, without jeopardising their social or economic relationship.

While it is tempting to believe that Jefferey's independence may have been influenced by the farmer–reformer alliance of the 1820s, there is no proof for such a suggestion. Yet it would be surprising to find that those stirring county meetings had not reinforced the characteristic independence of yeoman and tenant farmers. After all, one of the reformers' premier objects had been to open county meetings to freeholders and inhabitants; the success of the campaign must have contributed to the politicisation of the rural and middle classes. Certainly from the 1830s onwards the political opinions of the farmers and their changes of direction had a profound influence in East Cornwall. Their gravitation away from the politics of parliamentary reform, commutation of tithes and abolition of slavery, towards an insistence on the maintenance of agricultural protection, coincided with the swing back to the Conservatives – Lord Eliot being elected in 1837, Eliot and William Rashleigh, Jr, in 1841. Admittedly this was an accurate reflection of what was occurring nationally; nevertheless events in 1852, 1857 and 1868 confirm the impression of their power. Above all it is difficult to reconcile the outcome of the 1852 East Cornwall election, when the farmers and principal

---

[77] ?Sept. 1832, MSS Carew Pole CC/G3/7.
[78] Letters between Pole Carew and Jefferey, Mar., Apr. 1833, ibid.

landed gentlemen were on opposite sides, with any conception of a subservient, politically passive tenantry.

The extent to which landlords were prepared to countenance political independence is also questionable. When William Rashleigh heard that some of his tenants were actually canvassing for Lord Eliot's opponents (Sir Hussey Vivian and Sir William Trelawney) in 1837, he lost little time reminding Thomas Robins to give him, 'a list of my Tenants as they voted in Luxulyan & Roche (at your leisure) & should also wish to know, who is the principal Tenant there, whom I might occasionally consult or make the channel of communication at any time'.[79] Rashleigh had at least 250 tenants throughout his Cornish estates, was politically active, and always concerned that his influence might be used when he chose. But obviously neither he nor Robins kept too close a watch over the tenantry before this general election. That may be a clue to the attitudes of a widely respected landlord. Rarely were tenantry anywhere in the county marched in a body to the polling booths, and evictions for political intransigence were apparently non-existent.

Press accounts from both papers confirm that it was Cornwall's Conservatives who appear to have relied most heavily on landlord influence in county elections. But of course this refers only to East Cornwall; in the West there were no contests, so such influence was never tested. When there was the possibility of a vacancy in March 1851, the earl of Falmouth informed a fellow Conservative that in the event of the party finding a candidate 'I will take care that my tenants have timely intimation of my wishes and intentions – and I feel sure that Lady Basset & Mr Collins will act with me, though I am not so sure of Mr Gregor.'[80] At this point wishful thinking was always superseded by reality: the register remained heavily loaded in the Liberals' favour. No one on the Conservative side was prepared to spend money on a sustained campaign to eradicate the bad votes, or to enrol those who were eligible, so the Liberals had few worries about opposition.

The exertion of landlord influence relied on communication: effective communication relied on sound organisation. So piecemeal were many Cornish estates that the marshalling of landlord influence relied chiefly upon local agents, stewards or substantial tenant farmers. Without close supervision these men were subjected to many different pressures. Often they acted on personal preferences, and successful electioneering then became a matter of unravelling the networks of local agents, before endeavouring to establish whether landlord and agent were in political harmony. On many occasions they were not.

An example of this involving Basset property occurred in 1852 in East Cornwall when Claudius Hawker of Boscastle (an election agent for Robartes), wrote to Sir Thomas Acland about the Basset tenants in Stratton

79 Rashleigh to Robins, 15 Sept. 1837, CRO, MSS Rashleigh R 5330.
80 Dr Clement Carlyon to Kendall, quoting Falmouth, 26 Mar. 1850, MSS Kendall KL.

Hundred.[81] Lady Basset, although unwilling to give Robartes 'actual support', was not likely to oppose him. But Edward Shearm, a solicitor and one of the Basset estate's deputy stewards, was influencing the tenants to split their votes for Kendall and Pole Carew. Hawker's motivation for writing to Acland was that he understood the latter to be the patron of Mr Edmund Marriott, Lady Basset's steward. Therefore, if Acland could persuade Marriott to write a letter stating that Lady Basset wished her tenants to plump for Pole Carew, this would aid the re-election of Robartes. Probably this is what happened for Robartes's organisation was supremely efficient. The subversion of a land-lord's intentions by those involved in face-to-face canvassing was not unusual, and landlord influence therefore counted for little in such circumstances, unless those involved in party organisation were prepared to probe and manipulate. There is singularly little evidence that Cornwall's Conservatives were capable of this.

Recapitulation

To return to the themes discussed in this chapter, by far the most important is the continuing independence of East Cornwall's farmers. It arose from a combination of circumstances which produced a potent force in county politics. One was the farmers' frequent meetings to express their opinions and to petition parliament. These occasions were often chaired by members of the gentry, but in the best traditions of the earlier farmer–reformer alliance, all view-points were heard. Another circumstance was the unusually high number of farmer organisations: the Callington and Stratton Agricultural Associations, the Wadebridge, St Germans and St Austell Farmers Clubs, the Probus Ploughing Club and the Trigg, East Cornwall and Cornwall Agricultural Societies. All claimed to be apolitical. Yet on occasions they provided forums for contentious local and national issues to be discussed, for example protection in 1849–51, and it was farmers rather than gentry whose opinions counted. No doubt this was why articulate farmers soon came into prominence. Two of the more outspoken were the brothers William and Benjamin Snell, who from the mid 1840s argued that farmers should act independently of their landlords whenever their economic interests were being ignored. William Snell was one of those who spoke in favour of protection at the county meeting in February 1850, besides being the driving force behind the formation of the ECSPNI. Thomas Liddell, a tenant of Sir William Moles-worth at St Minver near Padstow, argued the merits of protection with John Tremayne, Sr, after Carew's election in 1845, and other farmers voiced their opinion at various times.[82] Most joined the committee of the ECSPNI, and shared a determination to see two protectionists elected for East Cornwall.

[81] C. C. Hawker to Sir Thomas Acland, 7 May 1852, MSS Acland 1148M/8/17.
[82] Elvins, 'Reform movement', ch. ix.

Although Robartes survived the attack, the farmers' defiance towards those landlords who ignored their concerns confirmed how outmoded the politics of influence had become. Hindered as well by organisational ineptitude, this meant the mid nineteenth-century county Conservatives were in danger of becoming politically irrelevant.

7

Parties, Organisation and Issues, 1847–1868

Liberal resurgence, Conservative decline

In the 'Age of Equipoise', that mid nineteenth-century era of semi-peace, prosperity and optimism, the features of Cornwall politics were clearly defined. East Cornwall's representation was shared by parliamentary parties, while the West continued to be a Liberal stronghold: between 1832 and 1880 there was not a single contested election in West Cornwall, despite occasional talk of a Conservative candidate challenging the *status quo*. Three small, single member boroughs, Launceston, Helston and St Ives, were more often than not the core of Conservative strength, the first a pocket borough, the remaining two subject to various forms of factional in-fighting and intrigues. The remaining boroughs, Bodmin, Liskeard, Truro and Penryn & Falmouth either sent Liberals to Westminster or were shared. Like Launceston, Bodmin was a pocket borough of a kind because after 1857 Thomas Robartes's nominee always occupied one seat. Liskeard remained as steadfastly Liberal as in the 1830s and 1840s, while only once between 1835 and 1868 (in 1857) did Truro deviate from electing a Liberal and a Conservative. As for Penryn & Falmouth, gradually the borough's Liberals gained the upper hand.

In terms of the total number of seats won at general elections, the Liberals slowly consolidated their position after the 1852 low point. Between 1832 and 1868 the only general elections at which they won less than half of all seats, were 1841 and 1852.

Another feature was the variation in the numbers of contested constituencies at each general election. 1857 and 1859 show very clearly how disorganised the local Conservatives were on the former occasion, and the much greater effort made two years later. Otherwise, usually less than half the constituencies were contested, this probably being an acknowledgement by the respective parties that it was pointless wasting money in Launceston, St Ives or Liskeard. What it also suggests is the number of candidates available to each party. Between 1852 and 1865, when the Liberal ascendancy was becoming firmly established, a total of thirty-two candidates stood for election, compared with twenty-one Conservatives. From the 1860s onwards, the Conservatives found increasing difficulty in attracting suitable candidates – probably both cause and outcome of the Liberal dominance. How then may we account for these emerging trends in the fortunes of major parties?

Table 15
General election results, Cornwall, 1832–68

	1832		1835		1837		1841		1847		1852		1857		1859		1865		1868 *	
	L	C	L	C	L	C	L	C	L	C	L	C	L	C	L	C	L	C	L	C
Counties	4	–	4	–	3	1	1	3	3	1	3	1	3	1	3	1	3	1	4	–
Boroughs	6	4	5	5	4	6	5	5	4	6	3	7	8	2	5	5	7	3	5	4
Total	10	4	9	5	7	7	6	8	7	7	6	8	11	3	8	6	10	4	9	4
Contested Constituencies	5		5		5		4		3		4		2		6		3		4	

* Bodmin lost 1 seat as a result of the 1867 Reform Act

Source: *McCalmont's parliamentary poll book.*

It is well-known that nationally the Conservatives experienced 'years of frustration' between 1841 and 1874, failing to win a single election.[1] Explanations for this range from the long-lasting effects of the Peelite split in 1846, indecisive leadership, and the undoubted popularity of Lord Palmerston. Certainly, according to one influential opinion, the party's organisation was not a reason:

> in the 1850s and 1860s, the central organisation of the Conservative Party, despite the even temper of political debate and the consequent decline in importance of national issues in the constituencies, operated as thoroughly and efficiently as it had in the days of Bonham.[2]

Of all the explanations for the Conservatives' 'years of frustration', this one must be open to questioning. In Bonham's era (the 1830s and 1840s), the Conservative revival was the outcome of closer attention to registration of voters in many constituencies, a rising tide of expectations among supporters generated by the party's gains in the 1835 and 1837 general elections, and effective party management linking Westminster and the localities.[3] A logical result of this was an increasing number of Conservative candidates willing to stand for election.

The 1850s and 1860s present a very different picture, not least because by then the energetic Conservative Associations found in many counties and boroughs thirty years earlier had become moribund or disappeared. Although there were occasional exceptions to this, the change meant that the Chief Whip, party agent and their helpers probably relied much more on bribery and nurturing candidates whose local influence could be decisive, than on encouraging wealthy Conservatives to attend to the annual registrations.[4]

---

1 Robert Blake, *The Conservative party from Peel to Churchill*, London 1972, title of ch. iii.
2 Stewart, *Foundation of the Conservative party*, 339.
3 Close, 'The general elections'.
4 Harvey, 'British general elections', 38.

Lincolnshire and Buckinghamshire, like Cornwall, were counties where parties' local organisations withered in these years.[5] This chapter explores several of the organisational problems evident in the mid nineteenth-century Conservative party led by Derby and Disraeli.

While the Conservatives continually struggled their rivals flourished, although the methods by which they achieved success were a combination of organisational dexterity, ideological appeal and electoral manipulation. Undoubtedly the characteristics of political modernisation were as obvious as they had been since early in the century – voters often did 'respond to party cues taken directly from debates and events in Westminster'.[6] Coexisting with them however, was the looming presence of local affairs or influences, which sometimes slowed the consolidation of the powerful nexus between Liberalism and Dissent.

The Williams family and Cornwall's Conservatives

Lack of leadership and unreliable information are the keys to understanding the problems of Cornwall's mid century Conservatives. With the exception of the Robartes and Trelawny families, and J. M. Williams, all Cornwall's major landowners before 1868 were Conservatives, so when measured by acreage the party's outward strength was immense. Why then were none of these families prepared to undertake the effort or expenditure necessary to revive the party's fortunes? Lack of interest seems to be one explanation: the sixth Viscount Falmouth (cousin of the second earl and fifth viscount) usually remained aloof from politics, members of the Basset family were often absent from the county, Earl Mt Edgcumbe marginalised himself by being one of Nicholas Kendall's supporters and Sir Richard Vyvyan was an incorrigible behind-the-scenes intriguer. Another reason was the deep rift resulting from Kendall's victory in East Cornwall: for so long as he remained an MP John Tremayne and Vyvyan were at loggerheads, as were many others in the party. Finally, there was the inability of almost all the families to provide parliamentary candidates. Few if any of these same families retained solicitors to act on the party's behalf at the annual registrations, adding to Conservative difficulties.

One way in which these difficulties might have been overcome would have been for the central party organisers to encourage an individual or family to take a dominant role, and this is what occurred in Cornwall. The Conservatives placed their hopes on the wealthy and prolific Williams family which, they believed, could reverse the party's electoral decline. Unfortunately little was achieved, but the machinations reveal a great deal about the party's organisation in Cornwall and elsewhere.

---

5 Olney, *Lincolnshire politics*, chs x, xi; Davis, *Political change*, chs viii, ix.
6 Phillips and Wetherell, 'The Great Reform Act', 434.

Table 16
Principal Cornish landowners, mid nineteenth century

Lord Falmouth	25,910 acres	F. Rodd	7,912 acres
Lord Robartes	22,234 acres	J. M. Williams	6,254 acres
G. M. Fortescue	17,208 acres	J. J. Rogers	6,214 acres
G. L. Basset	16,969 acres	earl of St Germans	5,961 acres
earl of Mt Edgcumbe	13,288 acres	Revd A. Molesworth-St Aubyn	5,888 acres
C. H. T. Hawkins	12,119 acres	Sir J. Trelawny	5,813 acres
Sir R. R. Vyvyan	9,705 acres	C. P. Brune	5,746 acres
Jonathan Rashleigh	9,252 acres	Edward Coode	5,632 acres
Col. A. Tremayne	8,823 acres	Col. S. M. Grylls	5,500 acres
Augustus Coryton	8,383 acres		

Source: *Returns of owners of land in England and Wales*, PP 1874 lxxii.

In the 1850s the Conservative party's Chief Whip Sir William Jolliffe (MP for Wells) had overall control of the central organisation.[7] Helping him to link the parliamentary party with the constituencies was Benjamin Disraeli's personal solicitor Philip Rose, of the firm of Norton, Baxter and Rose. Assisting Rose was Markham Spofforth, a junior member of the firm, who travelled widely around the country compiling lists of contact persons in many constituencies, and providing Rose with summaries of election prospects. Rose in turn forwarded this information to Jolliffe and Disraeli, although the Chief Whip also had his own network of contacts. One of them was Samuel Triscott, an employee in the Plymouth Naval Dockyard. Triscott wrote frequently about electoral prospects in Devon and especially Cornwall, with additional information also being supplied by Sir John Yarde Buller (later Lord Churston) MP for South Devon. Triscott's correspondence with Jolliffe in particular, together with entries in Jolliffe and Rose's election notebooks compiled from correspondence, plus Spofforth's observations, are very revealing.[8]

Triscott, and eventually Jolliffe and Rose, believed a Conservative revival in Cornwall could be led by the wealthy and prolific Williams family. Two branches monopolised the extensive commercial and mining interests; one was headed by Michael Williams, a Liberal MP for West Cornwall from 1853 to 1858, and the other by his brother William who was six years younger. Both had six sons, several of whom were interested in parliamentary careers.

---

[7] Stewart, *Foundation of the Conservative party*, ch. xvi.
[8] Jolliffe's election notebook, 1859, pts 1, 2; Sir Philip Rose's election notebook, 1859.

Extracts from Jolliffe's 1859 election notebook illustrate why the party was so optimistic about the family's involvement.[9]

BODMIN	'Mr [M] Williams has influence here, as in fact in all Cornish towns.'
FALMOUTH	'Mr M Williams has interest here.'
LISKEARD	'There is a respectable minority which can be turned into a majority if Mr M Williams is disposed to assist.'
TRURO	'There is a strong Cons. party in the Borough but as usual a stronger Cons mismanagement. The deciding power is with Mr M Williams of Trevince.'
CORNWALL, EAST DIVISION	'It is understood Mr Robartes retires and Mr Williams is anxious to support Lord Valletort who however I think will not start.'
CORNWALL, WESTERN DIVISION	'Last election [1857] Mr [M] Williams and Mr Davey started on the Liberal interest and Mr Tremayne on the Cons. Mr Williams was favourable to Tremayne'.

These notes were compiled after the 1857 general election when the Conservatives lost five seats in Cornwall, and before Michael Williams's death in June 1858, following which his eldest son John Michael (J. M.) was tempted to join the Conservatives, but finally resolved to remain a Liberal supporter. Triscott then assumed J. M. Williams's uncle, William, could play the same highly influential political role as his dead brother, a debatable proposition given that William Williams and his sons were at this time members of the Reform Club, and would therefore have to switch sides.[10] Despite this, Triscott proceeded to take an optimistic view of affairs. For example in February 1859 he and Lord Churston deliberated for three hours over the Conservatives' need to gain the support of the Williams family. Churston regarded it as the most important affair in the West, six seats depending on it.[11] Six days later Triscott informed Jolliffe that 'we must have Mr [W] Williams at any price. This will give us

2 seats for Falm °	1 if not 2 Bodmin
2 seats for Truro	1 Liskeard'[12]
1 Helston	

At the end of March Triscott remained optimistic, but now the eight seats would come from Falmouth, Bodmin, Liskeard (one each), two for Truro, and

9   Jolliffe's election notebook, 1859, pt 1.
10 Triscott to Jolliffe, n.d. [March 1859?], MSS Hylton DD/HY/24/19.
11 Triscott to Jolliffe, 17 Feb. 1859, ibid. DD/HY/24/17.
12 23 Feb. 1859, ibid. DD/HY/24/16.

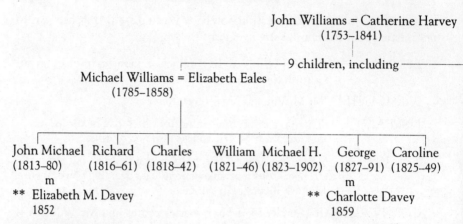

John Williams = Catherine Harvey
(1753–1841)

———————————— 9 children, including ————————————

Michael Williams = Elizabeth Eales
(1785–1858)

John Michael	Richard	Charles	William	Michael H.	George	Caroline
(1813–80)	(1816–61)	(1818–42)	(1821–46)	(1823–1902)	(1827–91)	(1825–49)
m					m	
** Elizabeth M. Davey					** Charlotte Davey	
1852					1859	

Williams, Foster & Co
Copper Smelters & Manufacturers
William Williams
F. M. Williams
E. Williams (nephew of Michael and William Williams)
G. Williams
Sampson Foster
* J. M. Williams

* He successfully petitioned in 1861 to dissolve the partnership, the defendants being the remaining directors, including his brother George.
** The Davey sisters were daughters of Stephen Davey whose brother Richard was Liberal MP for West Cornwall 1857–68. As mine agents Stephen and Richard were linked through business to the Williams family.

three for the two divisions of the county.[13] John Tippett, the party's agent in Truro, believed that the town would elect two Conservatives 'if the Williams are satisf ^{d} = Baronetcy'.[14] On the basis of these reports and letters the Conservative party had much to gain by pursuing the Williams, so who were they?

The family exemplified the rapid upward social mobility of those who were involved in highly profitable mining, smelting and banking activities. In 1822 John Williams (1753–1841) and several of his sons 'established a manufactory of copper and yellow metal at Burncoose, the firm being Fox, Williams, Grenfell & Co. and the partnership for twenty one years'.[15] Partners retired and were replaced, the firm's name changed to Williams, Foster and Co., and 'places of business' were opened in London, Liverpool, Birmingham, Swansea and Manchester. As the family tree shows, by 1857 two branches of the family (those headed by Michael and William) were

[13] Triscott to Jolliffe, 31 Mar. 1859, ibid. DD/HY/24/17.
[14] Jolliffe's election notebook, 1859, pt 2, 'Truro'.
[15] C. B. Boase, *Collectanea cornubiensia: a collection of biographical and topographical notes relating to the county of Cornwall*, Truro 1890, 1248–54.

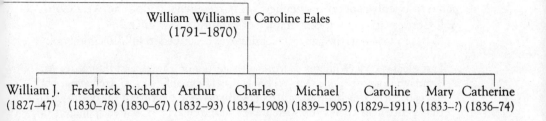

```
              William Williams = Caroline Eales
                  (1791–1870)


William J.  Frederick  Richard  Arthur   Charles   Michael   Caroline    Mary   Catherine
(1827–47)   (1830–78) (1830–67)(1832–93)(1834–1908)(1839–1905)(1829–1911)(1833–?)(1836–74)
```

Cornish Bank – Tweedy, Williams & Co
Truro – Falmouth – Redruth
W. Williams
Michael Williams
George Williams
* J. M. Williams
F. M. Williams
Robert Tweedy

* He retired in 1862, taking the Redruth branch as his share. It was re-named the West Cornwall Bank.

well-represented among the firm's partners, although day-to-day management was handled by Michael Williams and his eldest son.[16] The same two branches comprised a majority of partners in the Cornish Bank – Tweedy, Williams & Co, which also prospered. Geographically, most family members lived in the Gwennap–Redruth area, at least until 1854 when Michael Williams purchased Caerhays Castle in the Veryan district south-east of Truro. In the mid 1850s the family appeared to be united in commercial and political affairs, with Michael Williams's status as a county MP symbolising the kind of upward mobility enjoyed by the Lemon family a generation or so previously.

Where Sir William Lemon and his son Charles differed from Michael Williams was in their staunch adherence to Whig–Liberalism throughout their parliamentary careers.[17] Williams was different. Many Cornish Conser-

---

16 Ibid. 1249.
17 In the mid 1830s Sir Charles Lemon did waver, being inclined to support the Derby Dilly for a short period.

vatives were content to have him represent them, for his opinions were remarkably moderate and he was an appropriate spokesperson for the mining interest. In fact in 1857 when Sir Charles Lemon retired, Williams was prepared to openly support his nephew John Tremayne, giving the West Cornwall Conservatives their best chance of winning a seat since 1841.

What followed in the general election was described in Jolliffe's notebook:

> Last election Mr Williams & Mr Davey started on the Liberal interest & Mr Tremayne on the Cons. Mr Williams was favourable [sic] to Tremayne, but instead of splitting his votes with Mr Williams so as to prevent the necessity of that gentleman coalescing with Davey he [Tremayne] solicited plumpers & asked Cons who had before supported Williams to withdraw from him. Williams . . . was thus actually as he explained to me driven to split 1300 votes with Davey.[18]

Throughout these difficulties Michael Williams continued to maintain contact with the Conservatives, who were annoyed that Tremayne's efforts allowed a second mining man, Richard Davey, to succeed Lemon. This resulted in the agricultural interest not having 'their' MP, as they had when Lemon sat for West Cornwall.[19]

Early in 1858 Michael Williams's health began to fail. Later Triscott informed Jolliffe that if and when Williams died his eldest son would seek election – as a Conservative who would be an acceptable spokesperson for the West Cornwall landed interest.[20] This was a tall order for someone whose fortune had been amassed from commercial activities. Still, Triscott remained optimistic. His plans quickly unravelled immediately after Michael Williams's death, when the Liberals stepped in to claim the now vacant seat. John St Aubyn was their candidate, and he was sold to the Conservative squires as a man of moderate opinions, like his late predecessor.[21] J. M. Williams quickly abandoned his plans when he was told that, owing to Sir Richard Vyvyan's intervention, the entire Conservative interest had swung behind St Aubyn, who was eventually returned unopposed.[22]

Undeterred by this setback Triscott, Churston and Jolliffe continued to encourage J. M. Williams and his younger brother George, as well as William Williams and his sons, to join the Conservatives. Triscott never doubted that the family held the key to the revival of the party's fortunes in Cornwall. He therefore encouraged J. M.'s brother George to stand at the next general election, besides reiterating to Jolliffe the family's political importance. 'They are quite omnipotent in the West', Triscott wrote in August 1858, 'their power and arrangements astonish me: they laugh to scorn any attempt of the Tory

18 Jolliffe's election notebook, 1859, pt 1, 'West Cornwall'.
19 *Royal Cornwall Gazette*, 20 Mar. 1857, 4.
20 Triscott to Jolliffe, 2 June 1858, MSS Hylton DD/HY/24/17.
21 Ibid. 23 June 1858.
22 Ibid.

Squires or any combination to defeat them, or offer the slightest impediment to their success at the next general election.'[23] In writing this Triscott was conveniently overlooking the critical role of those same Tory squires only a month or so earlier. Ultimately Jolliffe was being made what seemed to be a very attractive offer, and finally the Chief Whip agreed to the arrangement, the details of which were finalised after haggling by both sides. Either George Williams or his uncle William would stand for West Cornwall, and other family members would contest several boroughs. The Williamses would also join the Carlton, their eventual reward being a baronetcy sometime after the next general election.[24]

What did the Conservatives gain from this pact? In the 1859 general election, nothing. Not a single member of the family risked a contest, even in the boroughs. According to Triscott William Williams had helped to win seats at Truro and Helston, but there is no evidence of this.[25] Frederick Martin Williams, William's eldest son, told Triscott that in future he would work for Lord Derby 'in purse and person', which he certainly did when he became one of Truro's MPs in 1863.[26] In the same letter Triscott referred to this as the poorer branch of the family, no doubt because of his disappointment that despite all his efforts J. M. Williams refused to desert the Liberals. After the dissolution of Williams, Foster & Co., then later his withdrawal from the Cornish Bank, J. M. Williams became the richest man in Cornwall, and in the years ahead he and his wife (Richard Davey's niece) worked hard for the county Liberal party.[27]

In August 1866, immediately after Lord Derby took office for the third time, William Williams received the long promised baronetcy. This suggests that the Conservative party was indebted to the family, in spite of the meagre dividend on their investment. It also leads to the conclusion that Triscott and Churston were impressed by Scorrier House, Trevince, Tregullow and Caerhays Castle, the family's various residences, and their assorted commercial activities. Michael Williams's election as a county MP, one of the most prestigious of public offices, must have convinced Triscott of the family's status and potential political importance. The reality was quite different, especially after J. M. Williams chose to remain with the Liberals, and initiated the dispersal of the family's great wealth. What then does the Conservatives' pursuit of the family reveal about the efficiency of party organisation in Cornwall and elsewhere?

[23] Ibid. 12 Sept. 1858.
[24] Ibid. 19 Mar. 1859.
[25] Triscott to Jolliffe, 31 May 1859, ibid. DD/HY/24/19.
[26] Triscott to Jolliffe, 31 May 1859, ibid.
[27] See Boase, *Collectanea*, for details of his wealth. Williams and his wife were instrumental in persuading Arthur Pendarves Vivian to succeed Richard Davey as Liberal MP for West Cornwall in 1868.

The Conservatives' organisational weaknesses

In the aftermath of the 1857 general election Triscott addressed a long memorandum to Sir William Jolliffe. From his observation point in Plymouth, where he could survey proceedings in Devon and Cornwall, Triscott concluded that the Conservatives were defeated not so much by the Liberals' efforts, 'as from the want of energy, unity, and harmony, amongst the Conservatives themselves; that in fact we have helped the Liberals to their present strength by our inaptitude [sic] to turn the progress of events to account'.[28] The party which had been split by the Corn Laws was, according to him, dispirited and careless, registrations were neglected, 'and all discipline abandoned'. After analysing the 1857 and 1859 general elections Caroline Harvey's much more recent assessment is very similar:

> In our period [1857 and 1859] the Conservatives central organisers were more successful in influencing elections by traditional means – principally bribery, and the fielding of candidates with local influence – than they were in encouraging local parties to affect the result themselves by paying attention to the registration of supporters.[29]

Both conclusions, one contemporary, one modern, and based on very different evidence (Harvey's was far more wide-ranging), point to several serious organisational problems.

One was the structure of the organisation, not at the top where the Liberals and Conservatives paralleled each other with the respective Chief Whips and Central Party Agents working together, and relying on information being channelled in from the constituency agents. For the Conservatives, at least in the south-west, there was an intermediate layer between Jolliffe and Rose and local agents such as George Mennie (Plymouth), Thomas Commins (Bodmin), John Tippett (Truro), William Carne (Penryn & Falmouth), John Brooking (Dartmouth), Thomas Hawker and John Beer (Devonport), and many others. Triscott and Lord Churston seemed to act as 'super agents', liaising between localities and centre, and therein was a weakness. The Carnes and Commins supplied them with information gathered in their boroughs, whereas Churston and Triscott's overview of electoral prospects was based on additional, and often unreliable sources, and coloured by their own prejudices.

In Triscott's case he seems to have been driven by personal ambition and a desire for greater status. Hawker of Devonport, mentioned above, explained this in a long letter to Jolliffe before the 1859 election:

> Do caution Mr Disraeli Lord Stanley (and I believe Lord Derby also) against writing confidential and important letters to our friend Mr Samuel Triscott of

[28] Triscott to Jolliffe, 5 Apr. 1857, MSS Hylton DD/HY/24/11.
[29] Harvey, 'British general elections', 38.

the Victualling Yard at this Port some men are unable to retain what is communicated to them, they must always know more than their neighbours – and their vanity prompts them to let the world know that they are on intimate terms and in confidential communication with the eminent leaders of a party.[30]

This inveterate name dropper bombarded Rose and Jolliffe with his opinions, grievances and demands for such offices as the governorship of Bermuda, or treasurer to the county courts of Devon and Cornwall. So persistent was he that in October 1858 Jolliffe wrote to Disraeli about 'a most awful correspondence with poor old Triscott', who had sent enough letters to fill 'three volumes'.[31]

In terms of electoral politics, and in particular providing advice to Jolliffe and Rose about the Conservative party's prospects in the south-west, Triscott's optimism often defeated his ultimate purpose. An example was his prediction of the number of seats which could be won by the party if the Williams family was encouraged to intervene. Another difficulty was his over-reliance on the politics of influence, and a tendency to give relatively little importance to the registers of voters. Churston was much the same. Both men gave the impression that they knew exactly what was happening in various constituencies, and sometimes they did. But how could they and Spofforth judge Bodmin to be 'anyone's borough', when at least one Liberal had been elected in the thirty-seven years since 1832.[32] Furthermore Spofforth had visited in 1855, 1856 and 1857, and reported 'Registration neglected'.[33] Triscott also wrote long letters about potential candidates whom he was encouraging: he spent months persuading Jolliffe that Sir Joshua Rowe, a Cornish-born former chief justice of Jamaica, could win one of the Truro seats.[34] In 1859 Rowe backed out at the last minute.

Spofforth too was a problem for the Conservatives. Hard-working though he may have been, like Triscott his focus was more often on the status and influence of individuals than the realities arising from the politics of registration. It was probably he who thought John Tremayne could win a Bodmin seat if prepared to stand; Spofforth also fancied the Conservatives' chances in the Liberal stronghold of Liskeard.[35] When he visited Helston in 1857, one of the party's local solicitors, Frederick Hill, hastily wrote to Sir Richard Vyvyan to ask who he was, so he was hardly well-known to the party faithful who supplied information to Jolliffe.[36] Like Triscott and Churston, Spofforth's observations seem to have been misguided; the election notebooks suggest his

---

[30] T. H. Hawker to Jolliffe, n.d. [Jan. 1859?], MSS Hylton DD/HY/24/17.
[31] Jolliffe to Disraeli, 8 Oct. 1858, Oxford, Bodl. Lib., MSS Disraeli B/xx/J/56a.
[32] Jolliffe's election notebook, 1859, pt 2, 'Bodmin'.
[33] Ibid.
[34] See series of letters from Triscott to Jolliffe, MSS Hylton DD/HY/24/17.
[35] Jolliffe's election notebook, 1859, pt 2, 'Liskeard'.
[36] Hill to Vyvyan, 5 Dec. 1857, MSS Vyvyan V 60/46/51.

achievement was to identify party agents in most towns, and encourage them to correspond with either himself or Jolliffe. Beyond that his usefulness was limited: in March 1859 T. H. Hawker wrote from Devonport that 'the list of candidates produced there by Mr Spofforth won't do', and 'Our party always unprepared – Whigs are prepared to win'.[37] All the letter-writing and hypothesising appeared to achieve very little, because too often Triscott, Spofforth and others spent their time searching not for voters, but for influential men who could swing elections. This organisational uncertainty, including confusion over candidate selection, was apparent in Truro where Jolliffe noted that, 'There is a strong Cons. party in the Borough but as usual a stronger Cons mismanagement.'[38] He thought Williams would induce Mr P. Roll a former MP for Greenwich to come forward. In Rose's election notebook is the entry (March 1859), 'It will not do to wait for the William's but some Gent^n should be requested to issue an address at once – unless Fred^k Williams of New Ham House Truro consents to stand without delay.'[39] Eventually the long-serving local agent John Tippett, who zealously attended the registrations (he was an exception, rather than the rule), persuaded Montague Smith to contest the borough – successfully.

Jolliffe, Rose and Spofforth were also fully aware of political machinations in Penryn and Falmouth, where they had little impact:

> The Cons member Mr Gwynn [sic] & Mr Freshfield, were at the last Genl Election displaced by Baring & Gurney. Libs – who by their lavish distribution of patronage & promises, induced two leading influential Cons to <u>Rat</u>; one Captain Fitzgerald was repaid by the Superintendency of ? another Mr Kinsman by three nominations for his sons to the R. Artillery the Navy & East India service. Mr Baring was returned without opposition when appointed Lord of the Admiralty, thro the utter ineptness of the Cons party & I am quite convinced from enquiry that had Sir T. Herbert started a majority of from 10 to 15 would have been secured but the latter hesitated in consequence of some application to Mr Gwynn & the chance was lost.[40]

Despite the best efforts of the shipping merchant William Carne, 'for 30 years the leading Cons', political behaviour in the borough was always erratic.[41] In 1859 Howell Gwyn showed that he was a flawed candidate inasmuch as he refused, even under extreme pressure from Jolliffe and Rose, to share his plumpers with a fellow Conservative John Foster – another last minute candidate.[42] Consequently, between them Gwyn and Foster failed to win one seat, when Triscott had earlier believed that the party would seize both.

Affairs in this dockyard borough were also affected by the availability of

---

37 Jolliffe's election notebook, 1859, pt 2, 'Devonport'.
38 Ibid. pt 1, 'Truro'.
39 Sir Philip Rose's election notebook, 1859, 'Truro'.
40 Jolliffe's election notebook, 1859, pt 1.
41 Ibid.
42 Triscott to Jolliffe, 31 May 1859, MSS Hylton DD/HY/24/19.

patronage. 'I shall feel obliged if you could let me have some small places to give away to the numerous applicants here', Gwyn requested of Jolliffe in April 1859.[43] This was not an isolated request – and it was not acted upon. The result, Triscott quickly pointed out to Jolliffe soon after the general election, was that the Conservative government did not win a single seat in any dockyard borough.[44] No places were given out at Falmouth, or at Plymouth in Devon where, despite pleadings from the Conservatives in 1858–9, the Liberals had virtually a free hand in manipulating employment in the dockyard. In May 1858 200 men were given employment by Mr Edge, master shipwright in Devonport Yard. Edge, it was pointed out, 'always selects his own partisans'.[45] No wonder Jolliffe was soon informed that, 'Our friends here in the yard & out of it are disheartened, & disgusted at a lack of want of feeling for them, as has been shown by those who now have the power to have given them their fair rights.'[46] Complete failure in the dockyard boroughs by the Conservatives demonstrates how ineffectual the government and Jolliffe were in mobilising patronage at the disposal of the Admiralty Board.

At this point there is a stark comparison between Bonham in the 1830s, and the party organisers of the 1850s and 1860s. After 1837 Conservative registration committees flourished in East and West Cornwall, particularly in the former division, and in 1841 their hard work brought its inevitable reward. Later the effort subsided. For the next twenty years there is very little evidence of the registers being attended to. In the West no-one was particularly interested. Conservative tactics revolved around securing a seat without contest, hopefully through some kind of alliance, as was briefly possible between Michael Williams and John Tremayne in 1857. In the East Nicholas Kendall made no secret of his refusal to spend money on registrations; the farmers had elected him, therefore they could undertake the task if they wished . . . and nothing was further from their minds. None of the Conservative aristocracy or wealthy gentry were likely to become involved, owing to their dislike of Kendall, so there matters remained until 1868.

In this respect the suggestion that Conservative party organisation was no less efficient after 1852 than in the 1830s and 1840s, can be queried. Generally Bonham dealt with political realities. Whenever possible influence favourable to the Conservative party was nurtured, but in the years after 1835 what gave Bonham, Sir James Graham and the central organisation more pleasure than anything else was the heartening news of favourable registration results. Besides the usual business of matching seats and candidates, these men realised that attention to the registers could swing vital seats their way, so they encouraged the development of local party organisations. That

---

[43] Gwyn to Jolliffe, 10 Apr. 1859, ibid. DD/HY/24/16.
[44] Triscott to Jolliffe, 31 May 1859, ibid. DD/HY/24/19.
[45] T. H. Hawker to Jolliffe, 22 Mar. 1858, ibid. DD/HY/18/16.
[46] Ibid. 8 May 1858.

rarely seems to have been the case after 1852 as Jolliffe's notebook clearly reveals:[47]

ASHBURTON   'Mr Caunter has influence.'

BARNSTAPLE   'Conservatives divided into two sections . . .' Triscott described it as a 'slippery place' and 'M Williams knows how to make "all right".'

DEVONPORT   registration not properly watched; 'at least one seat may be had provided some man of influence would stand'.

TIVERTON   'Mr Daniel who resides near is a very powerful supporter and is said to be able to carry one seat.'

These and many other entries, together with those for the Cornish boroughs listed at the beginning of this chapter, point to the deficiency in party organisation. Although the Chief Whip's election notebooks reveal there was no shortage of auctioneers, bankers, solicitors and others (the Mr Tippetts of the party), eager to serve, without forceful leadership, a willingness to spend money on registration and elections, plus suitable candidates, very little could be accomplished. Add a stream of misleading information being processed by Jolliffe and Rose, and the party's mid century weakness may be better understood.

Mid century party conflict

Whereas the Conservatives struggled to regain the ground once held in 1841, the Liberals' progression to becoming the dominant political party in Cornwall was built on solid foundations. Superior organisation was one, a more than adequate number of able candidates a second, and thirdly, amid the plethora of issues emerging in the 1850s and 1860s, there was the perception in predominantly Wesleyan Cornwall that the Liberal party was most sympathetic to the Dissenters. The first two went hand-in-hand due to the energetic activity of Thomas Robartes of Lanhydrock. Once he had consolidated his position as a county member, Robartes devoted himself to the task of strengthening Liberalism throughout Cornwall. He oversaw the gradual disappearance of internal tensions between moderates and radicals – Charles Buller died in 1848, Molesworth in 1855, while his own position in East Cornwall was unassailable after 1852. As a free trader and an outspoken supporter of the ballot and the abolition of church rates, his personal popularity steadily grew. Yet he never rested on his laurels: excellent organisation and astute planning were his hallmarks, and eventually he became patron of one of the Bodmin seats. Given the proximity of Lanhydrock to the town, and the extent of his popularity with those Liberals who placed principles before pocket, this was not surprising. E. F. Leveson Gower, his nominee from 1859 onwards, wrote some charming political reminiscences in which he confirmed the Robartes influence.[48]

In time that influence spread well beyond eastern Cornwall, so that, for example, his part in Liberal victories at Penryn & Falmouth and Helston was well publicised. 'The singular position of the Robortes [sic] property', one observer wrote, 'clearly points to the manner in which it was acquired, so much is it scattered over the county and so small are the portions that it has ever been a remark that "Robartes has a finger in every man's pie".'[49] There were few parishes in the county where the family did not have property of some kind, making it relatively easy for Robartes to mobilise support. Election agents were employed in the principal western towns, tenants were circularised about their landlord's preferences, supervision was constant and Robartes appeared on the hustings to support fellow Liberals such as Michael Williams, John St Aubyn and Richard Davey. Although privately shy, he was publicly forthright, articulate and always unequivocal in his opinions. Without doubt Robartes possessed political influence commensurate with his position as a great landlord, but whether this or his genuinely Liberal principles confirmed and sustained his pre-eminence among Cornwall's politicians, is difficult to judge.

While issues continued to generate passion and debate, none gripped the public imagination in the same way as parliamentary reform, agricultural protection, commutation of tithes or church rates had done in earlier decades. The 1852 general election was a requiem for agricultural protection, 1857 became a virtual referendum on Palmerston's China policy while two years later parliamentary reform was in the headlines. However none of them enjoyed great longevity. Furthermore, according to Professor Gash, 'After 1850 the old church–dissent conflict had degenerated into a welter of secondary issues: Maynooth, voluntaryism, church rates, ritualism, admission of Jews to parliament, clerical courts, ecclesiastical discipline, civil divorce, university entrance and burial grounds.'[50] Most enjoyed a fleeting prominence in Cornwall. As more and more church vestries refused to strike a rate, Dissenter anger was slowly blunted. The education issue never gained great support before the 1870s. As for the Permissive Bill sponsored by the teetotal United Kingdom Alliance, whose goal was for ratepayers in any locality to be given the power to ban the drink trade in their district so long as two-thirds of them agreed, it rarely played a decisive part in elections.

One question which did retain the capacity to arouse passionately-held opinions – at least until the end of the 1850s – was the Maynooth Grant. It

---

[48] Hon. F. Leveson Gower, *Bygone years: recollections by the Hon F. Leveson Gower*, New York 1905, 241–58.
[49] Sarah Gregor's memoirs, MSS Gregor G 1952, 70.
[50] Gash, *Aristocracy and people*, 335–6.

had always been linked with the outcries over Puseyism and Tractarianism in the Church of England, and all of these flared anew during the national 'papal aggression' crisis. In the years following, Richard Spooner's annual motion to reopen debate on the principle of endowment kept it before the public. Die-hard anti-Catholic Anglicans could never dismiss from their minds the dangers posed by the Church of Rome, and among Nonconformists Maynooth crystallised their opposition to government endowment of any religion. Despite this, gradually Maynooth lost its relevance, except in specific instances such as the 1859 Liskeard election when William Pole Carew's much earlier votes for the grant and his presentation of two Puseyites to the living of Sheviock caused him great embarrassment.

The Liberals' growing support was not just the continuation of a trend starting in the 1820s then gathering strength in mid century. In several towns it was also the outcome of change of an unusual kind in electoral politics, the occasional re-emergence of electioneering traditions more typical of the previous century. These had always coexisted with the upsurge of popular activism originating in the 1820s and 1830s, gradually being obscured but never quite disappearing. Now they reappeared in such boroughs as Launceston and St Ives, where they were almost as obvious as in the era of the First Reform Act.

Truro, by the 1850s the county's undisputed commercial centre, provides an excellent illustration of this change. The vigorous middle- and working-class activism so evident in the 1830s, much of it infused with Nonconformist zeal, continued to enliven town life. There was also a reforging of the former links between middle-class Liberals and the town's Radicals, an alliance broken in 1837. The reunion occurred in the wake of the Chartist agitation in London during April 1848, when the Truro townspeople requested the mayor to summon a public meeting so they could vote an address of loyalty to the queen.[51] Unhappy with the mayor's decision to hold the meeting at mid-day, the Chartist James Longmaid requested that it be delayed until 7.00 p.m., so that working men too might be permitted to express their viewpoint. In this he was supported by one of the town's most eminent businessmen, the banker William Mansell Tweedy. The evening meeting revealed the common bond between Liberals such as Tweedy and Humphry Willyams, and the working classes represented by Longmaid and his friends. Two tradesmen, James Salmon and John Jory, joined Longmaid in putting the Chartist viewpoint, particularly the working men's political grievances and their determination to secure universal suffrage. Although the West Briton criticised some of the abusive language used by speakers, the generally moderate tone of the meeting was maintained by Tweedy in particular, encouraging the men to use the existing constitution to secure their goals.[52]

The same blend of moderates and radicals was very much in evidence in

51 West Briton, 28 Apr. 1848, 2.
52 Ibid.

June, when an even bigger meeting discussed parliamentary reform. This time Willyams took the chair, expressing pleasure at this revival of pro-reform sentiments, and reaffirming his loyalty to that cause.[53] Several of those who spoke at the earlier meeting reappeared; furthermore George Clyma, Thomas Barlow, Charles Hawke and several others were proposed as the committee of the town's Reform Association. Many of these tanners, potters, grocers and rope-makers were Dissenters who had been active reformers since 1830.

Controversy continued to rage over the payment of church rates, reaching a new peak in September 1849 when several well-known working-class reformers were prosecuted for failure to pay their arrears – Richard Bassett draper, Thomas Barlow (mentioned above) printer and glazier, Nathaniel Gatley a cabinet-maker and Jacob Edwards an iron-monger. Bassett, Edwards and Barlow had voted for Tooke in 1832, and all four were die-hard reformers.[54] Defended by another Liberal, Henry Stokes, they appeared before three magistrates, one of whom, Dr Clement Carlyon, was a prominent Tory. Carlyon believed the case paralleled that of a steward neglecting to collect a landlord's rent from a tenant – it still had to be paid the following year. Barlow quickly attacked him for a fallacious argument in that the landlord–tenant link was voluntary and each benefited from the contract, whereas church rates were not a matter of choice.[55] Dissenters received nothing from the payment. The four defendants were irate about their 'selection' when so many others were in arrears, protesting that the value of their property seized and quickly sold was well above the amounts owed. It did them little good, and there was more than a suspicion of the defendants being victimised, not for their religion, but for having the temerity to display their political loyalties at every opportunity.

It was men of similar occupational background who were in the forefront during the 'papal aggression' meetings in November–December 1850. Methodist New Connexion, Baptist and Independent ministers all weighed in with their contributions, painstakingly delineating the grounds upon which Truro's Dissenters could assist the agitation without simultaneously acknowledging the queen's supremacy in religious matters.[56] By this time the church rates controversy was about to be channelled into a much more comprehensive disestablishment movement fostered by the British & Anti-State Church Association, encouraging many of the well-known activists to redirect their energies towards this goal. What gradually became clear in Truro was that several of the reformers who had supported Tooke and Willyams in the 1830s were now, twenty years later, the respected senior figures in their party. The followers had become leaders; during Edmund Turner's political career some of them had been disappointed by his moderation, but old divi-

53 Ibid. 16 June 1848, 2.
54 Ibid. 21 Sept. 1849, 4.
55 Ibid.
56 Ibid. 22 Nov. 1850, 2.

sions were now healed. Many of the middle-class Liberals of that era served on the town council in the 1850s. In addition, they in turn found themselves leading local agitations inspired by middle- and some working-class men.

With the single exception of the two years between the 1857 and 1859 elections the long-standing arrangement of Truro being represented at Westminster by a Liberal and a Conservative continued in mid century. As early as 1849 approaches were made by the Liberals to Augustus Smith ('The King of the Scilly Islands') to be a candidate and after being defeated in 1852 he finally succeeded in 1857.[57] The *Gazette* approved of Smith: apart from supporting the ballot he was judged to be a moderate who was supported by 'all parties'.[58] He was a diligent MP who looked after local interests – but within two years he was encountering familiar problems, elements among Truro's Liberals and Conservatives choosing to run a second Liberal, J. C. W. Vivian, a local man whose family had been connected with the borough since the early nineteenth century.[59] Vivian finished last in the poll, although trailing Smith by a mere twelve votes. Six years later, in 1865, it was the town's long-standing desire for MPs with a direct connection with Truro, together with the agreement between parties about shared representation which forced Smith to retire, allowing Vivian and F. M. Williams (Conservative) to enjoy an uncontested election.

Unlike Truro, the Conservatives gradually lost ground at Penryn & Falmouth. The well-known venality of Penryn's voters, coupled with government influence at Falmouth because of the presence of the naval dockyard, made the borough unique in Cornwall. Despite the unpredictability of elections from 1832 onwards the Liberals always held one seat, and in 1841, contrary to the national trend, won both. In the years that followed, however, there was a notable swing back to the Conservatives with signs towards the end of the 1840s that residents were being motivated by more than bribes and patronage.

Besides an impressively well-attended meeting on parliamentary reform in 1848, 'papal aggression' stirred the people of Falmouth.[60] Slowly, clear expressions of middle-class opinion emerged, and never were they more apparent than in 1852 when more than a hundred of the 'most influential merchants and tradesmen' formed a committee to pursue three goals: (1) elimination of bribery and other illegal practices; (2) a careful scrutiny of the selection of Liberal candidates; (3) defence of the principle of free trade.[61] The so-called 'purity committee' implored the electors to rouse themselves and cast off the old system, arguing that their motives were neither personal nor selfish. As in Truro, middle-class men were conspicuous: Richard Thomas

---

[57] On Smith see Elizabeth Inglis-Jones, *Augustus Smith of Scilly*, London 1969.
[58] *Royal Cornwall Gazette*, 3 Apr. 1857, 5.
[59] Ibid. 13 Mar. 1857, 4.
[60] *West Briton*, 16 June 1848, 2; 22 Nov. 1850, 2.
[61] CRO, DD.X 394/33.

victualler, Jacob Hamblen shopkeeper, Moses Jacob hardware merchant, and several members of the Quaker Fox family, wealthy merchants and shipping agents. However, it seems to be straining credulity to suggest that their choice of Baring, a former private secretary in the Board of Trade and the Home Office, was governed solely by chance. Somehow, they believed, Baring might be able to boost the port's trade. When he confronted Howell Gwyn and J. W. Freshfield, both vastly experienced in the ways of surreptitiously filling the electors' pockets, Baring had little chance, but he reaffirmed his intention of renewing his efforts at the next opportunity.[62]

His opportunity came in 1857, apparently the climax to a high-minded attempt to reimpose impressive standards of electoral purity. But this is only part of the explanation for the Liberal revival. From the beginning of 1853 the county MP Michael Williams took a careful interest in events, looming up out of the background whenever electioneering was in progress. It seems an unlikely coincidence that on 27 March 1857, when Baring and Gurney were nominated, Michael Williams 'happened' to be passing by and stopped to make a couple of spontaneous speeches boosting the Liberal cause.[63] As a county member, and as a banker connected with Falmouth (Tweedy, Williams & Co was one of the town's banks), he gave valuable support to a well-organised effort. The Conservatives admitted that Baring had established a claim in 1852, also agreeing that thereafter he was the logical successor to the ageing Freshfield whose connection with the borough began in 1826, and who was certain to retire. Nevertheless they were equally certain that much of the formerly illegal electioneering had simply been transformed into a more acceptable guise – 'patronage and promises'.[64] Supposedly it was this 'new' form of generosity which induced Fitzgerald and Kinsman 'to Rat' on the Conservatives, who later consoled themselves with the thought that 'Baring is very unpopular from his ultra purist professions, amongst the lower orders of voters; for having done nothing for them, and everything for the turn coats'.[65] Unpopular he may have been; nevertheless his opponents failed to take advantage of the situation.

Helston remained unique among the Cornish boroughs. Although the old ultra-Tory Sir Richard Vyvyan represented the town virtually without challenge from 1841, nevertheless a well-organised group of local dissidents who had been responsible for Arthur Buller's candidacy in 1837 continued to nurse intentions of electing a Liberal. As we have seen earlier, Vyvyan's response had been to buy off one of their leaders, Thomas Rogers. However, as soon as Rogers succumbed to a £250 annual retainer for his services, John Gilbert Plomer, another Liberal solicitor, replaced him.[66] Through all the

62 *West Briton*, 16 July 1852, 4.
63 *Royal Cornwall Gazette*, 3 Apr. 1857, 3.
64 Jolliffe's election notebook, 1859, 'Falmouth'.
65 Ibid.
66 John Vivian of Pencalenick to Vyvyan, 25 Nov. 1847, MSS Vyvyan, V 36/45.

solicitorial plotting and scheming Vyvyan was faithfully served by his agents, Frederick Hill and Glynn Grylls. In 1852 Vyvyan decided it was Plomer's turn to be rewarded. But the latter quickly spotted the trap:

> With regard to the Retainer which Mr Vyvyan has offered, you will permit me to say that I am sincerely attached to political tenets, differing widely, on some points, from your own; and you will therefore fully appreciate the reluctance which I feel to take a retainer from you on this occasion, when I shall be unable to render you any service, and when, had there been a contest in view, I should probably have been found in the ranks of your opponents.[67]

Soon afterwards Plomer overcame his reluctance – then found that a Liberal was standing. No wonder that Plomer and his friends quickly told him to go away.

The significant point about these convolutions is that Vyvyan employed the tactics of buying off the professional men who led Helston's Liberals – yet even he couldn't pay them all. While Plomer was temporarily neutralised, Thomas Rogers became disenchanted (particularly when his retainers dried up) and rejoined his former Liberal allies.[68] In fact the Liberal breakthrough in 1857 can be partially explained in these terms. Vyvyan retired – no retainers were issued – therefore Thomas Rogers, his solicitor son Henry, Plomer, James Wearne and several others who had introduced Buller to the voters twenty years earlier, now had the pleasure of seeing a Liberal elected by the townspeople. Whether they could have carried the day without the assistance of two usually Conservative solicitors, Christopher Popham and Reginald Rogers, third son of the late Canon Rogers, is a matter of conjecture.

Another circumstance which pushed the balance in their favour was summed up by the *Gazette*:

> It (Helston) depends for its prosperity on great Wheal Vor Mines, which have led to the expenditure within the last two or three years of enormous sums, and whose returns of £4,000 or £5,000 a month, are nearly all spent on the works, and mostly in the neighbourhood. Mr Trueman, the newly elected member, is one of the directors.[69]

The long-awaited Liberal victory therefore resulted from the coincidence of an improbable set of circumstances in which the issues of the day had little impact, so it would be difficult to repeat.

Within months of the election Trueman became involved in serious financial problems; prospective candidates descended in a horde on Vyvyan, the town's reputed patron – among them William Rashleigh's younger brother

---

67 Plomer to Vyvyan, 27 June 1852, ibid.
68 Correspondence between Thomas Rogers and Vyvyan, 1855–6, ibid.
69 *Royal Cornwall Gazette*, 3 Apr. 1857, 5.

Jonathan, Edwin Chadwick the sanitary reformer, and John St Aubyn.[70] Like many before them in Cornish boroughs, they came, weighed the prospects and disappeared when they realised their projected campaign would be fruitless. Trueman hung on until 1859, but when the late Canon Rogers's eldest son John made up his mind to be a candidate he attracted all the old Vyvyan cliques; being highly regarded as a landlord in the town, he had few problems. However only he or Sir Richard Vyvyan could manage this operation (i.e. the blending of the various disparate forces), and when Rogers retired in 1865 another Liberal victory was certain. The gloss was soon taken off it when a successful petition for bribery was brought against A. W. Young after his defeat of Major Grylls, who was the unwitting victim of Helston's usual factional intrigues.[71]

This election was also notable for support for Young from the teetotal and Dissenting groups, as well as from Robartes who was now the unchallenged doyen of Cornish Liberalism, and always used his interests on behalf of the party's candidates. But that would have been insufficient without the support of Helston's veteran middle- and working-class Liberals, Thomas Rogers and Thomas Edwards auctioneer ('Tom Cat' and 'Tom Rat' as they were scathingly referred to by their opponents), Plomer, William Chegwidden tailor, John Menadue iron-monger, and many others who had spent most of their lives trying to oust the succession of Conservative MPs.[72]

No two boroughs were less affected by changes originating in the 1820s than Launceston and St Ives. The duke of Northumberland's grip on Launceston was unyielding: he seized every opportunity to strengthen his interest. One example was the projected railway connecting the county with the world east of the Tamar. The planned route for the Cornwall Railway passed through Launceston, so in 1845 Northumberland wasted no time in explaining to Gurney what was required. In his proprietorial way he (the duke) regarded the Central line as the only choice, 'that would give me a sufficient control . . . for the benefit of the whole Borough'. He added:

> All that I must insist on is, that the line is the best for the Public & for the Inhabitants of the Borough generally. The Station must be in the most convenient spot for the public service. I shall be glad if the Station was on my Property because it would give me a control beneficial to the Borough.[73]

Actions such as these meant that the small coterie of Liberal faithful could do little more than grumble about their position, something the old Radical William Pearse certainly did in 1859 when yet another Northumberland nominee, T. C. Haliburton, was elected. During a provocative and very humorous speech on election day, Pearse implored the candidate to vote for

---

[70] Correspondence Nov. 1857–May 1858, MSS Vyvyan V 36/46.
[71] *Royal Cornwall Gazette*, 21 July 1865, 4.
[72] The activities of Rogers and Edwards were referred to in the *Gazette*, 25 Aug. 1868, 1.
[73] Northumberland to Gurney, 22 Dec. 1845, CRO, MSS Tregoning DD.TG 9/6.

the ballot and hoped his first vote in parliament 'will be for the abolition of this miserably rotten and miserable borough'.[74] Even the *Gazette* admitted the use to which Northumberland put his property at election time might be indefensible, but this was counterbalanced by the obvious superiority of the members. 'Who could compare for an instant Hardinge, or Bowles, or Haliburton, with the mob of metropolitan members, the Tittlebat Titmice of the reformed House of Commons.'[75] Nothing changed in 1864 when Northumberland sold his property to another Conservative, Alexander Campbell. Within a year he was the borough's MP, thereby reminding the hapless townspeople that no matter how strongly they felt about parliamentary reform, the Permissive Bill, church rates or any other topic, they had the misfortune (in a political sense) to live in a pocket borough.

At the western extremity of the county St Ives was little better, although unlike Launceston it was contested four times between 1841 and 1868. Even in the 1860s election results were governed by the preferences of various wealthy families (mostly Conservative), living in and near the town. When the Liberal, Geissler, decided in 1859 to challenge the Conservative hegemony, friends in London told him beforehand of the need to have a majority of the wealthy landlords at his side if he wished to be successful.[76] This was extremely difficult to manage, even for Cornish-born candidates.

Despite a situation where many of the voters, like their Launceston brethren, were pressured by the landlords or agents, there was a small 'reform' party. Leading it was the Wesleyan, William Docton, a man of indefatigable enthusiasm and energy. An opponent described him as 'this depraved and malignant scribbler', whose conduct was a combination of 'egotism, pride, obstinacy, radicalism, impertinence, overbearing dogmatism, and coxcombry as I never before witnessed'![77] It was Docton who in 1852 travelled to London, taking a requisition for Hussey Vivian, Jr, to stand on the Liberal interest.[78] Although Vivian eventually retired before the poll his presence in St Ives was an acknowledgment of the party's presence there, besides providing Docton and his friends with another opportunity to enlarge their numbers. But they also did much more. At each election they vigorously questioned the various candidates at public meetings and on the hustings, especially in 1859 when Geissler and the sitting Conservative Henry Paull were forced to express their opinions on the ballot, the Permissive Bill and franchise reform. Unfortunately Geissler assisted his eventual defeat by admitting he felt unable to vote for the bill – not the response teetotal Liberals hoped for.[79]

[74] *Royal Cornwall Gazette*, 6 May 1859, 1.
[75] Ibid. 13 Sept. 1859, 5.
[76] Ibid. 6 May 1859, 1.
[77] Hayden, 'Culture, creed and conflict', 141.
[78] *West Briton*, 14 May 1852, 4.
[79] *Royal Cornwall Gazette*, 6 May 1859, 1.

The liquor question was one with the potential to unlock St Ives from Conservative dominance. Since the 1830s both the temperance and teetotal movements had thrived among the ports' numerous Wesleyans, although as with the religious revivals, support fluctuated almost from year to year. St Ives was recognised by the United Kingdom Alliance as one English constituency where its parliamentary candidates had at least the glimmer of a chance of success.[80] This explains why in 1865 Edward Vivian, an Alliance vice-president since 1862, challenged Paull. The result was closer than usual (Paull 233 votes, Vivian 177), causing the Alliance's Executive Committee to report how Vivian, 'in the face of a considerable territorial interest, succeeded in evoking the goodwill of the inhabitants of the borough, and in polling a considerable number of votes, justifying sanguine hopes for the future'.[81] Vivian continued his association with St Ives, believing he had a real chance of victory at the next election. To the despair of the town's Liberals, when the time came in 1868 the Alliance refused to pay his expenses, forcing Vivian to withdraw. Docton and his friends then made overtures to a succession of prospective candidates, before finally persuading Charles Magniac, a rich merchant, to stand.[82]

Meanwhile with the election campaign being devoted to the usual combination of local and national issues – including the Permissive Bill – plus accusations from both sides of electioneering tactics more associated with the previous century, Vivian found the key to Liberal success. Before he retired he wrote to Arthur Pendarves Vivian, John St Aubyn's Liberal running mate for West Cornwall. Everything, he told his namesake depended on neutralising Mr Cornish, a Penzance solicitor, 'as [he] has hitherto been our principal difficulty being land agent for Mr Tyringham and Mrs Davies Gilbert's properties – the whole of whose tenants have been compelled to vote against me, although Liberal, Dissenters, Teetotallers and of all advanced civilisations'.[83] Once Vivian and John St Aubyn, the two West Cornwall Liberals engaged the firm of Rodd & Cornish as their agents, Vivian repeated his point: the tenantry of the two estates should be allowed an uncontrolled vote. Mrs Davies Gilbert had been willing in 1865 to allow her tenants to use their discretion, but Cornish's office issued instructions compelling them to vote for Paull.[84] This time judicious pressure on Cornish produced the breakthrough local Liberals had so eagerly sought since 1832.

West Cornwall, the jewel in the Cornish Liberals' crown, provides one final illustration of the ways in which factionalism, feuding and personalities often outweighed matters of public importance or debate. Much of it was on

---

[80] Alliance House, Westminster, 13th Report of the Executive Committee of the United Kingdom Alliance, 1864–5.
[81] Ibid.
[82] *Royal Cornwall Gazette*, 13 Aug. 1868, 5.
[83] Edward Vivian to A. P. Vivian, 12 June 1868, CRO, MSS Pendarves Vivian PV(290)1.
[84] Ibid.

the Conservative side, originating with the manipulative Sir Richard Vyvyan. Nevertheless this should not be allowed to obscure the Liberals' part in the process of maintaining their dominance. Throughout the thirty-five years between the First and Second Reform Acts the 'Lemon connection' was a cornerstone of their success. In 1865 John Rogers, who sometime earlier had been regarded as a possible county member for West Cornwall, explained to Vyvyan:

> It would be unkind to Col T. [Arthur Tremayne] to invite him to be a candidate on the 'only politics' which would make him desirable: as he could scarcely be requested to announce a candidacy (?) in direct opposition to Carclew. It may well be however, that, at a future time, he might be ready to stand a contest on the right side.[85]

The other ray of hope was that John Tremayne, 'a very staunch Conservative', might agree to come forward again in the future. After their uncle's death in 1868 both Tremaynes did so, successfully. With so few Conservative candidates available in West Cornwall, the Liberals owed much to Lemon for neutralising his relatives.

Unlike their opponents the Liberals had no shortage of eligible candidates, because they were far less concerned to confine the representation to well-established and respected gentry families. Successful miners and bankers such as Michael Williams were quite acceptable, and in 1857 another, Richard Davey, replaced Lemon when he retired, a move which enraged the *Gazette*. The paper acknowledged that Davey was a successful and wealthy mining adventurer; nevertheless the mining interest was already represented by Williams, so the agriculturists were being denied their usual seat. Besides, 'however influential in his own business and town [Redruth], he [Davey] has never taken the position or devoted himself to the duties of a county gentleman, and we know not of any pretensions he can advance to the distinguished trust of a County Member'.[86] In Conservative eyes Davey was being presumptuous, but he had been prominent in Cornish Liberalism for more than thirty years, made it clear he wished to see the church rates question settled and an extension to voting rights, and favoured 'a sound system of education'.[87] In almost every sense he was an ideal choice for West Cornwall – and like Williams and St Aubyn he could, if necessary, afford a contested election. Knowing this, and well aware of the predominantly Wesleyan complexion of the electorate, the Conservatives found themselves without a realistic chance of breaking the Liberal monopoly of West Cornwall.

The purpose of this chapter has been to expose those forces shaping the contours of mid century Cornwall electoral politics. One was the organisational debility of the Conservatives, whose greatest difficulty was leadership.

[85] Rogers to Vyvyan, 5 June 1865, MSS Vyvyan V 22M/80/36/46.
[86] *Royal Cornwall Gazette*, 20 Mar. 1857, 4.
[87] Ibid.

Another was the growing strength of the Robartes-led Liberals, who carefully watched the registrations, and in the tradition of the farmer–reformer alliance promoted debate on important national issues. Also, they rather than the Conservatives benefited from a situation in which, after 1850, 'the old church–dissent conflict degenerated into a welter of secondary issues'.[88] The point was that the ensuing controversies strengthened the Liberal–Dissenter alliance, which was based on the ideological affinity between them. Unfortunately for the Conservatives, with the possible exception of St Ives and Launceston, their reliance on the outmoded politics of influence was much less productive. This, as much as any factor, structured borough politics in the 1850s and 1860s.

[88] Gash, *Aristocracy and people*, 335.

8

Party Management and Public Opinion, 1868–1885

Liberals and Conservatives in county politics, 1868–85

By the end of the 1860s Cornwall was undergoing a protracted period of economic and social upheaval. The once proud toast, 'Fish, Tin and Copper', was leaving a sour taste, for the fishing and mining industries were slipping into a sad but inexorable decline. The deep water drifters had long since triumphed over the inshore seiners, and it was now the 'new middleman interest, the great fishmongers of London and other markets who, minimising the loss of deteriorated fish by the use of ice', were reaping most of the profits. Despite deliveries being speeded to markets by railway, and a growing customer demand, nothing could alter the reality of ever smaller seasonal catches. Agriculturists too were badly hit by the cattle plague of the mid 1860s, followed by the disastrous, protracted depression beginning in the 1870s. No wonder tenant right, the claim by farmers to compensation for any unexhausted improvements made by them, and remaining on their holding at the end of their tenancies, became such a topical issue in the county.

Meanwhile, deep in the Cornish granite the once productive copper seams were exhausted, throwing hundreds of men out of work. The tin mines were an obvious alternative, or the China clay works in the St Austell district, but unhappily relatively few found employment in either. As underground workings collapsed and mines flooded, only the gaunt, towering engine houses and smokestacks were left as forlorn sentinels. Many of the highly skilled miners emigrated to South Wales, Lanarkshire, Canada, South Africa and Australia, and soon 'there were to be as many Cornish miners in Johannesburg and Butte City as there were in Redruth and St Just'.[1] The impact on the county was dramatic, the population declining in each decade after 1861 when it peaked at 369,390: 1871 – 362,343; 1881 – 330,686; 1891 – 322,571. In the same three decades 1861–91, the percentage population increase for England averaged 13 per cent; in Cornwall it was obviously negative, including –9 per cent in 1871–81.[2] Overseas remittances were the only source of income for hundreds of families in the Camborne, Redruth and Liskeard areas. Tourism,

---

1 Rowe, *Cornwall*, 326.
2 See Johanssen, 'Demographic transition', 255–6, and *1891 Census of England and Wales: preliminary report and tables of population*, PP 1890–1 [C6422], xciv. 2.

holiday-making, china clay production or the commercial growing of vegetables and early blooming flowers may have seemed inferior substitutes for the old staples, yet they were the forerunners of the twentieth-century world.

In these circumstances it is not surprising that electoral politics regained a sharpness of definition lacking in the 1850s and 1860s. Issues were clearly presented, and more than ever before MPs were repeatedly made aware of the view-points of voters and non-voters. Demands for their presence at public meetings grew, and the sometimes irritating persistence of such pressure groups as the Liberation Society, the Farmers' Alliance, assorted temperance groups or the Sunday Closing Association, gradually restricted their former freedom, such as it was. Contacts between MPs and their electorates became much more frequent: as a result, more people were drawn into participation in electoral politics than ever before – helped of course by the franchise provisions of the Second, and later the Third, Reform Act. In turn this overflowed into party electoral organisation, something which soon become evident in Cornwall's two county divisions.

When the West Cornwall MP Richard Davey realised early in 1868 that he no longer had the desire to remain in parliament, his decision sparked an organisational upheaval among the Liberals. An equally important stimulus for change was the 1867 Reform Act, which gave the right to vote to £12 occupiers. Yet what followed was not new. Instead it bore several similarities to the East Cornwall Conservative revival of the late 1830s. However there were also important differences: then the Conservatives were determined to wrest back from the Liberals the two seats held by them since 1832. For the Liberals of 1868 their goal was to maintain their monopoly of the West Cornwall seats, while simultaneously overcoming the strong prejudice against an 'outside' candidate. What the process of change revealed in 1868 was the steadily increasing power of middle-class men in electoral politics, and, conversely, the declining role of the 'men of property and character'. Meanwhile in East Cornwall after 1870 the same process was much further advanced, and, because of the farmers, it continued.

As early as May 1868 West Cornwall Liberals had an inkling of Davey's impending retirement, which he confirmed the following month. The intriguing point about this is that Davey officially notified Henry Grylls, the chairman of his committee, on 6 June.[3] Grylls, a Redruth solicitor, in turn called a meeting at Camborne on 16 June to begin the search for a suitable successor. Meanwhile, behind the scenes the decision had already been made; the old reformer Humphry Willyams repeatedly refused to pay any expenses over and above subscriptions if his son Brydges contested the vacancy, so the search was already under way in late May. By 4 June Arthur Pendarves Vivian, a Welsh copper-smelter and nephew of Hussey Vivian, one-time MP for Truro and East Cornwall, had agreed to stand. The invitation was issued

---

3   Notice from Richard Davey to Henry Grylls, 6 June 1868, CRO, X, 529/26.

by J. M. Williams with the concurrence of Thomas Robartes and the fifth Viscount Falmouth, who was a political aberration in the normally Tory Boscawen family.[4] Immediately Vivian's telegrammed acceptance arrived at Caerhays Castle, Williams and his wife Elizabeth threw themselves into a campaign to ensure that there were no obstacles to his success. J. M. Williams began a painstaking tour of several critical districts – among them, Redruth, Camborne, Penzance – consulting with the principal Liberals, while Elizabeth used her influence with Mrs Gilbert of Trellissick and the Enys family near Penryn.[5] Grylls was apparently left in the dark until 8 June; then he informed Vivian that, 'It is deemed very desirable that nothing should transpire previous to our meeting on the 16 Inst that can be construed into the semblance of a wish on the part of a few, however influencial [sic] to dictate in the election of a Candidate.'[6] Probably it was the political sensibilities of the middle classes that made him offer this timely hint.

Vivian's selection was no more than a formality, nevertheless before 16 June he received plenty of advice on his future campaign, and on Cornish politics. Most revolved around four subjects; the drawbacks associated with being a non-resident, and the need therefore to establish a household in the county, the importance of consulting the principal mine managers and adventurers, making sure that Edward Heard, editor of the *West Briton*, was on-side, and finally, the necessity of securing Methodist support. On the last point Grylls believed that,

> a general declaration in writing to be read to the meeting, that you approve of Mr Gladstone's politics – specially with respect to the Irish Church, would be sufficient – on this latter point we are here very strong. All the Sections of the Methodist Body & other dissenters have these views, besides many good Churchmen.[7]

Most of the advice was taken, especially the significance of the Methodists to whom Vivian's attention was repeatedly drawn in the next few weeks. Thus, after visiting Helston in mid July, Vivian's principal election agent S. T. Downing explained:

> We have the great advantage in the 'South Country' that most of the farmers are Wesleyans and from the time that Mr W. Bickford Smith spoke at the great Camborne Meeting (on the 16 June) in the name of his father and the 20,000 male Wesleyans in the division . . . the Wesleyans have been with us to a man. I need not point out to you the vast importance of this fact.[8]

4 J. M. Williams to Vivian, 4 June 1868, MSS Pendarves Vivian PV(290)1.
5 Mrs E. M. Williams to Vivian, 5 June 1868, ibid.
6 Henry Grylls to Vivian, 8 June 1868, ibid.
7 Grylls to Vivian, 13 June 1868, ibid.
8 Downing to Vivian, 14 July 1868, ibid.

Vivian quickly absorbed the message and became a strong supporter of Irish Church disestablishment.

Equally important, before the end of June he had a committee (comprising predominantly wealthy middle-class men) hard at work, their initial priority being the forthcoming registrations. The basis of Vivian's organisation was local district, as opposed to parish, committees, with each appointing its own chairman and secretary. A decentralised system of local autonomy, carefully supervised, was to be the organisational structure employed by Vivian and St Aubyn for the next twelve years, time proving it to be remarkably effective.[9]

As early as 8 July Downing began a daily stream of letters, detailing the steps being taken to build up the register. The gist of these was that the decentralised committees mentioned earlier overlay a further organisational level. As he explained with regard to registrations:

> Committees are all very well in their way but with them it is much more talk than real work & on the other hand to rely on professional men solely is to pay very dearly for very little. But in every parish almost there can be found some man who at former Elections had done good service & who from being a parish officer or having been one in former years understands something of the business. These men for a very small sum will do everything we want & do it well too.[10]

Here once again is evidence of the critical role middle-class men were now playing in Cornwall's Liberal party. Among those upon whom Downing placed great faith were John Bottrall, printer and book-seller of Camborne, Mathew Courtenay, grocer and ship chandler in Truro, and Reuben Carne, assistant overseer in Kenwyn. In addition the Liberals also went to some lengths to utilise the influence of the most important landed families: Downing noted that 'all our large properties are being worked up by the Stewards and Lord Falmouth's rental alone will shew an immense number of new votes: the same may be said for Mr Robartes' property and that of others'.[11]

The most interesting aspect of this activity was the care required to avoid placing possible Conservatives on the register. As Downing was all too well aware, over-zealous committeemen could always fall into the trap of including, 'persons of doubtful politics with the hope that they will ultimately go right!'[12] He and his helpers therefore spent hours thrashing out lists of men who should be asked to claim, so that the 'right persons only' could be registered. Downing, a wily and experienced solicitor, well knew those landlords and businessmen whose politics were Conservative, and who might well pressure voters over whom they had any influence. Consequently the objective he took such pains to impress on his assistants, was to avoid registering

9 Downing to Vivian, 8 July 1868, ibid.
10 6 July 1868, ibid.
11 Ibid.
12 10 July 1868, ibid.

anyone who might conceivably vote against a Liberal candidate, i.e. 'persons of doubtful politics'.[13]

How accurately or how skilfully these operations were carried out is certainly questionable. With no contests in West Cornwall since 1832 there were no pollbooks from which agents or canvassers could glean the politics of thousands of individual voters, and after 1850–1 neither side had paid great attention to the registers, which must have been littered with bad votes. Furthermore the last serious canvass of the division had been carried out in 1857, the interval since then making those records outdated. So for all his confidence Downing must have been involved in more than a little guesswork; consequently it is not surprising that Vivian pressed him for the actual numbers likely to go onto the register from each district, rather than numerical estimates of influence, which left him unimpressed. Eventually Henry Grylls reported that their calculations were:

Total of New Claimants	3,876
Liberals	2,762
Conservatives	1,114[14]

These figures were roughly the difference in the official size of the electorate between 1865 and 1868; what is surprising about them is the number of Conservatives who registered, because none of their party's usual solicitors was engaged to attend to the registrations. Quite clearly the politicisation of the middle and working classes was proceeding rapidly, even in a county division where only one party had shown spasmodic interest in electoral organisation.

Turning to the Conservatives in both East and West Cornwall, the contrast with the Liberals is stark. Where the latter exhibited bustling activity and efficiency the Conservatives were lackadaisical, handicapped by the same weaknesses prevalent in the 1850s. While the Liberals made thorough preparations in 1868 for claimants' forms to be handed in to overseers by 20 July, their opponents in East and West were motionless. In conceding all four county seats to the Liberals, in 1868 the Conservatives endured a humiliation unequalled since 1835. Not surprisingly there was an immediate reaction in the East, the proven heartland of Conservative support, where the party had held at least one seat at every general election since 1832. A combination of firm leadership and some semblance of party unity meant that recovery was not out of the question, providing prominent Conservatives were willing to work with, and take notice of the farmers. When Kendall travelled to Gibraltar in February 1869 to take up the post of police magistrate, there was no reason for his farmer-opponents to refuse to support the party, so the revival could begin.[15]

13 Ibid.
14 Grylls to Vivian, 19 Aug. 1868, ibid.
15 The Kendall papers in the Cornwall Record Office reveal Kendall's persistent attempts in 1867–8 to find a remunerative public office.

Within a year the first step was taken: initiated by John Tremayne, a Conservative Registration Association was formed in East Cornwall. Late in 1871 several members believed it had been so successful in rebuilding the party's support on the register, that at least one seat could be contested at the next general election.[16] Prior to that, and long before anyone expected to be involved in the selection of a possible candidate, a crisis developed. For once it was not of the Conservatives' making. Brydges Willyams, one of the sitting Liberals, had for some years been having an affair with Lady Jolliffe, wife of Captain Jolliffe (MP for Wells), the eldest son of the Conservative party's former Chief Whip. The Jolliffes had been living in Cornwall because of the captain's health, but his discovery of the scandal brought that arrangement to an abrupt end.[17] Willyams quickly resigned from the local militia, and with rumours of divorce proceedings, it was generally assumed that there would soon be a vacant parliamentary seat. Such a move would have suited the grumbling farmers, for neither Willyams nor Trelawny had made themselves conspicuous at their meetings.[18]

In March 1871, soon after the Willyams–Jolliffe affair became public knowledge, John Tremayne telegraphed Kendall asking him whether he wished to stand. The answer was a firm 'no', which under the circumstances was wise, for the party was still torn between traditional, and (for the Conservatives) innovative electoral strategies. Tremayne followed his telegram with two explanatory letters, an extract from the first revealing a familiar dilemma:

> I have called a meeting of the Registration Committee for Friday next, when I propose to go carefully through the register and ascertain what our strength is – and 2nd decide whether the seat can be contested successfully, and if so who shall be selected as the Conservative Candidate. I have no doubt if you stand you can be returned – there is a very strong feeling in your favour, and that very class who turned you out in 1868 would I am sure be glad of the opportunity of restoring to you again a seat in Parliament.[19]

When the committee met Tremayne realised that calculations would have to be hard-headed and pragmatic. To him it was no use calculating party strength on the basis of Kendall's 1868 canvass, plus the increases in later registrations, which supposedly left the two parties even. Tremayne also argued that the £12 voters (and almost 2,000 of them were newly enrolled) had never been tested at a poll, so it was impossible to predict what their behav-

16 Report of Conservative meeting at Lostwithiel, 25 April, *Royal Cornwall Gazette*, 27 Apr. 1872, 4.
17 Thomas Olver to Kendall, 18 Feb. 1871, MSS Kendall KL.
18 William Geach to Kendall, 3 Feb. 1872, ibid.
19 Tremayne to Kendall, 1 Mar. 1871, ibid.

iour would be.[20] However, buoyed up by optimism about the register and the weakness of Charles Robartes, the likely Liberal candidate, the committee ignored Tremayne's analysis. Luckily they avoided another possible defeat, as Willyams chose to ride out the storm of public disapproval. One cynic told Kendall, when the divorce case was imminent, 'He [Willyams] has now paired off for some months so as to visit Utah – the land of the Mormons – where he can with impunity follow the example of Brigham Young to his heart's content!'[21]

Events took a new turn in 1872, immediately after Jolliffe's divorce was granted. Requisitions for Tremayne began circulating in East Cornwall, and the Rashleigh family's influence, briefly given to the Liberals in the 1860s, was now restored to the Conservatives by Jonathan, the late William Rashleigh's younger brother and heir.[22] Another hopeful sign was that Truro had recently been the scene of a highly publicised Conservative by-election victory. With the popular mood running their way, the Conservatives of East Cornwall were ready for action; no doubt due to Tremayne's cautions the leaders were also a wiser group than they had been in 1868. When a well-attended meeting was held at Lostwithiel in April 1872, and many of the principal landowners attended – among them the Tremayne brothers, Jonathan Rashleigh, the nucleus of the Registration Association and many leading farmers, William Pole Carew was appointed chairman.[23] It was the most significant gathering of its type since the 1840s, but why should it be regarded as a turning point in the party's fortunes?

Firstly, the importance and reliability of the Registration Association's figures were recognised. More than 500 Conservative voters had been added in a highly successful 1871 registration, prompting even the usually cautious Tremayne to admit that prospects were much brighter. Secondly, Carew, eleven years younger than his long-time rival, laid it firmly before the meeting, no doubt with some relish, that in his opinion Kendall was too old and not the best candidate. No-one disagreed. Thirdly, the former party leaders who constituted the Registration Association – men such as Fortescue, Prideaux Brune, Boger, Charles Gurney, Carew, Tremayne – at long last realised it was not for them to decide upon or impose a candidate on the party. The ways of the 1840s were being belatedly set aside in favour of more democratic processes. Fourthly, the farmers made it very clear that they insisted upon vetoing any prospective candidate whom they found unsatisfactory. On this issue the lead was taken 'by that glib & slippery political yeoman Mr William Snell', who, speaking on behalf of hundreds of his brother farmers, said they wanted to hear a candidate's opinions before pledging

20 5 Mar. 1871, ibid.
21 Edward Geach to Kendall, 3 Feb. 1872, ibid.
22 Ibid.
23 *Royal Cornwall Gazette*, 27 Apr. 1872, 4.

assistance.[24] After making themselves conspicuous in the early 1850s as the ECSPNI, the farmers had fallen back into the shadows until their year-long campaign against Kendall in 1868 once again demonstrated their political potency. Except in the lead-up to the 1841 election they had never been an integral component of either party. Now they were merging with the Conservatives, on their own terms.

Snell made it clear that to be acceptable, a candidate would have to agree to a reduction in local rates and the establishment of county financial boards, the rating of woodlands, plantations and dues on mines, and an alteration to the Game Laws so that occupiers could kill hares and rabbits.[25] For good measure he added that the farmers wished to popularise the Conservatives, transforming the party image into one of modern enlightenment, rather than outdated Toryism. As if the writing was not already on the wall, William Prynn, a tenant farmer from the south-eastern parish of St Stephens-by-Saltash, elaborated upon earlier arguments by announcing that there was a strong feeling among his friends that if they could not find a gentleman from among the 'territorial aristocracy' to represent their views, they would be reluctantly driven to bring forward one of their own class.[26] By this stage the farmers were dominating proceedings, so perhaps to avoid any further blood-letting John Tremayne was proposed as Conservative candidate for the next general election. After a long speech in which he satisfied the farmers on all points, then proceeded to attack Gladstone's foreign policy and later the Permissive Bill, which he dubbed tyrannical class legislation, Tremayne was selected.

Considering that the election was not due until 1874, the choice of a candidate by the Conservatives in April 1872 was an unprecedented step. Politically though, the significance of this meeting lay in the forcefulness with which the farmers asserted their position in the East Cornwall Conservative party. Not only that – they also made confident use of their electoral strength to influence the candidate's platform. This was change with a vengeance, and all that now remained was the testing of this new bond.

The opportunity came suddenly – in fact too suddenly – in January 1874, when Gladstone took everyone by surprise in calling a general election. In the interim the trend of events continued to favour East Cornwall's Conservatives. Willyams placed his future in the hands of a Liberal committee which decided that, 'under the circumstances', he ought not to stand for re-election.[27] Kendall's son-in-law Sir Colman Rashleigh, Sir Charles Sawle and Charles Robartes all refused invitations to be his successor, then the other sitting Liberal Trelawny announced his forthcoming retirement, prompting

---

24 Geach to Kendall, 3 Feb. 1872, MSS Kendall KL. Geach had a long-standing dislike of Snell, who at this time was taking a prominent stand on the iniquities of the Game Laws.
25 *Royal Cornwall Gazette*, 27 Apr. 1872, 4.
26 Ibid.
27 Ibid. 31 Jan. 1874, 4.

Willyams to continue to flirt with the opinions of the electors. Meanwhile Tremayne had consolidated his strength as the single Conservative candidate, there being cross-party agreement that he should quietly go forward and share the representation with a Liberal. Underlying this assumption was the confidence engendered by five years uninterrupted effort building up the register.

At the last minute apparent Liberal disarray caused the Conservatives to over-reach themselves. With no prospective Liberal candidate other than Willyams being spoken of at the end of January, they decided to bring forward a reluctant Carew – despite his and several colleagues' opinions that this would be a needlessly provocative step – causing the Liberals to retaliate. Maybe Tremayne would have calmed the hot-heads, but he was preoccupied with a sick wife in Cannes, leaving Carew as the only critic of the move, and his pessimism was mistaken for modesty.[28] By now the Game Laws and Tenant Right pre-empted most other issues, and as William Snell eulogised Carew's pro-farmer opinions on both, he was quickly adopted.

Soon afterwards Sir Colman Rashleigh reconsidered his decision not to stand for East Cornwall. He was quickly joined by Reginald Kelly, a Devon landowner who had an additional 3,000 acres in Cornwall. However loudly the Conservatives protested that they had decided upon two candidates only because they feared that the scandal-tainted Willyams might be successful in re-establishing himself, they could not escape the criticism that in bringing forward Carew they were acting provocatively.[29] It quickly became obvious, once the campaigning began, that Rashleigh's great personal popularity would carry him to victory. For Carew, on the other hand, there were constant reminders of the past. 'Sheviock' was continually raised at his meetings, while Snell's occasional presence on his platforms revived the bitterness of 1852 (Snell was one of Kendall's most fervent supporters).[30] The 1868 'Colvill Cry' also resurfaced, because Rashleigh was a member of the Gaol Committee which had made the initial recommendation to increase the governor's salary.

Yet the contest was much more than a parade of recriminations over past controversies. All the candidates wished to see some degree of change to the Game Laws – Tremayne and Carew favouring their abolition, and a strong law of trespass in their place, Rashleigh, believing the existing situation on Lord Mt Edgcumbe's properties (where tenants had rights to all but winged game), would soon be the law of the land – while both Liberals favoured some form of relief from local taxation, as well as agreeing on the principle of fair compensation to tenants for unexhausted improvements at the end of their

---

[28] Conservative meeting at Lostwithiel, 30 Jan. 1874, reported in the *Royal Cornwall Gazette*, 31 Jan. 1874, 4.
[29] Ibid. 21 Feb. 1874, 4.
[30] Report of the Callington meeting, ibid. 7 Feb. 1874, 4.

tenancies.[31] Finally, when the poll closed, the result was much as everyone except the most optimistic Conservatives had expected:

Sir Colman Rashleigh	Liberal	3,396
John Tremayne	Conservative	3,376
W. H. Pole Carew	Conservative	3,099
Reginald Kelly	Liberal	2,983

For Carew in particular it must have been a galling outcome – over £2,000 wasted on a contest he could ill afford, and one which resurrected unpleasant memories.[32] For Tremayne the opposite applied. After years of vacillating and start-stop candidacies he belatedly took the plunge – successfully. It was also significant that this was not a victory for his family name and past traditions, for he, of all the eastern Conservatives, had at long last realised the futility of engaging in electoral politics according to the rules of his father's day, when the influence of large landowners was so important. As for his party, there were clear signs of the need for further electoral education. Some Conservatives plumped for one candidate rather than splitting their votes, a certain sign of long-standing problems.[33] As one perceptive observer admitted, it was necessary to elect a Conservative Committee (as distinct from the Registration Association)

> which should have absolute power over the machinery of the party & even to the extent of nominating or withdrawing a candidate. It is the want of this unanimity and central power which has always wrecked the Conservative cause in East Cornwall. I believed we suffered from it in the late contest but all this had better be forgotten.[34]

In addition, some of the Conservative gentry still seemed ambivalent towards the undoubted power of the farmers.

Most of these weaknesses remained until 1880. Kept away from Cornwall by parliamentary duties, Tremayne could no longer superintend the registrations. The suggested Central Committee did not materialise, so when the next general election took place, most Conservatives hoped Tremayne could slip in without a contest, thereby concealing their weakness. Unfortunately for them, when the Liberals learned how unpopular he was in the Mevagissey district adjoining Tremayne's seat of Heligan, they quickly brought forward another Cornishman, W. C. Borlase, to partner Charles Robartes.[35] By then the farmers had learned to their cost that a Disraeli-led Conservative government promised far more than it delivered with regard to the Game Laws or

---

31 Ibid. reports of Liberal meetings at Calstock and Callington.
32 'Election 1874 – W. H. Pole Carew Esq. – election expenses', MSS Carew Pole CO/CC/26.
33 *Royal Cornwall Gazette*, 21 Feb. 1874, 4.
34 John Coode to Jonathan Rashleigh, 4 Mar. 1874, RIC, MSS Rashleigh, Rash 4/55.
35 Downing to Vivian, 25 Mar. 1880, MSS Pendarves Vivian PV (290) 7.

Table 17
Borough electorates, 1865, 1868

Borough	Voters 1865	Voters 1868
Bodmin	397	886
Helston	348	1,029
Launceston	371	749
Liskeard	434	881
Penryn & Falmouth	837	1,546
St Ives	486	1,514
Truro	567	1,435

Sources: *Numbers of electors, 1865–6*, PP 1866 lvii. 23; *McCalmont's parliamentary poll book*.

tenant right. This motivated them to perform yet another of their well-known U turns; the result was that Tremayne, like Kendall before him, was savaged by the tiger he once had firmly by the tail. Borlase in particular posed as the 'farmers friend', flirting with the Farmers' Alliance and ultimately being elected with Robartes.[36]

Continuity and change in borough politics, 1868–80

In the aftermath of the 1867 Reform Act the political life of Cornwall's boroughs underwent comparatively few changes. Bodmin, still the official county town, but rapidly declining in importance in comparison with Truro, lost one member; otherwise the most dramatic impact was in the sudden expansion of the electorates, now that urban householders were entitled to vote (see table 17).

Although the totals more than doubled, the general elections of 1868, 1874 and 1880 revealed few alterations to the political characteristics of several towns. For example the addition of almost 400 voters to the registers made little difference to the ability of the owner of the Werrington Park estate to control Launceston's representation. It remained one of the last pocket boroughs in England, steadfastly returning a succession of Conservative outsiders eager to enter the House of Commons. Amazingly, there was a complete absence of contested elections at Launceston from 1837 to 1874. Thereafter, step by step the Liberals gradually whittled away the Conservative majority. Bodmin shared Launceston's pocket borough status. Writing in 1905 Edward Leveson Gower recalled how, 'Through the intervention of Mr Hayter, the whip, Mr Robartes, the Member for the Eastern Division of

[36] *Royal Cornwall Gazette*, 26 Mar. 1880, 8.

Cornwall, offered to get me returned for Bodmin.'[37] Leveson Gower represented the borough from 1859 until 1885, relying as much on a network of powerful friends, foremost among them Thomas Robartes, as on the support of the voters. Among these friends were the Molesworths of Pencarrow and the Vivians of Glynn, substantial landowning families long influential in the town, together with Bodmin's chief constable, Colonel Gilbert, and Mr Hicks, head of the county asylum.[38] As a staunch Gladstonian Liberal, Leveson Gower managed to satisfy his principal supporters both within and on the outskirts of the town. His tenure was therefore never seriously threatened, although he was most unhappy about spending more than £1,000 to successfully defend himself against charges of bribery in 1868. Leveson Gower admitted that life would have been far tougher for him if a Cornishman had stood against him, but as none was forthcoming, he and his patron had few concerns.[39]

Nearby Liskeard remained the jewel in the Cornish Liberals' crown. When Sir Arthur Buller died in 1869 he was replaced by Edward Horsman, who, like Leveson Gower, was an outsider. This was one among several reasons why the Cornish-born Leonard Courtney unsuccessfully attempted to unseat him in 1874, and when Horsman died two years later, succeeded in his goal of becoming the town's MP. Courtney, born in Penzance in 1832, was a former Fellow of St John's College, Cambridge, and between 1872 and 1875 Professor of Political Economy at University College, London.[40] Because of these achievements his native county regarded him as one of its favourite sons (in 1906 he became Lord Courtney of Penwith), and certainly the Liskeard voters were prepared to overlook his occasionally idiosyncratic liberalism. At Helston Adolphus Young, antipodean carpet bagger and Liberal, finally beat off his rivals in 1868. Besides winning the praises of the town's many Nonconformists by promising his warmest support for a Permissive Bill and Irish church disestablishment, he also rode to victory on the backs of those voluble and stirring Liberal solicitors, Henry and Thomas Rogers who left nothing to chance in 1868.[41] The younger Rogers, Henry, marched the men in from nearby Trumpet Consols Mine, in processional order,

> and stood at the polling booth, calling out each man's name and telling them whom to vote for. We understand that not a man has been employed in the mine for months past unless he was on the list of voters, and each man was obliged to sign a book that he would vote for Young.[42]

---

[37] Leveson Gower, *Bygone years*, 243.
[38] Ibid. 246–9.
[39] Ibid. 245–6.
[40] *Who's who of British members of parliament*, II: *1886–1918*, ed. Michael Stenton and Stephen Lees, Hassocks 1978, 79.
[41] *Royal Cornwall Gazette*, 19 Nov. 1868, 5–6.
[42] Ibid. 5.

These and other ongoing forms of electoral chicanery led one knowledgeable West Cornwall solicitor to say of Helston and its inhabitants, 'Bribery and intimidation of all sorts on the part of both parties have always been resorted to in their miserable borough contests.'[43]

Like Helston, Truro too was, in its own way, unique. By 1868 the politics of convenient compromise had been polished by almost thirty years of continuous usage. So skilled were the participants that they could hoodwink innocent outsiders such as the Reform League which in that year seriously believed there were good prospects for one of its candidates being elected. Unfortunately the league's emissaries were befriended by a group of dissident Liberals who chafed at the alliance between the sitting members Captain J. C. Vivian and Sir Frederick Williams.[44] The candidate chosen by the league to break this deadlock, Passmore Edwards, was far too radical for the dissidents who quickly ditched him and plumped for Vivian. After this Liberal debacle the situation worsened to such a degree that in 1871, when Vivian was appointed Lord of the Treasury, the Conservatives seized the chance to overturn the compromise and replace him with an 'outsider', James Hogg, who did everything in his power to entice Truro's working men into his corner. Because the Liberals were completely unprepared for the surprise 1874 election, Hogg and Williams had no trouble in retaining their seats. Still, the Conservatives left nothing to chance. With their long-time solicitor P. P. Smith, and the actuary for the Truro Savings Bank, Thomas Chirgwin, in charge of their electoral organisation, there were few problems. Chirgwin was obviously John Tippet's successor, devoting his time to 'going through his books and making those arrangements and calculations so necessary to success'.[45] Apparently more thorough than his predecessor, he was acknowledged as the architect of this 1874 Conservative victory.

Six years later an obvious Liberal resurgence in the town caused a return to the familiar compromise, although not without an outburst of anger on the part of rank and file Conservatives. That a small coterie (Chirgwin and his allies) could make such a far-reaching decision, was, they believed, unacceptable.[46] They showed their disagreement with the decision by hastily bringing a succession of strangers to Truro. All the prospective candidates surveyed the local political scene, then left almost as quickly as they had arrived. The reality was that the Conservative leaders, relying on Chirgwin's carefully formed opinions, rightly concluded that a second candidate had no hope.[47] Thus Truro, as it had done throughout most of the nineteenth century,

[43] Downing to Vivian, 8 July 1868, MSS Pendarves Vivian PV (290) 1.
[44] See Messrs Coffey and Odger to Howell, 18 Aug. 1868, Bishopgate Institute, London, George Howell Collection, 'Election Reports 1868'; for reports on electioneering see Royal Cornwall Gazette, 3, 10 Sept.; 8, 29 Oct. 1868.
[45] Ibid. 7 Feb. 1874, 4.
[46] Ibid. 26 Mar. 1880, 4.
[47] Ibid. 12 Mar. 1880, 4.

mirrored more general changes taking place in Cornish electoral politics. The compromise of 1880 showed how this was so.

> Experience had proved that since the introduction of Household Suffrage the old system, which entrusted the management of a borough to a few men, who pulled the wires in secret . . . without consulting the bulk of the electors had not worked satisfactorily. The enlarged constituencies cannot be got at in this way; the opinions of the bulk of the people, and the reasons which influence their actions are not known, hence blunders are inevitable.[48]

This applied almost everywhere, even in Penryn & Falmouth and St Ives where previously election outcomes were generally determined by factors other than voters' preferences. During the 1870s and 1880s it became clear that old influences and the small conclaves of solid, middle-class men who managed the party organisations were being successfully challenged by a new wave of activists. Just as fifty years before borough candidates had courted middle-class voters, now it was unusual for them to fail to address the concerns of working men.

The resurgence of issues

If, as we saw earlier, issues subsided in importance in the decade or so before the Second Reform Act, following it they moved back into the spotlight as events in East Cornwall reveal. It was the same in 1868 in the west where Pendarves Vivian took great pains over his election address. After consulting with his advisers who, more than anything else were determined to maintain the Liberal–Methodist nexus, he spelt out his unwavering support for the disestablishment of the Irish Church, believing it would bring a measure of simple justice to the Irish people.[49] Cleverly combining a national and local focus, he also was in favour of abolishing whatever disabilities arose from religious beliefs and reductions in the level of local taxation. This was an approach adopted by many other sitting members and candidates. Six years later Pendarves Vivian stood on his and the Gladstone government's record, besides reaffirming his views on local finances. He went on, 'In politics and general legislation there will be much still to be done by the new parliament. The questions of local government and taxation, of the sales of spirituous liquors, of the relation of landlord and tenant, and of the present state of the game and land laws must all be considered and dealt with.'[50] These were the important issues to which all parliamentary candidates had to direct their attention in the 1870s and early 80s.

Potentially the Game Laws had the capacity to divide landlords and

---

48 Ibid. 2 Apr. 1880, 4.
49 Copy of printed address, MSS Pendarves Vivian PV (290) 1.
50 Copy of printed election address, 1874, ibid. PV (209), 16.

tenants into irate opponents; in reality the divisions were rarely so obvious. The arguments were based upon a landlord's feudal right to both winged and ground game, each of which could cause serious losses of crops if unchecked by gamekeepers, owner or, by special arrangements, the tenants. Enlightened landlords usually came to some amicable arrangement over the extermination of hares and rabbits, but always there were exceptions. And, obviously, winged game posed awkward problems too. Brydges Willyams, Nicholas Kendall and John Tremayne were among the Cornish landlords who were at various times roundly criticised for their attitudes or actions on this thorny topic. However its impact at Launceston was unsurpassed in a county where the Game Laws preoccupied every parliamentary candidate in the 1870s and 1880s.[51]

Colonel James Deakin purchased the Werrington Park estate in 1871; like previous owners he expected that the Launceston seat came with the property. So at the next general election he decided to stand as the Conservative candidate. However, between 1872 and 1874 the district's rabbit population had exploded, much to the concern of local farmers and the townspeople. Deakin, who lived in Manchester, was unaware of the problem, while his gamekeepers were profiting by shooting the rabbits and sending them to London for sale.[52] Deakin's Liberal opponent, Herbert Drinkwater, quickly exploited the issue by arguing for alterations to the Game Laws so that tenants would have the right to ground game. Faced with a candidate who exposed an embarrassing political weakness (his lack of interest in the Game Laws), plus angry farmers and townspeople, Deakin was forced to confront the topic. He did so in a unique way, announcing at the Launceston election meeting that tenants and townspeople could kill as many rabbits as they wished, and sell them – a significant alteration to the terms of the leases. Deakin's none-too-subtle form of bribery was soon exposed by a successful petition. In the course of the hearings it became clear how the Game Laws had dominated the election, and eventually Deakin was unseated, only to be replaced by another Conservative.

Whereas the liquor question was one among several minor issues raised by Cornish parliamentary candidates in the 1850s and 60s, after 1868 its significance increased. This was partly due to frustration arising from the failure of earlier campaigns for the Permissive Bill. It can also be explained by the broadening of the franchise in 1867: more Methodists were eligible to vote thus, as in the case of Pendarves Vivian, candidates and MPs tailored their policies in order to win support. The Permissive Bill could undoubtedly influ-

---

[51] Willyams and Kendall were repeatedly questioned on this at public meetings in 1868, Tremayne in 1874.
[52] *House of Commons, accounts and papers*, PP 1874, liii. 421–62 (Launceston). The following details are from this source and from E. L. O'Malley and H. Hardcastle, *Reports of the decisions of the judges for the trial of election petitions in England and Ireland, pursuant to the Parliamentary Elections Act, 1868*, i, London 1870

ence election outcomes in certain constituencies. At the 1869 Liskeard by-election following the death of Sir Arthur Buller two Liberals, Horsman and Lycett, competed to replace him. But, the latter lost vital Nonconformist support when it was alleged that his conversion to liquor reform was very recent – a damaging accusation in a temperance stronghold.[53] Even so, Nonconformity and good temperance candidates did not always go hand-in-hand, a point illustrated in the same town when in 1874 several prominent teetotal Wesleyans invited Leonard Courtney to oppose Horsman.[54] Neither at this time nor later did Courtney support the Permissive Bill, and as Liskeard's MP from 1876 to 1885 he resisted pressure to declare his backing for the Cornwall Sunday Closing Bill. In some ways Courtney's independent Liberalism paralleled that of Charles Buller, one of his predecessors.

By 1880 the Permissive Bill had been dropped by the United Kingdom Alliance, which preferred to push Sir Wilfred Lawson's Local Option alternative. The purpose of this was to hand to localities the power to deal with the licensing of public houses, rather than the more prescriptive prohibition. In the 1880 election nine of Cornwall's elected Liberals publicly favoured this new alternative.[55] Soon afterwards, in 1881, Pendarves Vivian initiated the Cornwall Sunday Closing movement – yet another variation on the temperance theme. The idea was simple – following the precedents of Scotland and Wales public houses should remain closed on Sundays. In Cornwall, according to Peter Heydon, the movement 'combined aristocratic and Anglican patronage with the zeal and numbers of Cornish Nonconformists'.[56] By 1882 Sunday Closing had generated a surprising degree of support: more than 100,000 inhabitants over the age of sixteen signed a petition, all town mayors except one approved of it and so did eleven of the thirteen members of parliament.[57] Despite this Pendarves Vivian and the earl of Mt Edgcumbe, who led the fight at Westminster, had no success. What the movement did prove was the strength of Nonconformity in Cornwall and its impact on the borough and county Liberals, all of whom willingly associated themselves with it.

One of the few national pressure groups of the period to make a conspicuous effort in Cornwall was the Farmers' Alliance. Formed in 1879, its objects were to secure better parliamentary representation for tenant farmers, improve the farmer's contractual relationship with his landlord, gain security for capital invested and improved acreage, and reform of the Game Laws.[58] Such a platform was certain to appeal to many Cornish farmers. Well aware of the political virility of the county's eastern agriculturists, James Youngman,

---

[53] Hayden, 'Culture, creed and conflict', 157.
[54] Ibid. 159.
[55] Ibid. 161.
[56] Ibid. 162.
[57] Ibid. 163.
[58] J. R. Fisher, 'The farmers' alliance: an agricultural protest movement of the 1880s', *Agricultural History Review* xxvi (1978), 15–25.

an Alliance committee-man, and W. E. Bear its industrious secretary, did their best during a visit in March 1880 to persuade the outspoken William Snell to come forward as an Alliance candidate in the forthcoming general election.[59] Snell, a veteran agitator for more than thirty years, regretfully declined the offer, however the Alliance's Callington and Liskeard branches formulated what became known as the 'Callington Platform' – in which tenant right was very prominent. Both Borlase (an Alliance member), and Robartes, the victorious East Cornwall Liberal candidates in 1880, made a point of giving the Platform their wholehearted support because they knew this was agreeable to the farmers, whose long tradition of independence usually took an anti-aristocratic, Liberal form. Elsewhere the Alliance was far less prominent, but there were few candidates for either party who disregarded the concerns of tenant farmers.

In the 1880s public issues continued to dominate electioneering, almost to the total exclusion of personalities. As an acknowledged area of Nonconformist supremacy Cornwall was graced by few candidates who ignored the activities of the Liberation society, or the temperance movement. For example the Liberationists' conference at Truro in 1884 resulted in a rapid revival of the disestablishment issue in western Cornwall. Two years earlier in East Cornwall the Liberals had made desperate efforts to swing a vital by-election their way, successfully pressuring the Gladstone government to provide for a second reading of the Cornwall Sunday Closing Bill. C. T. D. Acland's eventual victory over John Tremayne was generally attributed to this timely concession.[60] The farmers too forced MPs to think hard about their bases of support. By 1884 Borlase was an overt populist, intent on projecting himself to the lower-middle and working classes, and always concerned to satisfy their demands.

After the Third Reform Act such voters commanded a respect in proportion to their numbers. Some, of course, were quick to profit by that realisation.

Conversely, with only one or two exceptions, the powerful landed and commercial families could no longer promote particular candidates with total disregard for voters, or manipulate election outcomes. Nor did they play a meaningful role in party organisation. Yet they continued to provide candidates for public office because family members had the income and time to be members of parliament. This is why a glance at McCalmont's parliamentary poll book suggests little change over the century. The two Tremaynes, John and Arthur, were MPs in the 1870s and the Robartes name was similarly prominent. So were the Williams, Acland, St Aubyn, Molesworth-St Aubyn, Willyams and Praed families. Together they satisfied one of the most enduring needs of the Cornish – for locally born MPs who could identify with the

59 *Royal Cornwall Gazette*, 5 Mar. 1880, 4.
60 MSS Pendarves Vivian PV (290) 24, 29, contain details of the Cornwall Sunday Closing Movement.

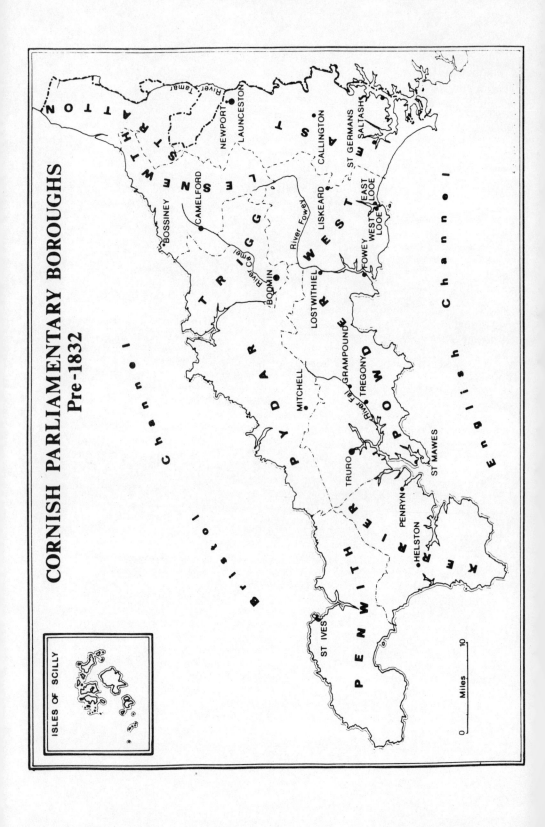

CORNISH PARLIAMENTARY BOROUGHS
Pre-1832

STRATTON

NEWSLEY

TRIGG

EAST

WEST

POWDER

PENWITH

KERRIER

ISLES OF SCILLY

Bristol Channel

English Channel

River Tamar

NEWPORT
LAUNCESTON
ST GERMANS
SALTASH
CALLINGTON
LISKEARD
EAST LOOE
WEST LOOE
FOWEY
BOSSINEY
CAMELFORD
River Camel
BODMIN
LOSTWITHIEL
River Fowey
MITCHELL
GRAMPOUND
TREGONY
River Fal
TRURO
ST MAWES
PENRYN
HELSTON
ST IVES

Miles
0   10

county. Even so, this outward continuity was deceptive. In most respects electoral politics in the 1880s bore little resemblance to the much earlier era of patronage.

Working men's politics in Camborne, 1885

The new face of electoral politics may be seen in the most controversial of all the 1885 elections in Cornwall, that for the Camborne or Mining division. It demonstrates how much the political culture of the western part of the county had altered since the 1860s, for besides the familiar combination of local and national issues, and the undeniable importance of Methodism, the election also exposed the importance of working men's votes. This election, and others in Cornwall, apparently reinforce the generally held view of 1885 as a watershed in English electoral politics.

According to such an interpretation the 1883 Corrupt Practices Act, the significant alterations to the franchise one year later, together with the redistribution of seats in February 1885 resulted in dramatic changes. This appears to be undeniable; one and a half million voters were added to the registers, a total greater than the combined additions of the 1832 and 1867 Reform Acts. Counties, most of them Conservative strongholds, were divided into several single seat divisions, following acceptance by Gladstone's Liberal government of the Conservative opposition's principle, 'that seats should be occupied according to population'.[61] Together the three acts produced a fundamental transformation; henceforth the voting power of the rural and urban working classes could never be neglected. Cornwall too underwent a dramatic metamorphosis: in 1884 26,000 electors returned thirteen members for nine constituencies. As table 18 reveals, the number of electors doubled in 1885, while the number of seats was almost halved.

Such a transformation seems to support the contention of some historians that this was the dawn of the era of mass politics, of widespread political participation characteristic of the twentieth century. But was it really the dawning of mass politics, because there is also a plethora of opinions about when various changes first appeared.

The Camborne election and Cornwall politics generally may clarify the impact of the Third Reform Act through the consideration of several questions. For example, did the aristocracy and gentry retain an important measure of control over candidate selection and party organisation? What were the most notable changes in party organisation and who initiated them? Should the frequently made suggestion that 1885 heralded the emergence of new electioneering methods remain unchallenged? And was there a heightened level of public debate about major issues?

---

[61] C. Seymour, *Electoral reform in England and Wales: the development of the parliamentary franchise, 1832–85*, Newton Abbot 1970, 513.

Table 18
Cornwall, 1885 general election

Constituency	Electors	Voters	Turnout %
Bodmin division	9,158	7,355	80.3
Camborne division	7,139	5,563	77.1
Launceston division	9,297	7,277	78.5
St Austell division	8,860	6,647	75.0
St Ives division	7,606	5,889	77.4
Truro–Helston	8,825	6,699	75.9
Penryn & Falmouth	2,562	2,239	87.4
Totals	53,447	41,609	78.8% average

Source: *British parliamentary election results, 1885–1918*, ed. F. W. S. Craig, London 1974.

Total population of Cornwall in 1885 = 330,686

Each of these questions must be answered in the context of the greatly increased number of registered voters in Cornwall: among those enfranchised were numerous working miners, farm labourers and semi or unskilled workers employed in small manufacturing enterprises in the Redruth–Camborne area. Many were staunch Methodists; most possessed the typically Cornish independence of outlook. Growing concern at loss of jobs, extension of voting rights, the egalitarian nature of Methodism, all contributed to greater participation in electoral politics by working-class men and women. In 1884–5 in west Cornwall there were repeated references to a new element, the 'lower stratum', the 'irresponsible new element', the 'violent party' and the 'working miners'.[62] By their participation and political behaviour did they and others like them bring a new element into electoral politics?

Greater public involvement in electoral politics

Conjecture surrounds the degree to which England's landed class was actively involved in late Victorian county politics. Yet almost all the conclusions derive from the prior assumption that in the mid 1880s significant change was occurring in the role of those referred to by one historian as 'natural leaders'.[63] This was not so in Cornwall, because there the aristocracy and wealthy gentry conceded their political weakness and irrelevance long before the

[62] See particularly the election reports in the *West Briton* between May and December 1885.

[63] J. Howarth, 'The Liberal revival in Northamptonshire, 1880–1895: a case study in late nineteenth-century elections', *Historical Journal* xii (1969), 80.

beginning of the 1880s. Indeed in 1852, if not earlier, Nicholas Kendall's victory provided unmistakable evidence that the Conservatives' natural leaders had lost the right to elect their nominees. Never again did those families seriously attempt to regain their previously influential role, a point illustrated by their loss of both East Cornwall seats in 1868. The reaction to that defeat was a party revival, but despite being initiated by the gentry the farmers were the real catalyst, and they maintained their pivotal role in electoral politics up to and beyond the Third Reform Act.

As we have seen, developments in West Cornwall were different. The absence of contested elections between 1832 and 1884 meant that the Liberal stranglehold was complete, representation usually being shared between the agricultural and mining interests. The two MPs were chosen after consultation among the 'natural leaders', many of whom had a hand in each of the major forms of economic activity. In 1868 Vivian was the chosen nominee of three of the county's richest men, J. M. Williams, Thomas Robartes and Viscount Falmouth, the selection process being outwardly similar to earlier decades. There was, however, one important difference: the genuine concern to prevent Vivian's candidacy being seen as the wish of an influential few. The middle-class men who now dominated the party's organisation would not tolerate such unilateral action if they heard of it – and to antagonise them could be fatal. East Cornwall politics proved the point.

The mood for change gathered pace in the 1870s; not only were the aristocracy and gentry pushed aside, the middle-class party managers were being pressured by voters and non-voters. By 1879–80 St Aubyn and Vivian knew that the restlessness in West Cornwall was partly due to economic tensions, as well as being stimulated by their reluctance to appear more regularly at meetings of various organisations.[64] Simultaneously, the Liberal organisation was criticised for its tendency to keep party activity to a minimum in order to avoid provoking possible Conservative opposition. The hegemony of the party managers began to weaken; the growth of working men's associations and Joseph Chamberlain's radicalism also played a part, the result in 1883–4 being a divided Liberal party.

Growing public involvement in electoral politics is demonstrated by the candidate selection procedures in June 1885 for the Camborne division. Several Liberal Associations (for example, Redruth, Camborne, St Agnes) had been in existence for almost a year; by February 1885 it had been agreed that all parishes within an association should be consulted when likely candidates were considered. In May, 10 per 1,000 population was agreed upon as the basis for calculating a parish's representation on the Liberal Central Committee.[65] As for the final selection of a Liberal candidate, after a process dubbed by some as 'a competition in loquacity' it was carried out at a public

[64] Jaggard, 'Patrons, principles and parties', ch. vii.
[65] *West Briton*, 14 May 1885, 6.

meeting in Camborne's Assembly Rooms. Almost 500 delegates voted on behalf of their parishes, the result being Vivian 250 votes, Conybeare 191. Amid great argument the latter then refused to accept the decision, insisting that he would go to the poll.[66]

When comparing these public procedures (which were almost identical in the adjoining Truro–Helston division) with those of 1868, it is obvious that a private, almost furtive party organisation dominated by men of social and financial standing, had been overturned. By 1885 the Liberal party's organisation was more broadly based, embracing both Whig and Radical wings. Parliamentary candidates were now publicly evaluated, but Vivian was slow to realise the changes of strategy this required. One of his friends bluntly told him he needed enthusiasm and energy in his campaign:

> Instead of this there has been the old dry-as-dust plan of picking out a man here and there who perhaps has more money or employs more men or for some other equally useless reason and the reins thus seem to have been dropped into the hands of those who are doubtless clever at laying plans and industrious too in working them but who fail to see the real point.[67]

This was that the attitude of the electorate had changed; the new political milieu required the predominantly middle-class men around Vivian to work co-operatively with representatives of the working classes.

Growing public activism, 1880–5

As with many English counties in the late Victorian years, the level of organised political activity in Cornwall fluctuated markedly between decades. More often than not the parties depended on a handful of dedicated loyalists, their identity sometimes remaining hidden from public view. In Cornwall the changes which appeared after 1880 did not arise from the legislation of 1884–5. Instead they resulted from very different pressures which shaped the patterns of county politics from the start of the decade.

Towards the end of the 1870s in West Cornwall there were persistent demands for the introduction of public meetings at which the two MPs, St Aubyn and Vivian, could speak on the issues of the day.[68] This occurred well before similar requests in such counties as Lincolnshire and Northamptonshire, and was probably symptomatic of growing economic tensions in the county. Criticisms were voiced about the members' seeming lack of interest in the electorate's concerns, without being translated into public opposition to their position.

Privately, St Aubyn was disturbed by these signs. He had no doubt that he

66 Ibid. 18 June 1885, 14.
67 John Thomas to Vivian, 19 Aug. 1885, MSS Pendarves Vivian PV (290) 126.
68 Jaggard, 'Patrons, principles and parties', 388.

and Vivian would be re-elected without difficulty in 1880, 'but I don't feel quite so sure about the next Election afterwards and trouble then is more likely to come from our side than from the other'.[69] Two inferences can be drawn from this opinion, the first, that the Liberals, a majority of whom were undoubtedly Methodists, were now dividing, the radicals being the divergent group. The second was that a possible reason for this splintering was the Liberal organisation, dominated by men of wealth and smug respectability who prided themselves on spending little money on electioneering and registration expenses, and who had now alienated many rank-and-file supporters. Just as these middle-class party managers had previously usurped the aristocracy and landed gentry, now their leadership was under attack. Elements among the working classes, increasingly confident in their radicalism, and stirred into action by such issues as church disestablishment and the local option, pressed for a change of political status. The growing public clamour signified instability, which in turn foreshadowed change. How to reconcile the dissident Methodists to a Liberal party organisation in need of rejuvenation, was a critical question for all concerned.

Early in 1881 William Grylls, one of the party's solicitors, summarised the problem:

> The Methodist bodies are often spoken of as almost the key of the position in West Cornwall – I believe there is some exaggeration in this – but speaking more particularly of the old Wesleyans Society the most important in number & influence, if they work unitedly it will be on behalf of the Liberal and not the Conservative section of the party, supposing both such exist, and this should not be lost sight of in introducing new members to the General Committee. Their preachers and people may now be depended on, much more than 25 years ago, as Liberals – and I am certain will not be so tied down by the influence of some of their leading members.[70]

Therefore Grylls suggested that Vivian should create the impression of being identified with the liberal wing of the party. Soon afterward Vivian was also urged to broaden the party's organisational membership by including younger men at different levels in the structure – even if they were not voters.[71]

Apparently this was not successful for the predicted rupture happened in 1883–4, despite the efforts of Vivian and St Aubyn to control the situation. The Liberal party fractured because of what St Aubyn saw as 'the extreme, and I am afraid violent, party about Redruth and Camborne'.[72] Among them were town labourers and the miners in the adjoining parishes, men who were staunch Wesleyans and radical in their politics. The party organisers wished to keep their heads down and tinker with the tried and trusted methods,

---

[69] St Aubyn to Vivian, 1 Feb. 1880, MSS Pendarves Vivian PV (290) 7.
[70] Grylls to Vivian, 21 Jan. 1881, ibid. 8.
[71] Vivian's correspondence, Feb. 1881, ibid.
[72] St Aubyn to Vivian, 27 Feb. 1884, ibid. 11.

hoping they would prevail, while the bulk of the party's followers wanted much more; they were better informed than in the past, 'and like to talk and feel they are nearer their Representatives'.[73] One outcome was that early in 1884 Liberal Associations were formed in Redruth, Camborne and Truro. After the electoral redistribution of 1885 the Liberals initiated consultation among all parishes within associations before parliamentary candidates were chosen.

West Cornwall's Conservatives underwent a very different metamorphosis. Although active and successful in the three western boroughs, St Ives, Helston and Truro, where their organisational networks were traditionally strong, at the county level after 1868 they remained a negligible force. The aristocracy and landed gentry had lost interest in active involvement, particularly at the annual registrations which they had shunned for years. In 1880–1 however, a change of outlook was noticeable. Possibly it was a response to the same problems (the demand for public meetings) worrying St Aubyn and Vivian. Any disenchantment with the sitting members could help the Conservative cause, so they began to stir themselves.

The driving force was a middle-aged Truro solicitor, John Chilcott, who sought and received support for his initiative from fellow solicitors elsewhere in West Cornwall.[74] The next step was the long overdue formation of a Conservative Association in May 1881, together with the systematic spreading of rumours about the influence of Viscount Falmouth. Publicly pro-Liberal for years, Falmouth was now allegedly informing farmers near Truro that he would soon change his political views.[75] Such a *volte-face*, which would have been of great assistance to the Conservatives, so alarmed Vivian and St Aubyn that the former met with Falmouth to seek reassurance of his support. He duly received it.[76]

The newly formed Conservative Association was a public reunion of several hitherto divided gentry families – among them the Tremaynes, Vivians, Rogers and Rashleighs. Besides busying itself attending to county registrations, more importantly the association agreed upon a candidate for West Cornwall – Carew Davies Gilbert, a young man with substantial estates near Truro. Gilbert was then encouraged to canvass the division, and according to an unsurprised St Aubyn, more than five-sixths of the electors west of Penzance signed a Conservative requisition for him. To Vivian he admitted:

My own belief is that from one cause or another the purely agricultural districts would show a tory majority – and that it is the Liberal feeling in the urban districts which will save the seats. . . . The truth is that a large number of

73 David Bain to Vivian, 1 Mar. 1884, ibid.
74 Chilcott correspondence, CRO, MSS Rogers RO 8155–220.
75 Various correspondents to Vivian, 14–26 May 1881, MSS Pendarves Vivian PV (290) 8.
76 Ibid.

those who depend exclusively upon land (of <u>all</u> classes) are getting thoroughly frightened – and of course they will express their feeling by their votes.[77]

It was an astute move by the Conservatives to take advantage of this mood, thereby exacerbating divisions among the Liberals. Unhappily for his supporters, Gilbert proved to be a woeful public speaker, so after five months of spasmodic activity he retired, and in 1883 peace returned for a few months.

Chilcott was not prepared to sit back and watch the Liberals fight among themselves. He rightly believed that the dissension would be aggravated by the appearance of a fresh Conservative candidate, consequently in February 1884 another Truro meeting was called. Although headed by familiar gentry names such as Tremayne, Williams, Collins and Rashleigh, some of whom had represented or been candidates for various Cornish seats, those attending were a curious mixture of religious and economic interests. Among them were Anglican clergymen, six prominent Nonconformists, lawyers, shopkeepers, accountants, farmers, spirit merchants, a forage dealer and a butcher.[78] The gentry and their usual allies, including the clerics, were decisively outvoted. H. J. Atkinson of Hull, a Wesleyan and prominent member of Conference, was chosen to contest West Cornwall. This was a remarkable decision for as a Conservative Wesleyan Atkinson could expect little support from Cornish Nonconformists, most of whom were Liberals. 'It is amusing', wrote one of Vivian's followers, 'to think of the old Tory aristocracy cheek by jowl with a political adventurer they would not have touched with a 9 foot pole under other circumstances – "How are the mighty fallen".'[79] Nor was the choice likely to maintain unity among the predominantly Anglican Conservatives. Nevertheless Atkinson quickly began a speaking tour in districts west of Truro, in the course of which he provoked such strong reactions that the political passivity long characteristic of the division finally disappeared.

Atkinson's electioneering took him far and wide in West Cornwall. Obviously a decision was taken to embarrass the Liberal MPs, who studiously avoided such exposure. The initial round of public meetings ended with him being shouted down in May at Penzance.[80] He then made intermittent speeches until October, without convincing anyone that he would be prepared to contest an election. However what Atkinson did succeed in demonstrating was that there was a demand for open meetings, something the radicals remembered in the months ahead.

One final point should be made about the West Cornwall Conservatives. Proof of their continuing determination to influence the course of electoral politics after the redistribution came in the course of their successful appear-

---

[77] St Aubyn to Vivian, 12 Apr. 1882, ibid. 9.
[78] A lively description of those attending may be found in William Lidgey to Vivian, 11 Feb. 1884, ibid. 11.
[79] John Thomas to Vivian, 13 Mar. 1884, ibid.
[80] David Bain to Vivian, 8 May 1884, ibid.

ance before the visiting Boundary Commissioner in December 1884. The Conservatives were happy with the suggested formation of a Western (St Ives) division. Conversely, they were very concerned about the possible union of Camborne with Helston and Redruth with Truro, in two further divisions.[81] In each of the old parliamentary boroughs they had strong support; that would be swamped by an influx of radical voters. It would therefore be preferable to have a separate (and obviously Liberal) mining division and link Truro–Helston where their chances of success were much greater. Because of their representations and the failure of the Liberals to make a persuasive case, this is what happened.

What is now clear is that the organisation of both parties underwent important changes in the 1880s, particularly before 1885. Internal divisions produced alterations to the Liberals' structure, partly due to the Liberal–radical split, and partly as a reaction to years of manipulation by a small but powerful group. The radicals quickly realised that electoral support was as much about public presentation of candidates as about registration, a lesson learned from the Conservatives early in the 1880s. As for the latter, their organisational revival was a timely response to disagreements among the Liberals, the result being much greater party activity in West Cornwall than in earlier decades.

Popular politics in Camborne

The outstanding features of the 1885 Camborne election were the strenuous campaigning of the candidates, together with the often vicious verbal and press attacks on Pendarves Vivian. Even before the Liberal Central Committee endorsed him in June as their candidate, the *West Briton* declared:

> For days and even weeks past, there has been an outpouring of political speeches, such as even the proverbial oldest inhabitant – let his memory cover ever so long a period – cannot remember. Places, at which for years, and even for generations – until the advent of Tory-Wesleyan Mr Atkinson – deliverances on political topics had not been made, have been visited, and stirred into life by the energy and zeal of Mr Vivian, Mr Conybeare and Mr Barker.[82]

What was the effect of this political education? According to the same source, 'The number of those who take an interest in politics is ever increasing, and men who have hitherto, perforce, been "dumb dogs" in regard to the government of this country, are now everywhere making their voices heard.'[83] Whether this was accurate is difficult to judge. Certainly the energetic promotion of political literacy by the radicals of West Cornwall was

81 *West Briton*, 5 Feb. 1885, 4; 23 Feb. 1885, 2.
82 Ibid. 11 June 1885, 2.
83 Ibid. 25 June 1885, 4.

new. Prior to this the Liberals had persuaded them to avoid such tactics for fear of Conservative retaliation. Therefore, in order to win support from these newly enfranchised 'dumb dogs', did the radicals adopt tactics previously unknown in the county?

In fact they were very familiar, although the audience was different: almost every aspect of electioneering employed in Camborne had been used in East Cornwall nearly twenty years earlier, by middle-class farmers. When they turned on Nicholas Kendall he sought support through widespread public meetings. From July to October 1868 he continuously addressed gatherings in towns and villages, hoping to change the minds of the yeomen, tenant farmers and townspeople. Although his efforts ended in failure, Kendall showed how opinions could be shaped by direct appeals to the people. In a highly politicised electorate such as East Cornwall there was always pressure on members to frequently appear in public, just as there was in Camborne in 1885.

This was demonstrated again in the East in the 1880 election and afterwards. Through the efforts of the second Liberal, Borlase, the party won both seats. Borlase's appeal was that of a stirring populist. Posing as the farmers' friend, for he was a forthright member of the Farmers' Alliance, Borlase, like Kendall before him, spent as much time in small villages as he did in larger towns.[84] His campaign strategy, having more in common with the twentieth than the nineteenth century, was closely followed by Conybeare and his advisers in Camborne. Soon after Borlase's victory, St Aubyn confided to his fellow West Cornwall MP, 'In my opinion holding political meetings will be taken (being a new thing) as a sign of weakness, will directly throw out a challenge to the opposition which they can hardly decline.'[85] With such an attitude, and with Borlase's public posturing being reported in the local press, it was not surprising that long before 1885 there was persistent agitation for public meetings in West Cornwall. After all, similar tactics were being applied by the East Cornwall Liberals. In that context St Aubyn and Vivian's dislike for Borlase is readily understandable.

West Cornwall's MPs had another reason for their antipathy. By 1884 the *Western Daily Mercury*, published in Plymouth, regularly attacked them, while openly supporting their East Cornwall Liberal counterparts Borlase and Acland. St Aubyn became annoyed about this, explaining to Vivian that 'Borlase is intimately mixed up with the management and, as you know, Northy [sic] (who writes one of the letters on Monday) is his head man and chief adviser in E. Cornwall.'[86] Borlase persuaded the *Mercury* to encourage the western radicals to pressure their MPs. As for Northey, a well-known political activist, he and Thomas Allanson, a St Columb manure merchant, had orchestrated Kendall's downfall in 1868. There was no guile in their

84 Jaggard, 'Patrons, principles and parties', ch. viii.
85 St Aubyn to Vivian, 26 Aug. 1881, MSS Pendarves Vivian PV (290) 8.
86 St Aubyn to Vivian, 27 Feb. 1884, ibid. 11.

tactics: they appeared at all of Kendall's meetings, interjecting, questioning, shouting and exposing his political weaknesses.[87] Dirty politics were nothing new to Northey, and the *Mercury* provided him and Borlase with an excellent forum for their views, as well as appealing to the radicals of Redruth and Camborne.

There was another way in which the unfortunate Kendall provided a model for future election campaigns: his re-election prospects in 1868 were ruined by a relatively minor local matter – support for a small increase in salary of a county official. The anti-Vivian forces applied the same techniques in the first six months of 1885, though with less success. Vivian had always been on shaky ground in West Cornwall, because he was the first non-Cornish MP to represent the county. To counter the criticism Vivian purchased a succession of Cornish properties including Glendorgal, an imposing residence near the north coast town of Newquay. Unfortunately, during his years as owner he chose to restrict public access to footpaths on his property, much to the disgust of the town's residents. In political terms the local meetings about this were a storm in a teacup.[88] But the episode was recalled later when he bought the Bosahan estate on the south coast, decided to renovate the residence and unwittingly snubbed Silvanus Trevail, a Truro architect who was a close friend of Northey. Between them Trevail and Northey concocted two scurrilous pamphlets which were widely circulated in West Cornwall in February and April 1885.[89] Vivian's personal behaviour and political beliefs were smeared in a way strongly reminiscent of the outcry against Kendall in 1868. Trevail's bitterness led him to remark of Vivian, 'I'll have my knife in him.'[90] He did so with a vengeance; by June 1885 Vivian's re-election prospects for the Camborne division were seriously weakened.

Insofar as electioneering was concerned, 1885 was not a watershed in Cornwall electoral politics. The often controversial speaking tours, the personal smears and the manipulation of the press were all familiar, especially in East Cornwall and several of the more hotly contested boroughs. The main difference was the appearance of a radical candidate whose campaign was imitative, cleverly conducted and, judging by the result, very effective.

The importance of issues

The final question concerns the extent to which issues influenced the 1885 election outcome. Francis Channing, who witnessed the election in Northamptonshire, thought the issues were obscure and tangled. Liberal success

---

[87] Reports of Kendall's meetings appear in the *West Briton*, July–September 1868.
[88] Series of letters to Vivian, Oct. 1881, MSS Pendarves Vivian PV (290) 8.
[89] Ibid. 13. Both pamphlets cited Vivian's apparent contempt for the people of Newquay during his ownership of Glendorgal.
[90] Northey to Vivian, 31 Oct. 1885, ibid.

owed much to 'the delight of the new voting power'.[91] Howarth's conclusion for the same county was that voting 'was influenced less by particular election issues than by a more generalised impression of what the parties stood for'.[92] In Camborne the election was about the way in which various issues clarified the Liberal and radical standpoints and, importantly, the differences between them. This may be illustrated by entries in the diaries of John Oates, a school-master at Blackwater, several miles north-east of Redruth.[93] Oates, a radical, was personally acquainted with several of the so-called 'Nobs' who ran the Liberal party's West Cornwall organisation. He became a Conybeare sup-porter in 1885, attending many of his meetings and sometimes travelling around the constituency with him. Throughout the six months of campaign-ing Oates, a thoughtful and articulate man, only occasionally mentioned the salient issues because for him, as a radical republican, they were already clear. More important was the reality of meetings in villages such as Blackwater, Mithian, Illogan and at various mines in the division. Oates was overjoyed to see electoral politics being brought to the working man in a way that had never happened before in West Cornwall.[94]

The Cornish miners appreciated the sharp differences on issues between Conybeare and Vivian. The candidates had directly opposing view-points on the abolition of the House of Lords and the Game Laws, free education for all, female suffrage and the payment of MPs. So clear were the contrasts that the voters readily identified with one side or the other. But new and old voters were also swayed by the simple fact of a candidate being prepared to speak to them face-to-face. Oates's description of a working men's meeting in September at Illogan was typical:

> One man said, 'Maaster Vivyan is a nice man and I respect Maaster Vivyan as a man; but wudn vote for n ef he was my own father' – Isaac Jenkin said, 'They do say we are revolutionised and want to turn things upside down, well [thats] exactly what we want to do. They've been wrong side up long enough for me.'[95]

Such comments were indicative of the opinion of many voters. Whereas in East Cornwall from 1852 issues had mobilised the farmers (protection and the county rate are two examples), Camborne's working-class voters were moved by various forces, issues being one among them. There was one strik-ing similarity between the two divisions in 1868 and 1885. Just as the middle-class farmers confirmed in 1868 that they would not follow their social superiors, so the working classes now rebuffed Camborne's middle-class Liberals. Encouraged by Conybeare, class clashed with class. In mining terms

---

91 Howarth, 'Liberal revival', 110.
92 Ibid. 98.
93 Diaries of John Oates, 1885, CRO, X, 629/4.
94 Ibid.
95 Entry for 30 Sept. 1885, ibid.

Table 19
Cornwall, 1885 general election, Camborne division

Electors	Turnout	Candidates	Party	Votes	%
7,139	77.1	C. A. V. Conybeare	Ind.L	2,926	53.2
		A. P. Vivian	Lib.	2,577	46.8

Source: *Parliamentary election results*, 239.

it was a contest between the 'count house' (management) and the 'dry' (workers). On 1 June the *West Briton* made a similar point: 'there exists a strong antipathy to the principle of landlordism. It is unfortunate for Mr Vivian that from the social position in which he is placed he must, to a certain extent, be affected by that prejudice.'[96] After more than a half century of being disregarded by the wealthy political wire-pullers of West Cornwall (Liberals and Conservatives), the working classes exulted in their new-found influence.

There was another way in which election issues helped Conybeare rather than Vivian. In mid November at one of the farmers' meetings Oates, the schoolmaster, noticed a number of men who had worked overseas. These, he felt, personified the broadening effect of travelling, 'especially in Republican countries'. Later the same month the *West Briton* reported that American influences were working in Conybeare's favour, with telegrams of support arriving from the USA.[97] According to John Rowe, 'Politics acquired in America and encouraged by Cousin Jacks still in the States' contributed to Conybeare's success. Miners who returned to Cornwall demanded the franchise for all adult males, besides holding the belief that in politics one man was just as good as another to represent people's interests in parliament.[98] Such straightforward arguments were frequently heard during electioneering.

When the outcome of the Camborne election was known there were complaints of wholesale 'ratting' by voters, and rule by a 'howling mob'.[99] Full of bitterness, Vivian attributed his defeat then and in later years to the tactics of his opponent, together with the treachery of some who professed to support him.[100] Never did he allude to the issues in either general or specific terms. Nor did the press. Inevitably some believed that radicalism had conquered Liberalism; indeed there were obvious policy differences between Vivian and Conybeare, which in turn produced polarities of opinion among voters and

[96] *West Briton*, 1 June 1885, 3.
[97] Diaries of John Oates, entry for 13 Nov. 1885; *West Briton*, 30 Nov. 1885, 2.
[98] J. Rowe, *The hard-rock men: Cornish immigrants and the North American mining frontier*, Liverpool 1974, 292.
[99] G. Robinson and J. R. Daniell to William Rich (Vivian's election agent) 5, 7 Dec. 1885, MSS Pendarves Vivian PV (290) 12d.
[100] Vivian to John Tremayne, 16 July 1895, ibid. 14.

non-voters. However during almost six months of campaigning they became submerged beneath discussion of personalities, generalities and Conybeare's electioneering tactics.

1885: changes in Cornish electoral politics?

In the 1885 general election Cornwall's county divisions, particularly Camborne, exhibited several characteristics identified with electoral politics in other counties. R. J. Olney found that in Lincolnshire 'It was no longer enough to dispense friendly nods in the market place and swallow an ordinary dinner with the farmers. Tradesmen and labourers who were unable to attend ordinaries expected to hear their Members at evening meetings.' Village meetings were now essential and time-consuming; worse were the town ones, 'where heckling and rowdiness were becoming more common'.[101] The same applied to Northamptonshire; few if any village meetings were held before 1885. Consequently villages had to be introduced to party political controversy and electioneering; face-to-face contact between voters and candidates was essential.[102] Cornwall was no different from Lincolnshire and Northamptonshire, because this style of electioneering had appeared in 1868, if not earlier.

As for the working class, Davis has suggested that until 1885 in Buckinghamshire they 'did not play a creative role in politics'.[103] William Hayes found evidence illustrating how from the 1870s the working class grew in political awareness and self confidence. Thus, 'the political centre of gravity tended to move downward on the social scale'.[104] This is confirmed by members of the working class of West Cornwall who were already developing a sense of political awareness by the end of the 1870s. It was heightened in the years prior to 1885, produced a split within Liberalism in West Cornwall, and was taken to its logical extreme in May 1885 when Conybeare was invited to address the Liberals of Camborne, as a prelude to becoming their candidate.

According to D. C. Moore another feature of the late Victorian period of transition was the transferral of the right to nominate, 'from the hands of the various elites who enjoyed their powers in respect of their "property and character", into the hands of committees most of which were formally elected'.[105] Olney differed from Moore on this, for the former found that in the early months of 1885 new constituencies appeared susceptible to old

---

101 Olney, Lincolnshire politics, 219.
102 Howarth, 'Liberal revival', 93–4.
103 Davis, Political change, 11.
104 W. A. Hayes, The background and passage of the Third Reform Act, New York 1982, 13–14.
105 D. C. Moore, 'The gentry', in G. E. Mingay (ed.), The Victorian countryside, London 1981, ii. 380.

interests. Only when those interests failed to supply sufficient candidates were they usurped or their powers eroded.[106] Evidence from Northampton-shire is contradictory, but there is the suggestion that landed control of county politics continued into the 1880s. There is no uncertainty about where control lay in Cornwall. In East Cornwall farmers effectively con-trolled one seat from 1852; in the West, admittedly very different in econ-omic complexion from Lincolnshire or Northamptonshire, the elites of 'property and character' were onlookers by 1880.

There is, therefore, enough evidence to question the assumption that in 1885 the transition to more public forms of electoral politics was relatively abrupt. Many of the characteristics of electoral politics elsewhere were dis-played in Cornwall during the general election, but not for the first time. Because of the relative political weakness of Cornwall's landed elite, political power began to slip from their grasp as early as the 1850s. Soon afterwards party organisations experienced new stresses producing changes in structure and control: selection of candidates became more open, electioneering far more widespread within constituencies. As political power moved down-wards towards the base of the social pyramid, the shift 'was manifested in the new classes of people, such as the agricultural labourers, becoming politically active, and in the more aggressive viewpoints expressed'.[107] Cornwall typifies this. The first general election following the legislation of 1884–5 confirmed that as so often before the deep rooted populist vitality evident in the county structured electoral politics.

---

[106] Olney, *Lincolnshire politics*, 218.
[107] Hayes, *Third Reform Act*, 14.

Conclusion

In the aftermath of the Third Reform Act Cornwall's parliamentary representation was reduced to seven, a stark contrast to the forty-four in 1790 when this study commenced. Interestingly, among the seven after 1885 was a St Aubyn, member of the same family which had supplied several eighteenth-century county MPs.[1] Another link to an earlier era was the fact that four of the remaining six parliamentarians had strong ties to the county or the south-west, evidence of the enduring desire of many of the Cornish to be represented by their own people.[2] Both these connections with the past were more obvious five years earlier, for at the 1880 general election members of the Robartes, Tremayne, Praed, Willyams and Molesworth families were among the candidates. Indeed, for almost a century after 1790 half or more of Cornwall's MPs were recruited from among the county's aristocratic and gentry families, including new arrivals in those ranks. What such domination did not equate with was political power, for one of the characteristics of Cornwall politics after 1820 was the way in which such power was claimed by elements among the rural and small town middle classes, then later by the working class.

Cornwall electoral politics in the Victorian era and beforehand also exhibited an unusual diversity of behaviour. After 1832 the two county divisions were as different as chalk and cheese: West Cornwall provided the Liberals with their safest seats, always without contests. A perceptive explanation for this was offered in 1842 when Lord Boscawen Rose retired:

> Sir Richard Vyvyan, who was applied to in the first instance, continues to adhere to his resolution of not giving up Helston, and the very few gentlemen of our party [the Conservatives] in this Division, who could have the smallest chance of success, are deterred from coming forward, from various family and other reasons; so that Sir Charles Lemon, who has thrown himself into the arms of the Radical Party, has every chance of walking over the course.[3]

Except for the years between 1835 and 1847 East Cornwall also witnessed a weak and divided Conservative Party, but in contrast to the West contests

---

[1] Sir John St Aubyn, MP for West Cornwall 1858 to 1885, St Ives division 1885 to 1887 when created Baron St Levan.

[2] W. Bickford Smith (Truro division), W. C. Borlase (St Austell division), and Leonard Courtney (Bodmin division), were descendants of long-established middle-class families in West Cornwall. C. T. D. Acland (Launceston division), was from a Devon-based landed family whose extensive estates were spread across Devon, Somerset and Cornwall.

[3] Gregor to Peel, 29 Jan. 1842, BL, MS Add. 40501, fo. 130.

were frequent, the farmers played a decisive part, and the Liberals' organisation was highly efficient.

The seven small boroughs were equally diverse, though all had less than 900 voters in 1832 and remained below that benchmark in 1865.[4] Liskeard, an open borough, was as different from the pocket borough of Launceston as Truro with its compromises was from the factional intrigues of Helston. Despite this, beginning early in the nineteenth century issues and principles were paramount in several towns, important in others, and evident everywhere. Counterbalancing them were deeply ingrained electoral traditions most obvious in the eighteenth century: bribery and treating, the decisive influence of nearby landowners, and others. As a result, the pace of political modernisation was uneven – relatively rapid in the 1830s when innovative forms of party organisation temporarily smothered traditional modes of electoral behaviour, then much slower in the next two decades when organisational impetus waned, before regaining momentum after the Second Reform Act. If late Victorian voting was influenced much more by the perception that particular interests were damaged or promoted by government action, one caveat is that this was also evident in the 1830s, and even earlier in several boroughs.[5]

Along with the distinctively different political behaviour exhibited in the boroughs was at least one point of uniformity: throughout the years from 1790 to 1885 they were among the smallest towns in England to enjoy the privilege of parliamentary representation. As late as 1881 five still had populations of less than 10,000, and nowhere did the number of voters exceed 2,300.[6] Yet size did not mean political insignificance, for after 1832 similarly small towns in England and Wales elected almost one-third of the membership of the reformed House of Commons. Together with the counties it was these constituencies which frequently decided the outcome of general elections. In 1872 twenty-seven English boroughs had less than 1,000 voters, seventy-seven fewer than 2,000, underlining the point that small towns were a crucial element in the mid nineteenth-century electoral system.[7] This study has shed further light on that system, as well as exposing several powerful forces which combined to produce a political culture different in some ways from the remainder of England.

Foremost among these forces was the county reform movement which began in 1805 and petered out in acrimony soon after the 1832 Reform Act, having been a catalyst for intra-elite friction and farmer independence which later resurfaced. Led by Colman Rashleigh it had its origins in the campaigns for parliamentary reform in the 1780s and 1790s, long-standing and continu-

4 McCalmont's parliamentary poll book.
5 J. P. Parry, The rise and fall of Liberal government in Victorian Britain, New Haven 1993, 222.
6 McCalmont's parliamentary poll book.
7 Parry, Rise and fall, 217.

ous tensions between the greater and lesser gentry, and a sense of shame at the way in which Cornwall's twenty-one boroughs failed to represent the interests of the people. Instead they brought little but notoriety to the county. Being lesser gentry the reformers faced formidable opposition from within their own class; they overcame this through persistence, building a political alliance with the farmers, and opening county meetings (their favourite forum) to inhabitants as well as freeholders. Those who attended the meetings and signed petitions for parliamentary reform gave the movement a weight of support which made the predominantly Tory aristocracy and wealthy gentry wary of publicly challenging them. This was exacerbated by the events surrounding the 1826 county election when one of their nominees, John Tremayne, was forced to retire in favour of the reformer Edward Pendarves.

Besides leaving their imprint on county elections, politicising the farmers, and turning their newspaper, the *West Briton*, into a widely circulating rival to the Tory *Royal Cornwall Gazette*, the reformers were one of the catalysts for growing political activism in towns. Even the tight control exercised by many patrons over their parliamentary boroughs could not stifle the upsurge of public debate which became evident after the Napoleonic Wars. Reformers such as Pendarves, Rashleigh and Walker encouraged this by their reformist stance towards the abolition of colonial slavery and their consistent support for Catholic emancipation. In turn this brought the small town middle classes into the political arena, adding to the existing undercurrent of opposition to patrons such as the Boscawen family. Ultimately the county reform movement politicised important segments of the rural and urban middle classes, with far reaching consequences for Cornwall electoral politics.

A second force was Methodism, and the eventual identification of Methodism with Liberalism. Despite the spasmodic nature of the revivals with their accompanying decline in support afterwards, the Methodists steadily increased in numbers from the beginning of the nineteenth century. Together with the widespread presence of Methodism, old Dissent was strong in most boroughs. As a result, as early as the 1820s Whigs and Dissenters were frequently allies and the numerous anti-slavery societies which sprang up during the decade were one manifestation of this. Catholic emancipation certainly tested the embryonic alliance, but after the 1830s it was generally rock-solid. Dissenters knew the only hope for redressing their numerous grievances lay with Whig–Liberal governments. They also regarded Conservatives and the Church of England as a unity, and although many Wesleyans professed a strong attachment to the latter, at the end of the day their loyalties lay with their own denomination. And no matter how hard they rationalised their position they could not escape the truth that the state discriminated against them. Although the Whig–Liberals were far from being iconoclasts, they were certainly willing to modify the privileged position of the Established Church.

The 1851 religious census confirmed what many already knew: the numerical strength of Dissent in Cornwall meant that the Church of England, and in turn the Conservative Party, were on the defensive. By the 1850s it was obvious that this religious factor meant that the Conservatives could succeed in sending representatives to Westminster only when the electoral system was in some way subverted, an issue such as agricultural protection gave the party a natural advantage, or their organisation was more efficient than usual.[8] In the wider sphere of county politics there is no reliable way of estimating Methodism's importance – at least until 1868. But there are enough clues to suggest firstly that a number of the wealthier Dissenters were drawn into the Liberal organisation. For example they were among the committee-men of the West Cornwall Reform Association, which drew heavily on Truro's principal activists. And it was that shrewd observer of the Cornish electoral scene, Sir Richard Vyvyan, who believed in 1864 that the overwhelming prevalence of Dissent was a formidable barrier to any Conservative candidate. The party's prolonged inactivity was often due to lack of leadership and funds, but we cannot avoid the conclusion that the Conservatives were also cowed by the Methodists, who comprised a substantial proportion of the county's electorate.

As demonstrated by the parliamentary career of Arthur Pendarves Vivian, the Wesleyans were a much more obvious electoral force in the West after 1868, but it is doubtful whether their impact on mid century politics in East Cornwall was as great. If we employ the criteria of candidates' addresses and speeches from the hustings, then we may safely assume that Nonconformity was sufficiently strong to be courted at various times by men of both parties. Liberals, and even one or two Conservatives (East Cornwall's Nicholas Kendall being a notable exception), certainly sympathised with, and supported their complaints of religious discrimination. However most of the voters were first and foremost farmers, Nonconformist opinions being submerged beneath economic questions in their political consciousness. If it had been otherwise, Kendall's sixteen-year stint as a county MP would be almost incomprehensible.

Agricultural politics was the third force, one notably powerful in East Cornwall and several eastern boroughs. The politicisation of Cornwall's farmers began during the heyday of the farmer–reformer alliance in the 1820s, when their concerns ranged across tithes, agricultural protection, currency and parliamentary reform. Despite their links with Rashleigh and company the farmers were never particularly radical, self-interest being their principal motivating factor. It was this which finally splintered the alliance in the 1830s, when agricultural protection seemed to be under attack: irrespective of farmers' religious affiliations it was the hip-pocket nerve which guided them. Hence from 1837, when the Conservatives regained one East Cornwall seat, to Nicholas Kendall's victory in 1852, the farmers occupied centre stage,

8 As we have seen subversion of the system was the most frequent choice – and the most successful.

as they did in a number of predominantly agricultural English counties. So determined were they to safeguard their own interests that during the same period they completed a remarkable transition: between 1837 and 1845 they were happy to allow the county's traditional (aristocratic and gentry) leaders to choose the parliamentary representatives and oversee party organisation. By 1852, driven by the imperative of agricultural protection, they rejected these traditional leaders, organised themselves as the East Cornwall Society for the Protection of Native Industry and elected their own protectionist candidate. It was a remarkable turnabout, having long-lasting effects throughout the county.

The most important result was the political demise of the Conservatives' long-time aristocratic and gentry leaders. Their hegemony had been seriously challenged by the county reformers, but with the stimulus of the free-trade scare, their fortunes revived towards the end of the 1830s. However the 1852 slap-in-the-face was the final straw, especially as Kendall defeated their nominee. Wisely perhaps, the wealthy Conservatives steered well clear of the farmers until 1868, when they were made fools of yet again. Not surprisingly this was almost the end of their political road, and hastening their downfall was the prolonged feuding resulting from Kendall's victory. It prohibited the Conservatives from making a serious challenge in either county division, with such political influence as they possessed after 1820 being dissipated in byzantine internal struggles. Together Methodism and the farmers devastated the county Conservatives, apart from a brief flicker of life in the 1870s.

The patterning of borough electoral politics was partly shaped by notable characteristics of the unreformed system. As O'Gorman and Phillips have found elsewhere, even before the 1820s several of the larger boroughs exhibited vigorous political debate arising from certain national and local issues, and it continued throughout the nineteenth century in all of them.[9] However, underlying this was the continuation of earlier forms of electoral behaviour resulting from the degree of patronal control, the numerical size of borough electorates, and peculiar local factors, for example the excessive venality of Penryn voters. So, irrespective of the organisation of parties, the level of ideological debate between them and the growing, partisanship of voters, the pace of political modernisation was partly determined by hangovers from the unreformed system. This is why Launceston and St Ives remained pocket boroughs; the control of patrons or local landowners was not seriously disturbed by the extension of the franchise in 1832. They could therefore retain their roles without undue inconvenience. The reverse applied in Truro, Bodmin and Liskeard, one-time Corporation boroughs. In each the patron-dominated Tory cliques controlling the towns' parliamentary representation aroused such opposition that, after 1832, a substantial increase in voters ensured the Whig–Liberals of at least one seat. Helston

9 O'Gorman, *Voters, patrons and parties*; Phillips, *The Great Reform Bill.*

politics were long beset by corporation and solicitorial factionalism dating from the duke of Leeds's heyday, and Penryn & Falmouth demonstrated how venality and government influence could produce curious election results. In one form or another most of these hallmarks which endured until at least the 1860s, if not longer, were observable elsewhere in England during the same period.

Finally, analysing Cornwall politics over a broad sweep of time leads to the conviction that although it fluctuated in importance, localism was too powerful a force to be ignored. In county politics one sign of this was the network of families connected to the Lemons of Carclew; their long-lasting influence reduced the likelihood of good Conservative candidates being persuaded to stand. Localism was more evident in the small boroughs where old traditions or attitudes died hard: compromises between the two parties at Truro, and the determination of Liskeard's voters to fight the return of a Tory hegemony – an attitude whose origins lay in early nineteenth-century resistance to the Eliots. Localism manifested itself in another way. From John Lemon's years as a Truro MP at the beginning of the nineteenth century to Sir John St Aubyn's successful switch from West Cornwall to the St Ives division in 1885, Cornish-born candidates had a pronounced advantage. There is no reason to disbelieve the *Gazette* when it suggested in April 1880 that the Conservatives' William Molesworth-St Aubyn defeated Adolphus Young at Helston because he was the 'popular scion of a local family', had made his mark in the world and, most important, had succeeded in persuading the post office authorities to extend the telegraph to the nearby town of Porthleven, where Young had failed.[10]

If these were the internal forces patterning Cornwall politics in the age of reform, among the most important external forces were the succession of Reform Acts in 1832, 1867 and 1884. Each increased the electorate significantly, so that the 10,800 of 1832, more than two-thirds of them county voters, had been translated into almost 54,000 by 1885. In 1832 sections of the industrious middle classes and some of the better-off working men gained the vote. By 1885 all the middle-class and many working-class men enjoyed what once had been regarded as a privilege derived from ownership of property. As direct participation in electoral politics increased, so did the numbers of Wesleyans, a simplistic yet logical explanation for the Liberal's clean sweep in 1885. Yet simple statistics demonstrate this was not the dawn of 'mass politics', or even the beginning of democracy: fewer than one in six people in Cornwall were registered electors, and an even smaller proportion actually bothered to vote. There was increasing participation in electoral politics by working-class men and women, but with no means of quantifying this, a more accurate alternative to mass politics might be public politics. For example, parliamentary candidates were frequently selected at public gather-

10 *Royal Cornwall Gazette*, 9 Apr. 1880, 5.

ings of voters instead of by surreptitious conclaves among aristocracy and gentry; candidates and MPs had to spend much more time attending public meetings in small, once politically moribund villages, because voters and non-voters wished to meet candidates face-to-face; the process of political literacy also had to begin in these villages. From the 1860s onwards popular pressure gradually forced electoral politics more into the public domain.

Since 1790 political power had been moving inexorably downwards towards the base of the social pyramid, and after 1885, although a degree of personal influence was still retained by one or two MPs, public politics were soon evident in most constituencies. Despite the temporary confusion of party allegiances caused by Home Rule, middle- and working-class people, especially the latter in a division like Camborne, were now the political centre of gravity. Their religion, their opinions and the state of their pockets dictated the swings of the political pendulum, just as did parliamentary patrons one hundred years earlier. Why and how the movement from the heyday of the patrons towards the mass political parties of today occurred in Cornwall, has been one object of this study. In a wider sense, its purpose has been to reinforce the view-point that only through understanding the local and particular may national history of this kind be written.

Bibliography

Unpublished primary sources

Record offices, libraries and museums
Exeter, Devon Record Office
  Acland of Killerton MSS

London, Bishopgate Institute
  The George Howell collection

London, British Library
  Add. MSS (Peel papers)

London, Greater London Record Office
  Papers of the Liberation Society

Oxford, Bodleian Library
  Disraeli MSS
  Sir Philip Rose's election notebook

Selborne, Gilbert White Museum
  Holt White MSS

Taunton, Somerset Record Office
  Hylton (Jolliffe) MSS
    Jolloffe's election notebook

Truro, Cornwall Record Office
  Buller MSS
  Carlyon MSS
  Clifden MSS
  Coode and French (solicitors) MSS
  Coulson correspondence
  Gregor of Trewarthenick MSS
  Hawkins of Trewithen MSS
  Howell of Ethy MSS
  Kendall MSS
  Paynter and Whitford (solicitors) MSS
  Pendarves MSS
  Pendarves Vivian MSS
  Pridwaux Brune MSS

Rashleigh of Menabilly MSS
Rashleigh of Stoketon MSS
Rogers (solicitors) MSS
Treffry MSS
Tregoning MSS
Tremayne MSS
Prideaux Brune MSS
Vyvyan of Trelowarren MSS
Diaries of Davies Gilbert, John Oates, Richard Tyacke
Borough records: Bodmin, Helston, Liskeard, Penryn, Truro
Sir John Coleman Rashleigh, 'Memoirs of Sir John Colman Rashleigh Bt.: in
    four parts (1772–1847)' (typescript)
[X = miscellaneous collections; FS = facsimile collections]

Truro, Royal Institution of Cornwall
Hawkins of Trewithen MSS
Rashleigh of Menabilly MSS
Jenkin letterbooks
Journals of Christopher Wallis

Westminster, Alliance House
Papers of the United Kingdom Alliance

Private collections
Bodmin, Pencarrow
Molesworth MSS, by courtesy of Lt Col. J. A. Molesworth-St Aubyn, MBE

Marazion, St Michael's Mount
St Aubyn papers, by courtesy of Lord St Levan

Torpoint, Antony House
Carew Pole and Buller MSS, by courtesy of Sir John Carew Pole Bt, DSO, TD,
    and the late Mr P. L. Hull, MA, county archivist, Cornwall Record Office

Published primary sources

Official publications (in date order)
House of Commons, sessional papers: number of electors, PP 1833 xxvii. 21; 1834 ix.
    604; 1836 xliii. 373, 421; 1837–8 xliv. 553; 1840 xxxix. 187; 1843 xliv; 1846
    xxxiii. 145; 1857 (2) xxxiv. 83; 1864 xlviii. 227; 1866 lvii. 23; 1880 lvii. 53;
    1884 lxii. 213
*First report of the Commissioners on the Municipal Corporations of England and
    Wales*, PP 1835 xxiii/2
1851 Census of Great Britain: numbers of inhabitants, 1801–51, PP 1852–3 [1691]
    lxxxv

1851 Census of Great Britain: religious worship (England and Wales): reports and tables, PP 1852–3 [1690] lxxxix

House of Commons, accounts and papers (15), PP 1868–9 xlviii. 24–35 (Bodmin, 1868)

House of Commons, accounts and papers (19), PP 1874 liii. 421–62 (Launceston, 1874)

House of Commons, sessional papers: returns of owners of land in England and Wales . . . 1872–3, PP 1874 lxxii

1891 Census of England and Wales: preliminary report and tables of population, PP 1890–1 [C6422], xciv

Newspapers
Cornubian
Leeds Mercury
Morning Chronicle
Royal Cornwall Gazette
Sherborne Mercury
West Briton
Western Daily Mercury

Books
Allen, J., *History of the borough of Liskeard and its vicinity*, Liskeard 1856

Benson, A. C., *The life of Edward White Benson sometime archbishop of Canterbury*, London 1899

Campbell, Lord John, *Lives of the lord chancellors and keepers of the Great Seal of England from the earliest times till the reign of King George IV*, Boston 1875

Collins, Wilkie, *Rambles beyond railways: or notes in Cornwall taken a-foot*, London 1851

A complete parochial history of the county of Cornwall in four volumes, Truro 1867

The correspondence and diaries of John Wilson Croker, ed. Louis J. Jennings, London 1885

The correspondence of George, prince of Wales, 1770–1812, ed. A. Aspinall, New York 1964–8

Courtney, W. P., *The parliamentary representation of Cornwall to 1832*, London 1889

Defoe, Daniel (intro. G. D. H. Cole), *A tour through the whole island of Great Britain*, London 1927

The diocese of Exeter in 1821: Bishop Carey's replies to queries before visitation, ed. Michael Cook (Devon & Cornwall Record Society n.s. iii, 1954)

Fraser, Robert, *General view of the county of Cornwall with observations on the means of its improvement*, London 1794

Grego, Joseph, *History of parliamentary elections and electioneering in the old days*, London 1892

The journeys of Celia Fiennes, ed. Christopher Morris, London 1947

The letters of the Revd John Wesley, A.M., ed. John Telford, London 1931

Leveson Gower, Hon. F., *Bygone years: recollections by the Hon. F. Leveson Gower*, New York 1905

Llanover, Augusta, Lady, *The autobiography and correspondence of Mary Granville, Mrs Delany*, London 1862

Matthews, J. H., *A history of the parishes of Saint Ives, Lelant, Towednack and Zennor in the county of Cornwall*, London 1892

Mills, Thomas H., *A week's wanderings in Cornwall and Devon*, London 1863

Oldfield, T. H. B., *An entire and complete history, political and personal of the boroughs of Great Britain*, London 1792

—— *The representative history of Great Britain and Ireland*, London 1816

Parliamentary papers of John Robinson, 1774–1784, ed. William Thomas Laprade, London 1922

Truro: further account of election proceedings in this borough . . . together with a copy of the poll, Truro 1833

Wallis, John, *The Cornwall register: containing collections relative to the past and present state of the 209 parishes*, Bodmin 1847

Warner, Revd Richard, *A tour through Cornwall in the autumn of 1808*, Bath 1808

The Wesleys in Cornwall: extracts from the journals of John and Charles Wesley and John Nelson, ed. John Pearce, Truro 1964

White, Walter, *A Londoner's walk to the Land's End and a trip to the Scilly Isles*, London 1851

Winskill, Peter T., *Temperance standard bearers of the nineteenth century*, Manchester 1897

Worgan, G. B., *General view of the agriculture of the county of Cornwall*, London 1811

Wyvill, Christopher, *Political papers chiefly representing the attempt of the county of York, and other considerable districts to effect a reformation of the parliament of Great Britain*, York 1794

Directories and works of reference

Biographical dictionary of modern British radicals, I: 1770–1830, ed. J. O. Baylen and N. J. Gossman, Hassocks 1979

Boase, C. G., *Collectanea cornubiensia: a collection of biographical and topographical notes relating to the county of Cornwall*, Truro 1890

British parliamentary election results, 1885–1918, ed. F. W. S. Craig, London 1974

Burke's landed gentry

Burke's peerage, baronetage and knightage

Dod, Charles R., *Electoral facts from 1832–1853 impartially stated, constituting a complete political gazeteer*, ed. H. J. Hanham, Brighton 1972

English historical documents, XI: 1783–1832, ed. A. Aspinall and E. A. Smith, London 1971

Kelly's directory of Cornwall, 1856, 1873, 1883

McCalmont's parliamentary poll book: British election results 1832–1918, ed. J. Vincent and M. Stenton, Brighton 1971

Namier, L. B. and J. Brooke, *The House of Commons, 1754–1790*, London 1964

O'Malley, E. L. and H. Hardcastle, *Reports of the decisions of the judges for the trial of election petitions in England and Ireland, pursuant to the Parliamentary Elections Act, 1868*, London 1870

Pigot & Co's new commercial directory for 1824

Thorne, R. G. (ed.), *The House of Commons, 1790–1820*, London 1986

Who's who of British members of parliament, II: *1866–1918*, ed. Michael Stenton
and Stephen Lees, Hassocks 1978
Williams's commercial directory of the principal market towns in Cornwall 1847

Secondary sources

Books

Alexander, Boyd, *England's wealthiest son: a study of William Beckford*, London
1962

Armstrong, Anthony, *The Church of England, the Methodists and society,
1700–1850*, London 1973

Aspinall, A. (ed.), *Politics and the press, c. 1780–1850*, London 1949

Bateman, J., *The great landowners of Great Britain and Ireland*, 4th edn, London
1885

Bebbington, D. W., *The nonconformist conscience: chapel and politics, 1870–1914*,
London 1982

Blake, Robert, *The Conservative party from Peel to Churchill*, London 1972

Brett, R. L. (ed.), *Barclay Fox's journal*, London 1979

Brock, Michael, *The Great Reform Act*, London 1973

Brooke, John, *The House of Commons, 1754–1790: introductory survey*, London
1964

Brown, H. Miles, *The Catholic revival in Cornish Anglicanism: a study of the Tractarians of Cornwall, 1833–1906*, St Winnow 1980

Brundage, Anthony, *The making of the new poor law: the politics of inquiry, enactment, and implementation, 1832–1839*, London 1978

Cannon, John, *Parliamentary reform, 1640–1832*, Cambridge 1973

Christie, Ian R., *Wilkes, Wyvill and reform: the parliamentary reform movement in
British politics, 1760–1785*, London 1962

———— *Myth and reality in late-eighteenth-century British politics and other papers*,
Berkeley–Los Angeles 1970

Clark, J. C. D., *English society, 1688–1832: ideology, social structure and political
practice during the ancien régime*, Cambridge 1985

Coate, Mary, *Cornwall in the great civil war and interregnum, 1642–1660*, Oxford
1933

Colley, Linda, *Britons: forging the nation, 1707–1837*, New Haven 1992

Craig, F. W. S. (ed.), *British parliamentary election results: 1832–1885*, London
1977

Crosby, T. L., *Sir Robert Peel's administration, 1841–1846*, Newton Abbot 1976

———— *English farmers and the politics of protection, 1815–1852*, Hassocks 1977

Davis, R. W., *Political change and continuity, 1760–1885: a Buckinghamshire study*,
Newton Abbot 1972

Derriman, James P., *Records of Talland and West Looe, 1574–1869*, I: *Parliamentary
election returns, West Looe*, privately printed 1975

Douch, H. L., *The book of Truro: a portrait of the town*, Chesham 1977

Du Maurier, Daphne, *Vanishing Cornwall: the spirit and history of Cornwall*, Harmondsworth 1978

Edsall, Nicholas C., *The anti-poor law movement, 1834–44*, Manchester 1971

Eltis, David and James Walvin (eds), *The abolition of the Atlantic slave trade: origins and effects in Europe, Africa, and the Americas*, Madison 1981

Evans, Eric J., *The contentious tithe: the tithe problem and English agriculture, 1750–1850*, London 1976

Fawcett, Mrs, *Life of the Right Hon. Sir William Molesworth, Bart., MP, FRS*, London 1901

Foster, Ruscombe, *The politics of county power: Wellington and the Hampshire gentlemen, 1820–1852*, New York 1990

Fraser, Derek (ed.), *The new poor law in the nineteenth century*, London 1976

—— (ed.), *Urban politics in Victorian England: the structure of politics in Victorian cities*, Leicester 1976

Gardiner, A. G., *The life of Sir William Harcourt, II: 1886–1904*, London 1923

Gash, Norman, *Politics in the age of Peel: a study in the technique of parliamentary representation, 1830–50*, 2nd edn, Hassocks 1977

—— *Aristocracy and people: Britain, 1815–1865*, London 1979

Ginter, Donald E. (ed.), *Whig organization in the general election of 1790: selections from the Blair Adams papers*, Berkeley 1967

Glubb, A. de C., *When Cornwall had 44 MP's*, Truro 1934

Gooch, G. P., *Life of Lord Courtney*, London 1920

Goodwin, Albert, *The friends of liberty: the English democratic movement in the age of the French Revolution*, London 1979

Graham, Winston, *The four swans: a novel of Cornwall, 1795–7*, London 1976

—— *The angry tide: a novel of Cornwall, 1798–9*, London 1977

Haig, Alan, *The Victorian clergy*, Beckenham 1984

Halévy, Elie, *A history of the English people in the nineteenth century: England in 1815*, London 1964

Hamer, D. A., *The politics of electoral pressure: a study in the history of Victorian reform agitations*, Hassocks 1977

Hanham, H. J., *Elections and party management: politics in the time of Disraeli and Gladstone*, Hassocks 1978

Harrison, Brian, *Drink and the Victorians: the temperance question in England, 1815–72*, London 1971

—— and Patricia Hollis (eds), *Robert Lowery: radical and Chartist*, London 1979

Hartley, Dianna, *The St Aubyns of Cornwall, 1200–1977*, Chesham 1977

Hay, Douglas and others, *Albion's fatal tree: crime and society in eighteenth-century England*, New York 1975

Hayes, William A., *The background and passage of the Third Reform Act*, New York 1982

Hechter, Michael, *Internal colonialism: the Celtic fringe in British national development, 1536–1966*, London 1975

Hempton, David, *Methodism and politics in British society, 1750–1850*, London 1984

Hirst, D., *The representative of the people?: voters and voting in England under the early Stuarts*, Cambridge 1975

Hobsbawm, E. J. and George Rudé, *Captain Swing*, London 1969

Hole, Robert, *Pulpits, politics and public order in England, 1760–1832*, Cambridge 1989

Hollis, Patricia (ed.), *Pressure from without in early Victorian England*, London 1974

Hovell, Mark, *The Chartist movement*, repr. Manchester 1966

Hudson, Derek, *A poet in parliament: the life of Winthrop Mackworth Praed, 1802–1839*, London 1939

Inglis-Jones, Elizabeth, *Augustus Smith of Scilly*, London 1969

Jenkin, A. K. H., *News from Cornwall*, London 1951

Keast, John, *The story of Fowey (Cornwall)*, Exeter 1950

Kinnear, Michael, *The British voter: an atlas and survey since 1885*, London 1968

Lawrance, W. T., *Parliamentary representation of Cornwall: being a record of the electoral divisions and boroughs of the county from 1295 to 1885*, Truro 1925

Lawrence, Jon and Miles Taylor (eds), *Party, state and society: electoral behaviour in Britain since 1820*, Aldershot 1997

Leifchild, J. R., *Cornwall, its mines and miners*, new impression, New York 1968

Machin, G. I. T., *The Catholic question in English politics, 1820–1830*, Oxford 1964

———— *Politics and the Churches in Great Britain, 1832–1868*, Oxford 1977

Mingay, G. E., *The gentry: the rise and fall of a ruling class*, London 1976

Mitchell, Austin, *The Whigs in opposition, 1815–1830*, Oxford 1967

Mitchell, L. G., *Charles James Fox and the disintegration of the Whig party, 1782–1794*, London 1971

Moore, D. C., *The politics of deference: a study of the mid-nineteenth century English political system*, Hassocks 1976

Moore, Robert, *Pit-men, preachers & politics: the effects of Methodism in a Durham mining community*, London 1974

Namier, Sir Lewis, *The structure of politics at the accession of George III*, 2nd edn, London 1957

Neale, J. E., *The Elizabethan House of Commons*, London 1976

Nossiter, T. J., *Influence, opinion and political idioms in reformed England: case studies from the north east, 1832–1874*, Hassocks 1975

O'Gorman, Frank, *Voters, patrons and parties: the unreformed electorate of Hanoverian England, 1734–1832*, Oxford 1989

Olney, R. J., *Lincolnshire politics, 1832–1885*, London 1973

Orme, Nicholas (ed.), *Unity and variety: a history of the Church in Devon and Cornwall*, Exeter 1991

Owen, John B., *The eighteenth century, 1714–1815*, Totowa, NJ 1975

Parry, J. P., *The rise and fall of Liberal government in Victorian Britain*, New Haven 1993

Patterson, M. W., *Sir Francis Burdett and his times (1770–1844)*, London 1931

Payton, Philip, *The making of modern Cornwall: historical experience and the persistence of 'difference'*, Redruth 1992

Pelling, Henry, *Social geography of British elections, 1885–1910*, New York 1967

Pennington, R. R., *Stannary law: a history of the mining law of Cornwall and Devon*, Newton Abbot 1973

Perkin, Harold, *The origins of modern English society, 1780–1880*, London 1969

Phillips, John A., *Electoral behaviour in unreformed England: plumpers, splitters and straights*, Princeton, NJ 1982

———— *The Great Reform Bill in the boroughs: English electoral behaviour, 1818–1841*, Oxford 1992

Porritt, E. and A. Porritt, *The unreformed House of Commons: parliamentary representation before 1832*, Cambridge 1903

Prest, John, *Politics in the age of Cobden*, Toronto 1977

Probert, John C., *The sociology of Cornish Methodism* (Cornish Methodist Historical Association, Occasional Publication viii, 1964)

Rowe, John, *Cornwall in the age of the industrial revolution*, Liverpool 1953

—————— *The hard-rock men: Cornish immigrants and the North American mining frontier*, Liverpool 1974

Rowse, A. L., *Tudor Cornwall: portrait of a society*, New York 1969

—————— *A Cornish childhood: autobiography of a Cornishman*, new edn, London 1983

Russell, A. K., *Liberal landslide: the general election of 1906*, Newton Abbot 1973

Sack, James J., *The Grenvillites, 1801–29: party politics and factionalism in the age of Pitt and Liverpool*, Urbana 1979

Sellers, Ian, *Nineteenth-century nonconformity*, London 1977

Seymour, C., *Electoral reform in England and Wales: the development of the parliamentary franchise, 1832–85*, Newton Abbot 1970

Shaw, Thomas, *A history of Cornish Methodism*, Truro 1967

Shorter, A. H., W. L. D. Ravenhill and K. J. Gregory, *Southwest England*, London 1969

Speck, W. A., *Tory & Whig: the struggle in the constituencies, 1701–1715*, London 1970

Spring, David (ed.), *European landed elites in the nineteenth century*, Baltimore 1977

Stewart, Robert, *The politics of protection: Lord Derby and the protectionist party, 1841–1852*, Cambridge 1971

—————— *The foundation of the Conservative Party, 1830–1867*, London 1978

Taylor, T., *The Celtic Christianity of Cornwall: divers sketches and studies*, London 1916

Thompson, E. P., *The making of the English working class*, Harmondsworth 1976

Thompson, F. M. L., *English landed society in the nineteenth century*, London 1963

Todd, A. C., *Beyond the blaze: a biography of Davies Gilbert*, Truro 1967

Toy, H. Spencer, *The history of Helston*, London 1936

—————— *The Cornish pocket borough*, Penzance 1968

Trinder, Barrie, *Victorian Banbury*, Chichester 1982

Vernon, James, *Politics and the people: a study in English political culture, c. 1815–1867*, Cambridge 1993

Walvin, James (ed.), *Slavery and British society, 1776–1846*, London 1982

Ward, W. R., *Religion and society in England, 1790–1850*, London 1972

Articles

Beales, Derek, 'Victorian politics observed', *Historical Journal* xxi (1978), 697–707

—————— 'The electorate before and after 1832: the right to vote and the opportunity', *Parliamentary History* xi (1992), 139–50

Bebbington, D. W., 'Nonconformity and electoral sociology, 1867–1918', *Historical Journal* xxvii (1984), 633–56

Beer, Samuel, H., 'The representation of interests in British government: historical background', *American Political Science Review* li (1957), 613–50

Bromund, Ted, ' "A complete fool's paradise": the attack on the Fitzwilliam interest in Peterborough, 1852', *Parliamentary History* xii (1993), 46–67

Coleman, B. I., 'Southern England in the census of religious worship, 1851', *Southern History* v (1983), 154–88

Davis, R. W., 'The Whigs and the idea of electoral deference: some further thoughts on the Great Reform Act', *Durham University Journal* n.s. xxxvi (Dec. 1974), 79–91

——— 'Deference and aristocracy in the time of the Great Reform Act', *American Historical Review* lxxxi (1976), 532–9

Drescher, Seymour, 'Public opinion and the destruction of British colonial slavery', in Walvin, *Slavery and British society*

Dunbabin, J. P. D., 'British elections in the nineteenth and twentieth centuries: a regional approach', *English Historical Review* xcv (1980), 241–67

Eastwood, David, 'Toryism, reform and political culture in Oxfordshire, 1826–1837', *Parliamentary History* vii (1988), 98–121

Edwards, M. S., 'Bible Christians, political radicals and Cornish Methodism', *Journal of the Cornish Methodist Historical Association* ii (1967), 151–3

Fisher, J. R., 'The farmers' alliance: an agricultural protest movement of the 1880s', *Agricultural History Review* xxvi (1978), 15–25

——— 'Issues and influence: two by-elections in South Nottinghamshire in the mid-nineteenth century', *Historical Journal* xxiv (1981), 155–65

——— 'The limits of deference: agricultural communities in a mid nineteenth-century election campaign', *Journal of British Studies* xxi (Fall, 1981), 90–105

Fitzmaurice, R. M., 'A chapter in Cornish banking history', *Journal of the Royal Institution of Cornwall* n.s. ii (1991), 12–46

Hayden, Peter, 'Cornish Methodists and the general election of 1885', *Journal of the Cornish Methodist Historical Association* v (1978), 55–62

Heesom, Alan, ' "Legitimate" *versus* "illegitimate" influences: aristocratic electioneering in mid-Victorian Britain', *Parliamentary History* vii (1988), 282–305

Holderness, B. A., ' "Open" and "close" parishes in England in the eighteenth and nineteenth centuries', *Agricultural History Review* xx (1972), 126–39

Howarth, J., 'The Liberal revival in Northamptonshire, 1880–1895: a case study in late nineteenth-century elections', *Historical Journal* xii (1969), 78–118

Jaggard, E., 'Cornwall politics, 1826–1832: another face of reform?', *Journal of British Studies* xxii (1983) 80–97

——— 'The parliamentary reform movement in Cornwall, 1805–1826', *Parliamentary History* ii (1983), 113–29

——— 'The 1841 British general election: a reconsideration', *Australian Journal of Politics and History* xxx (1984), 99–114

——— 'Farmers, nabobs and county politics in Cornwall, 1832–1868', *Southern History* vii (1985), 145–61

——— ' "The age of Derby" outside parliament: new orthodoxy for old?', *Journal of The Royal Institution of Cornwall* n.s. x (1986–7), 62–83

——— 'Political continuity and change in late nineteenth-century Cornwall', *Parliamentary History* ii (1992), 218–34

——— 'Liberals and Conservatives in West Cornwall, 1832–1868', *Cornish Studies* i (1993), 14–30

Jennings, P., 'Notes on the parliamentary history of Truro, part iv (1761–1787)', *Journal of the Royal Institution of Cornwall* xix (1913), 230–40

—— 'Part v (1787–1820)', *Journal of the Royal Institution of Cornwall* xix (1914), 433–9

—— 'Part vi (1820–1832)', *Journal of the Royal Institution of Cornwall* xx (1915), 95–106

Joyce, Patrick, 'The factory politics of Lancashire in the later nineteenth century', *Historical Journal* xviii (1975), 525–53

Lambert, John, 'Parliamentary franchises past and present', *Nineteenth Century* xxvi (1889), 942–62

Lucas, B. Keith, 'County meetings', *Law Quarterly Review* lxx (1954), 109–14

Luker, David, 'Revivalism in theory and practice: the case of Cornish Methodism', *Journal of Ecclesiastical History* xxxvii (1986), 603–19

McQuiston, Julian R., 'Tenant right: farmer against landlord in Victorian England 1847–1883', *Agricultural History* xlvii (1973), 95–113

Miller, N. C., 'John Cartwright and radical parliamentary reform, 1808–1819', *English Historical Review* lxxxiii (1968), 705–28

Moore, D. C., 'The other face of reform', *Victorian Studies* v (1961), 7–34

—— 'Is "the other face of reform" in Bucks an "hallucination"?', and R. W. Davis, 'Yes', *Journal of British Studies* xv (1976), 150–61

—— 'Some thoughts on thoroughness and carefulness suggested by comparing the reports of the Aylesbury meeting of 24 February 1830 in *The Times* and the *Bucks Gazette*', and R. W. Davis, 'Rebuttal', *Journal of British Studies* xvii (1977), 141–4

—— 'The gentry', in G. E. Mingay (ed.), *The Victorian countryside*, London 1981

North, Christine, 'The Trists of Veryan', *Journal of the Royal Institution of Cornwall* n.s. viii (1980), 191–223

O'Gorman, Frank, 'Electoral deference in "unreformed" England: 1760–1832', *Journal of Modern History* lvi (1984), 391–429

—— 'Reply: the electorate before and after 1832', *Parliamentary History* xii (1993), 171–83

Overton, Mark, 'The 1801 crop returns for Cornwall', in Michael Havinden (ed.), *Husbandry and marketing in the south west, 1500–1800*, Exeter 1973

Parry, J. P., 'Constituencies, elections and members of parliament, 1790–1820', *Parliamentary History* vii (1988), 147–60

Phillips, John A., 'The structure of electoral politics in unreformed England', *Journal of British Studies* xix (1979), 76–100

—— and Charles Wetherell, 'The Great Reform Act of 1832 and the political modernisation of England', *American Historical Review* c (1995), 411–36

Pounds, N. J. G., 'Population movement in Cornwall, and the rise of mining in the 18th century', *Geography* xxciii (1943), 37–46

—— 'The social structure of Lostwithiel in the early nineteenth century', *Exeter Papers in Economic History* xii (1979), 31–42

Prince, H. C., 'The tithe surveys of the mid-nineteenth century', *Agricultural History Review* vii (1959), 14–26

Prothero, Iorweth, 'Reformers, radicals, and class in England', *Journal of British Studies* xxxiv (1995), 542–6

Rowse, A. L., 'The duchy of Cornwall', *Nineteenth Century* cxxi (1977), 43–56

Rule, John, 'Some social aspects of the Cornish industrial revolution', *Exeter Papers in Economic History* ii (1970), 71–106

—— 'Methodism and Chartism among the Cornish miners', *Bulletin, Society for the Study of Labour History* xxii (1971), 8–10

—— 'Wrecking and coastal plunder', in Hay and others, *Albion's fatal tree*

—— 'Richard Spurr of Truro: small town radical', *Cornish Studies* iv/v (1976/7), 50–5

Sack, James J., 'The House of Lords and parliamentary patronage in Great Britain, 1802–1832', *Historical Journal* xxiii (1980), 913–37

Simon, Alan, 'Church disestablishment as a factor in the general election of 1885', *Historical Journal* xviii (1975), 791–820

Trinick, Michael, 'A new acquisition: a portrait of William Lemon', *Journal of the Royal Institution of Cornwall* n.s. ii, i (1992), 121–7

Walvin, James, 'The public campaign in England against slavery, 1787–1834', in Walvin, *Slavery and British society*

Wilson, Kathleen, 'Whiggery assailed and triumphant: popular radicalism in Hanoverian England', *Journal of British Studies* xxxiv (1995), 118–29

Unpublished theses

Bradfield, B. T., 'The public life of Joseph Thomas Treffry (industrialist) of Place, 1810–1850', BA(Hons) diss. Birmingham 1955

—— 'Sir Richard Vivyan and Tory politics with special reference to the period, 1825–46', PhD diss. London 1965

Chesher, V. M., 'Some Cornish landowners, 1690–1760: a social and economic study', BLitt. diss. Oxford 1957

Close, D. H., 'The general elections of 1835 and 1837 in England and Wales', unpubl. DPhil. diss. Oxford 1967

Comber, Michael, 'The Cornish boroughs and parliamentary reform, 1800–1832', MA diss. Exeter 1976

Elvins, W. B., 'Aspects of parliamentary representation in Cornwall before the Reform Bill', BA(Hons) diss. Birmingham 1957

—— 'The reform movement and county politics in Cornwall, 1809–52', MA diss. Birmingham 1959

Harvey, Caroline F., 'The British general elections of 1857 and 1859', DPhil. diss. Oxford 1980

Hayden, Peter, 'Culture, creed and conflict: Methodism and politics in Cornwall, c. 1832–1979', PhD diss. Liverpool 1982

Jaggard, E., 'The 1841 general election in England and Wales', MA diss. Western Australia 1977

—— 'Patrons, principles and parties: Cornwall politics, 1760–1910', PhD diss. St Louis 1980

Johannson, Sheila Ryan, 'The demographic transition in England: a study of the economic, social and demographic background to mortality and fertility change in Cornwall, 1800–1900', DPhil. diss. Berkeley 1974

Luker, D. H., 'Cornish Methodism, revivalism and popular belief c. 1780–1870', DPhil. diss. Oxford 1987

Index